FORD MUSTANG RESTORATION

1964½–1973

David Stribling

CarTech®

CarTech®

CarTech®, Inc.
6118 Main Street
North Branch, MN 55056
Phone: 651-277-1200 or 800-551-4754
Fax: 651-277-1203
www.cartechbooks.com

Edit by Bob Wilson
Layout by Connie DeFlorin

ISBN 978-1-61325-416-5
Item No. SA421

Library of Congress Cataloging-in-Publication Data Available

Written, edited, and designed in the U.S.A.
Printed in China
10 9 8 7 6 5 4 3 2 1

All photos are courtesy of David Stribling unless otherwise noted.

DISTRIBUTION BY:

Europe
PGUK
63 Hatton Garden
London EC1N 8LE, England
Phone: 020 7061 1980 • Fax: 020 7242 3725
www.pguk.co.uk

Australia
Renniks Publications Ltd.
3/37-39 Green Street
Banksmeadow, NSW 2109, Australia
Phone: 2 9695 7055 • Fax: 2 9695 7355
www.renniks.com

Canada
Login Canada
300 Saulteaux Crescent
Winnipeg, MB, R3J 3T2 Canada
Phone: 800 665 1148 • Fax: 800 665 0103
www.lb.ca

CONTENTS

Acknowledgments

This book wasn't created by the efforts of one individual, as the efforts of the contributors, in most cases, went above and beyond providing a photo or two. Personal and business relationships were the driving forces behind this book.

First, thank you to those who provided their cars for this project: Bob Coulston, Ron Dickerson, Delonzo Rhyne, Bruce Faucett, Bill Abrams, Jenny Routh, Earl Batker, Mark Houlahan, Jose Mujia, Tim Laakso, Chris Rockwell, Dene Mattocks, Thomas Bruening, Chris Jones, Billy Carrol, Rick and Seth Nichols, Doug and Dean Hvidston, Steve Schonegg, Don Bierman, Jeremy Feller, and Thomas Beeler. I want your cars—all of them.

I am forever indebted to those who contributed technical help for this project: Ken Bramblett, Jim Cunningham, Kevin Tetz, Jeff Ford, Mark Houlahan, Dennis Woody, Delonzo Rhyne, Brett Ward, and Don Gould.

Thank you to Larry Jewett, the former editor of *Mustang and Fords* magazine, who gave me my first chance with a wild idea 20-plus years ago. In addition, thank you to the editors of *Mustang Monthly* and *Mustang and Fords* who kept me going: Don Farr, Mark Houlahan, Jeff Ford, and Rob Kinnon.

Thank you to my wife, Melissa, who's tolerance of me knows no bounds. Thank you for believing in me and supporting me in my endeavors.

Thank you to my children: Kayla and Caleb Surber, Kara and Jordan Stribling, and Andrew and Ryley Dougherty. You make the long hours worthwhile. In addition, thank you to Jesus Christ, who has saved me where stamped steel and petroleum products cannot.

Introduction

"Why do we need another book about how to restore a Mustang?" This was the first question I asked myself after CarTech requested that I write this book. As the owner of a restoration shop, I have a bookshelf full of how-to books and restoration books. Some are helpful, some are basically just advertising for various products, and some are out of date. However, none of them contain all of the necessary information.

Therein lies the answer to my question: not any single book provides every piece of information that you need, including this one. Teaching you how to paint a classic car in a single chapter would take much more than the space that is available here.

The obvious answer to my question relates to the quantity of Mustangs that were produced. Ford made 1 million Mustangs by the middle of the second year of production and a total of nearly 3 million during its first-generation run. In 1966 alone, Ford sold more than 600,000 units.

To this day, the styling of the original pony car remains popular, and younger generations of people are discovering the classic Mustang as a car that can be driven and as a car that can be a show piece. It's no wonder that so many Mustangs become parent-child restoration projects. The Mustang is certainly one of the most desirable collector cars, and many reside in automotive collections around the world.

Since it is always cheaper to buy a car that has been restored than

Two first-generation Mustangs are shown: a 1964-1/2 coupe (left) and a 1973 Mach I (right). Bob Coulston of Indianapolis, Indiana, restored both of these cars to the Mustang Club of America's concours level, and each required a different path for the restoration. The challenge of writing this book is to help restorers on both ends of the spectrum.

restore one yourself, why restore one yourself? For some, it's the family car that is passed down to the next generation. Even if it costs more than what it's worth, the result is priceless. Some people can't afford to buy a restored car, but they have the time and skills to do the job themselves. Some people simply enjoy the restoration process and tinkering with an old car, and some with a big skill set may find the right car and pocket some money for their effort.

The target audience for this book varies considerably—from the kid with his or her first driver's license to the lifelong Mustang enthusiast who may be on his or her third complete restoration. The information must be applicable to a wide audience. There is nothing more frustrating than buying a book that doesn't help you.

The first-generation Mustang evolved greatly in design and function over the first 10 years. So, taking photos of a 1966 convertible restoration may or may not help the owner of a 1973 coupe who needs help. The two cars are simultaneously similar but different.

The goal for this book is not to provide a step-by-step process for restoring your classic Mustang. The goal is to take you through all of the steps in restoring these vehicles and provide tips and tricks that I (and my associates) have learned over the years to help you keep the process out of the nightmare realm.

I cover when and how to seek help if you get stuck. Hopefully, the tips and tricks in this book help you decide whether certain tasks fit within your skill set. Although I primarily deal with restoring cars to their original state, some of the techniques apply to all levels of restoration. I cover every aspect of the restoration project—from cleaning up the engine compartment to a full teardown of the body and drivetrain.

I am trying to be the Boogeyman on purpose by telling you all of that information up front. I want you to succeed and not create yet another project car that gets sold for less than you have into it.

Having restored numerous cars myself and having helped many others achieve their goals through my shop, it is satisfying when the finished product is sitting there or driving along my favorite route. The satisfaction of restoring a piece of automotive history may be one of the most satisfying projects that you can take on.

This book covers the basics to bring your Mustang back to original condition. Depending on the intended use, consider upgrading the car in various areas for safety and driveability. In other cases, you may build a concours car that won't get driven at all. My goal is to share tips and procedures that have been developed over the years, instead of step-by-step procedures to perform certain tasks that may not apply to your car. In addition, knowledge that I've learned from other experts is shared to keep you out of trouble when restoring your car.

CHAPTER 1

THE BASICS

The 1964½ Mustangs were offered in coupe and convertible versions and are sought out by collectors due to the early generator-style charging systems and other unique features. This convertible was built in June 1964 and is finished in Wimbledon White. It is owned by Ron Dickerson and features a 260-ci V-8 engine and an automatic transmission.

This chapter covers what you need to know before deciding to restore a Mustang. Knowledge is king. For veteran restorers, I aim to remind you of any previous pitfalls so that you can avoid repeating them.

Rule 1: Know What You Have

It is important to understand what you are starting with before beginning a restoration. A car with a lot of rust will drive restoration costs upward. Many of my customers have bought cars at auctions and discovered that what they purchased wasn't what was advertised. If you have received a car as a family heirloom, carefully inspect the car so that you know what you have. Even if you restore the car for sentimental reasons, you need to know exactly what you have and what to expect before purchasing parts.

Knowledge is king. Educate yourself on the trouble spots for your choice of Mustang for corrosion and availability of replacement parts. If you are thinking of restoring a higher-end car, such as a Shelby or Boss, educate yourself on the particular model and year. As the value goes up, so does the expectation on a restoration. Research parts availability for the level of restoration that you are looking to complete. Don't be afraid to get on your back and lay on the ground to inspect the car. When making a big purchase, take someone knowledgeable with you when looking at the car.

Rule 2: Buying a Restored Car is Usually Cheaper than Restoring One

Car values fluctuate, but parts and labor always increase. The more work that it takes to get to your objective, the less cost effective it becomes (see Rule 1).

A complete teardown and rebuild restoration can be more than 2,000-plus hours, depending on the condition of the car. If you multiply a professional's hourly rate by 40 to determine the cost of just one week in a shop, the cost can quickly get out of control. In almost every case, you may need some professional help (paint and engine work are the most common areas). Doing the work yourself can certainly help you save some cash, but if you have to pay a professional, the cost increases dramatically.

The cost of replacement parts is always increasing. In your situation, you may not have a choice on parts, but when looking for a restoration project, the less you have to do, the better. Original parts are getting scarce, and as supplies dwindle, the value of those that are still available increases. Some original parts have been carted around to so many swap meets and passed around so much that even though they are new, they need to be refurbished before being used.

Rule 3: Double the Budget

I say this with full seriousness. Items that you were going to reuse may break or may not survive the restoration process. When fresh paint goes on, those chrome pieces that you were going to reuse may not make the grade anymore.

Fifty-year-old cars don't always cooperate with budgets. In addition, you may have overestimated your capabilities, and you may need help to fix what you just did. Jobs that should only take an hour may take a day or more. Anticipate cost overruns because they will happen.

Rule 4: Ford Parts Fit Better

Almost every Mustang part is available from aftermarket suppliers, including complete, brand-new bodies. Although most aftermarket parts fit the first-generation cars, the originals fit much better.

It may not be practical or even possible to use original parts, but the quality of aftermarket parts varies considerably. Some aftermarket parts are good, but some are copies of copies, and the fitment of the part or the performance of the part may be inferior. Some aftermarket parts can be downright dangerous. Just because the part has a Ford-approved logo printed on it does not make it suitable for use. For example, a rear trunk latch for 1969–1970 vehicles is currently being marketed through the major parts suppliers. The part looks good until you try to use it because it is drilled for metric hardware.

If you have to pay someone to fix or modify a part to fit, the cost increases substantially (see Rule 3). This is especially true when making poorly designed sheet metal fit properly, which is a labor-intensive job. Back when fenders were still available from Ford, I had a friend who couldn't justify spending $400 for a new 1965 fender from Ford, so he bought cheap $120 fenders from a swap meet. By the time the shop had reworked the fenders to fit, he could have bought the Ford fenders and bolted them on the car. Paying a professional to make poorly fitting parts fit can easily gobble up any savings over buying new old stock (NOS) parts, even if those parts are outrageously priced. Not all aftermarket sheet metal is bad, but original Ford parts fit much better.

Rule 5: Know Your Capabilities

Unless you own a machine shop or paint booth, expert help will be needed at some point during the restoration. In some states, it may be illegal for you to paint your own car in your garage due to regulations. If you are not an experienced welder, trying to install body panels on your dream car may not be the best place to learn. I have installed headliners myself, but I currently pay someone else to do them because they have more experience and the specialty tools to install them perfectly.

Tools to do the job properly also drive up the cost. Although this book shows you how to build a rotisserie, what do you do with a rotisserie after you are done with it?

I don't perform my own engine work, I usually farm that out. It's not that I can't do engine builds; I have built many motors. I don't have the equipment to do the machining, and the savings that I get by assembling the engine myself is canceled out by the warranty that I get by having the machine shop do all of the work.

This is especially true with high-performance engines. The more complex the engine, the more that you want an expert to handle it. I know that if I have a problem, I will be covered. A reputable shop is less likely to forget something—like I did once, and guess who paid to have it redone? Understand your capabilities, what knowledge is needed, and what tools you will need. Engine building is fun, and many books are available about rebuilding to help you through the experience.

Rule 6: A Disassembled Mustang Takes up a Lot of Space

A lot of space is needed to keep sheet metal from getting damaged after disassembly and before installation. Organizing parts so that you know where they are when you need them requires shelves and bins. Your other cars, tools, lawn mowers, and pretty much anything in your garage may need to find a new place to reside. Some options include renting a storage unit or setting up another shed. Renting or storing in non-climate controlled buildings (or your neighbors barn) can cause freshly restored parts to degrade, requiring them to be reconditioned at a later date. Think about how you will store parts until they are needed. See Rule 3.

Rule 7: Restore the Body Correctly

The body is where many projects go wrong. You can always change your mind on how to use your Mustang (as a show car or daily driver). A properly repaired and prepped chassis can be used for almost every application. You may change your car from a daily driver to a show car if the body was repaired correctly. However, a poorly restored body won't fare as well as one that has been done properly, and the value will be reflected.

First-Generation Mustang Details

First-generation Mustangs are divided into four categories: 1964½–1966, 1967–1968, 1969–1970, and 1971–1973. Within these categories, alterations occurred from year to year that change the outlook regarding how the cars are restored compared to the other versions. The following lists provide some of the significant changes from each year of production. However, these are not all-inclusive lists, and there are exceptions to every rule when dealing with changes.

1964½

- These cars were produced from March 9 to July 31, 1964
- No official fastback models were produced
- Production began in Dearborn, Michigan; production in San Jose, California, was added on July 10, 1964
- Cars were equipped with generator charging systems
- Backup lights were optional
- Sideview mirrors were optional
- Rear passenger seat belts were optional
- Depending on the delivery destination, cars were equipped with either road draft tube or a positive crankcase ventilation (PCV) system

1965

- The fastback bodystyle was added to the lineup
- Alternator charging systems were incorporated
- Production in Metuchen, New Jersey, was added on February 1, 1965
- The GT Mustang package was added in February 1965
- The Interior Decor Group, or "Pony," interior was added in March 1965
- Road draft tubes were phased out in March 1965

1966

- Backup lights became standard equipment
- An automatic transmission was added for the 289 Hi-Po
- Emissions control began on engines destined for California and other regulated regions
- The 1965 GT-style five-dial instrument cluster became standard

1967

- The engine compartment and suspension were redesigned to accommodate the 390 FE engine
- Crash padding was added to the steering column and dash
- An optional folding glass rear window was offered on convertible models
- Speed control was an option
- "Spinner" wheel covers had tines that laid back for safety regulations
- An overhead console was introduced
- Optional shoulder seat belts were available (I've never seen one, though)
- A hood with integral turn signal indicators was available
- The tilt wheel option was available
- A dual-reservoir brake master cylinder was standard
- First availability of radial tires
- A seat belt warning light was optional
- A torque box was added to coupes and fastbacks on the driver's side (convertibles still used them on both sides)
- Emergency flasher controls were moved to the steering column
- Power disc brakes were available for the first time

1968

- Safety side-marker lights and reflectors were standard
- Optional shoulder belts became mandatory mid-production
- A collapsible steering column was standard
- First factory use of fiberglass on non-Shelbys (428 Cobra Jet hood scoop)

Many cars that are for sale used to be show cars. The problem is that they were restored back when things such as flanged welds were acceptable. The value of these cars, even though they are pretty, is not as good as an owner might think because a smart buyer knows that a complete teardown and rework of the original repairs is required to make the car show-worthy with today's standards. This was evident after the 2009 economic mess. If you watched the auctions, the top cars were still selling for good money. It was the middle-of-the-road cars that took the biggest hits. Buyers got smart and realized that these cars required complete restorations to be acceptable, and their value fell dramatically.

Rule 8: Do It Right the First Time

Somewhat different from Rule 7, half of my business is fixing work that other people performed incorrectly, and it costs much more to fix it correctly the second time. Cutting corners using worn parts on a freshly restored car usually doesn't work for very long.

- Optional front-seat headrests were offered
- Locking seat backs were standard
- Torque boxes were standard on both sides for all models
- Wrap-around shock-tower bracing on late big-blocks
- Optional rear window defogger was available

1969

- Side vent windows were eliminated
- The "Drag Pak" option included an oil cooler to help reduce warranty issues (not for drag racing)
- Staggered rear shocks were offered on performance 4-speeds (to reduce wheel hop)
- Shaker hood scoop was introduced
- Grande luxury model was introduced with additional sound deadening and deluxe options
- Last year for the GT option
- First year for the Mach 1 option
- Intermittent wipers were available
- Only year for the four-headlight design
- 6-cylinder cars came with 5-lug wheels

1970

- Featured a locking steering column and key on steering column
- Evaporative emissions controls on gas tank (non-vented cap and system to pull vapors into engine) on California vehicles
- Some engines equipped with a throttle modulator to retard timing on cold start-up
- Optional headlights on warning buzzer
- 4-speed cars were equipped with Hurst shifters and aluminum T-handles

1971

- Gas tank was strapped under trunk floor
- Rear defrost was available
- Power windows were available
- Backup lamps were incorporated into rear taillamps
- Side-impact rails were installed inside doors
- Recessed outer door handles
- Windshield wipers hide under the hood for extra visibility
- Locks could be set without engaging the outer door handles
- Optional side body protective moldings for some models
- Only year for the 429 Cobra Jet/Super Cobra Jet

1972

- Compression ratios were lowered and an exhaust gas recirculation (EGR) valve was installed to meet Clean Air Act requirements
- Midyear change only allowed ram-air option with 351-2V engines
- The Sprint option was offered for one year only
- Redesigned seat belts, retractors, and warning system
- Dual color-keyed mirrors were standard
- A round, black shifter knob replaced the T-handle on Hurst shifters.

1973

- The urethane-covered impact front bumper met the new standards
- The rear bumper stuck out farther from the body (bumper guards were optional)
- Last convertible Mustang until 1983
- Brake size was increased, and disc brakes were standard on convertibles ■

For example, as I wrote this book, I was working on a car that was beautifully restored. However, the engine had not been rebuilt, and when I found a rear engine seal leak, I pulled the oil pan and found a head-gasket problem that was spewing coolant into the oil. Well, I had to pull the engine and ruin all of the beautiful detailing work that was done. It's a very costly mistake.

Just because some parts may look like originals doesn't mean they work as well as the originals. I have had friends who had their cars damaged by using inferior parts, and it was expensive to repair the damage. Some of the restoration parts are inferior to original parts (see Rule 4). A reproduction battery will not last or function as well as a new-technology battery. Parts that are stamped to look like production-line pieces are often inferior to the originals.

Rule 9: Understand the Final Objective

It is important to understand the final objective. If you plan to show the car, know what to expect because different organizations have different standards. I once built a car, and a group complained that it didn't have enough orange peel in the paint. The next group gave high praise for the same paint job. Different judging criteria may be used even by similar organizations, such as the Mustang Club of America (MCA) and Shelby American Auto Club (SAAC).

When building a daily driver, know the capabilities of the parts you are using. Likewise, you can't build a thoroughbred car from a catalog, and some concours parts are impractical for cars that are driven, such as bias-ply tires. Seriously consider updating safety equipment for daily drivers. Objectives frequently change, so apply Rule 7 and Rule 8, and you can change your mind freely.

Rule 10: Organize and Document

One of the top priorities when restoring a car is to become organized and to document. Documentation is the key to success, and photography is one of the most important tools. Get used to taking photos of everything (there is more regarding this subject in Chapter 2). Take photos of components before you remove them to note their orientation for reinstallation. If you find a body-mark paint daub, take a photo. After getting the car back from the paint shop, a lot of knowledge will be forgotten. Documenting the parts helps you avoid having to look on the internet to figure out how the part should be assembled.

Parts organization is critical. Bolts and other parts tend to walk off, and throwing them all in a bucket together is even worse. Especially during a concours restoration, sorting hardware into different categories to be replated or coated is required. It's important to know which bolts go where and how to sort them after plating. Organize the parts so that you know where they are when you need them. The better your organization is, the less frustrated you will be.

Shelbys, Bosses, and Other Limited Editions

Although most of the tips and techniques cross over to high-end Mustangs (Shelbys, Bosses, and other limited editions), some differences should be considered. Most of these cars, for average people, are becoming less practical to own. They are generally very expensive to own and insure, and because most of them are performance based, they are expensive to

The most exotic (and most prized) first-generation Mustangs are the Boss 429s, which were produced in 1969 and 1970. Instead of installing the Boss engines into Torinos, Ford stuffed them into Mustangs and created a legend. This is a 1970 version in Grabber Blue and is owned by Ron Dickerson. Only 499 Boss 429s were produced in 1970.

operate. Parts for rare, and desirable cars tend to be expensive.

Since enthusiasts tend to gravitate to these cars, a lot more information is known about them than some of the more common cars. This means that if you plan to restore for show, you better know your stuff because the knowledgeable enthusiast base won't let you slide in quality. If you build to drive, the enthusiast base will criticize you for building the car in any way other than their way. I call these knowledgeable enthusiast bases "snobs."

In the case of Shelby Mustangs, as the cars evolved, they included more and more fiberglass in their construction, so additional knowledge of fiberglass work may be required when rebuilding them. The rarer the car, the more difficult it is to obtain parts. Only 1,300 Boss 429s were produced, so spares are very rare. The rarest regular-production, first-generation car was the 1964½ Mustang pace car coupe, as about 190 examples were built. Items such as factory cruise control for a 1967 Mustang are rare. Only a handful of actual cars received this option, and finding all of the correct parts today is extremely difficult.

Restomods and retromods are two of the most popular categories for modified cars. Restomod cars generally feature upgrades for safety and reliability and have the look, feel, and performance of a newer car. Retromod cars feature upgrades for safety and reliability, but they retain many of the styling cues, the feel, and the road feedback of what the car was like when it was new. The* Thunder Hawk *certainly has its own styling cues, but they flow with the original styling, and the feedback is what you would feel driving a performance car in the 1960s. This car is owned by Triple R Mustang Ranch.

Modified Cars

Although I focus on restoring cars to their original condition, let's cover Mustang modifications. Most people who drive their Mustang do some form of modification. Most modifications, when done correctly, do not generally reduce the car's value. The following are a few pointers regarding Mustang modifications.

It's your car with your name on the title, so build the car the way you want it. Never build a car to please someone else—unless the purpose of your build is to sell the car.

The values on vintage Mustangs are generally based on low-mileage, unrestored, original cars. Modifications to any car, regardless of the change, may limit the number of potential buyers because those potential buyers may not like the change. Additionally, the more modifications, the more limited the buyer base becomes. It doesn't mean that the value necessarily decreases, but the next buyer may or may not like the modifications that you performed. In some cases, modifications may increase the car's value. For example, if some of the safety issues are eliminated on a car that is driven (see "First-Generation Mustang Safety Issues" in this chapter). Modifications that need to be reversed for the next owner may reduce the value of the vehicle.

If you plan to do bolt-on modifications, keep the original parts if you plan on selling. You may want to use a nice aftermarket aluminum intake and Holley carburetor, but the next owner may want to put the car back to its original condition. If you keep the original parts, it makes the car desirable to buyers who like the new setup as well as those who want to change it back to the original configuration.

Do the modifications correctly. The money invested in modifications may be recouped upon the sale if the modifications have been done well, but poorly done modifications will deter some buyers. For example, if your 5-speed overdrive conversion is clean and looks like it came that way, you will reach more buyers than a car that has been hacked up to make room for the shifter.

Engines

There were 28 different engines installed in first-generation Mustangs. Although some of the engines are nearly identical (for example, there are several versions of the 351 Cleveland), the engines are listed here as Ford designated them. Additionally, with all parts running through the first-generation cars, there are year-to-year changes within those base motors.

6-Cylinder Engines

The base motor for all Mustangs was the reliable straight-6 engine, which was a holdover from the Falcon line. In 1964, it was 170 ci and had only four main bearings. In 1965, the motor size was increased to 200 ci, and it had seven main bearings. This version was used until 1970. The 250 straight-6 was introduced in 1969 and was the base engine after the 200 engine was phased out.

Small-Block Windsor V-8

The small-block Windsor engine was synonymous with early Mustang performance and was used throughout the first-generation run. In 1964, the 260 2-barrel engine was used along with the 289 4-barrel and 289 Hi-Po engines. In 1965, the 260 was dropped, and a 289 2-barrel replaced it. In 1967, with the introduction of the FE big-block to the Mustang, the 289 Hi-Po was slowly phased out. In 1968, the 289 engine line was replaced with the new 302 engine. The 302 4-barrel lasted only one year, as the midsize 351 came online in 1969. The 302 2-barrel remained in the lineup through 1973.

Boss 302

The Windsor-on-steroids Boss 302 engine was created to be used in

Ford's 289 small-block engine was the early performance leader in the pony-car wars, and the 289 Hi-Po was the top dog. Rated at 271 hp, it came with goodies, such as a solid-lift camshaft, higher compression, and sturdy bottom end. This Hi-Po is installed in a 1967 Shelby GT350, which was one of the last of the era.

Ford's reliable 6-cylinder inline engines provided good torque with good fuel economy. In addition, they are a breeze to work on compared to some of the larger V-8s. The integral intake manifold is not extremely efficient, but issues were minimized with a nonremovable manifold. This is a 200-ci 6-cylinder installed in a 1967 coupe.

The Boss 302 engines were developed for road racing and took advantage of the new canted-valve technologies that were used on the Cleveland small-block engines. Everything about the Boss engine was high-end, with the Boss 302 winning the Trans-Am racing series in 1970. This is the 1969 version with chrome valve covers and slightly larger valves. The 1969 Boss 302 is rarer than the 1970 version.

racing, such as the Trans-Am series, and was inserted in a select number of 1969 and 1970 Mustangs. Dimensionally a small-block Windsor, it incorporated the canted-valve heads from the 351 Cleveland engines, had a revised four-bolt block, and utilized other information that was gathered from the 302 tunnel-port program.

Small-Block 351 Windsor

The 351 Windsor is a taller and wider version of the small-block Windsor, and it allowed for a 1/2-inch stroke increase in the engine and a closer bore-to-stroke ratio. In 4-barrel versions, it made the same rated horsepower as the Boss 302. The 351 Windsor remained in production through 1973.

351 Cleveland

In 1970, the Cleveland was introduced in the Mustang and incorporated canted-valve heads to allow for big valves and big ports. These motors were built with RPM in mind. The original 4-barrel heads had huge ports, which were great for high RPM but not so much for low-end torque. The two-valve version had smaller ports and worked well as a conversion head for Windsor small-blocks. The 351 Boss engine incorporated all that Ford had learned from its other engine programs. Although it was an exceptional engine, it only lasted one year due to emissions regulations. The 351 H.O. and Cobra Jet versions tried to carry on the legacy, but the horsepower wars were being stamped out in 1972. The Cleveland engines were available from 1970 to 1973.

FE Engine

Part of the 1967 redesign was to allow for the wider and larger 390 FE engine to be installed in the pony car. The introduction of the big-block saw the elimination of the Hi-Po as the performance engine of choice. The 390 was available in 4-barrel versions through 1969, and a 2-barrel version was available in 1968 (very limited).

Several versions of the 428 were available. The only multiple-carbureted Mustang to ever come from the factory was the 428 8-barrel Shelby GT500 in 1967. This was the police interceptor version with a more stout bottom end. In

The 351 Windsor was taller and wider than the 302 Windsor but retained much of the same technology. It gave Ford a platform with a more balanced stroke-to-bore ratio and is still the base platform used by Ford NASCAR engines today. This 351 is a 4-barrel version, which makes 290 hp in a 1970 Mach 1.

The 351 Cleveland was available in 2-barrel and 4-barrel versions, with the 4-barrel having much larger ports and valves. This 2-barrel is in a 1972 convertible and came with ram air, which in 1972 was only available with 2-barrel engines and a single exhaust.

As the horsepower wars heated up, Ford responded by installing big-block 390s and 428s into the small engine bay of the Mustang. Changing the center spark plugs is a difficult task. The biggest and baddest FE engine was the 428 Super Cobra Jet, which was installed from 1969–1970. With its big Le Mans rods, high compression, and oil cooler, it was a torque monster that helped the Mustang stay on top of the horsepower heap. This is a 1969 Super Cobra Jet ram-air engine in a 1969 Mach 1 with 3:91 gears.

The Boss 429 engine is unique with the hemispherical aluminum heads. Many of them made their way from the showroom to the track. This one is in a 1969 Boss 429 and makes more than 700 hp with some exotic parts courtesy of Holman-Moody.

1968, the dual 4-barrel carburetors were dropped for a 4-barrel version in the GT500.

In late 1968, the 428 Cobra Jet replaced the police interceptor and was installed in standard Mustangs and Shelbys. It used cylinder heads that were similar in design to the 427 medium-riser engine as well as other improvements to make it a capable competitor in the performance wars of the 1960s. There was also a Super Cobra Jet version that was designed for use with gear ratios of 3:91 and 4:30, which included big 427 Le Mans rods and an oil cooler. The last FE was installed in Mustangs in 1970.

Boss 429

NASCAR required Ford to sell 500 units with the Boss 429 engine installed to qualify the engine for competition. This big hemi-head engine required special work to squeeze into the Mustang's engine bay. Only 1,300 examples were produced in 1969 and 1970, and they are revered as the epitome of Mustang performance in the 1960s and 1970s.

429 Cobra Jet/Super Cobra Jet

Only used one year, the size of the 429 Cobra Jet and Super Cobra Jet engines was one of the reasons for the redesign of the Mustang body in 1971. The 429 Cobra Jet and

The 1971 Mustang was enlarged in part to accommodate this engine: the 385-series big-block 429 Cobra Jet. With a modern design, canted valves, and huge ports, the 429 was more than capable of moving the bigger Mustang around rapidly. It was only available in 1971 in Cobra Jet or Super Cobra Jet versions. (Photo Courtesy Scott Serlenski)

Super Cobra Jet used a canted-valve head that was similar to the Cleveland and was the response to Ford's "if big is better, let's go ridiculous" performance mentality. The 429 Cobra Jet is arguably the fastest first-generation Mustang by industry testing, although some had the Boss 351 posting the fastest time.

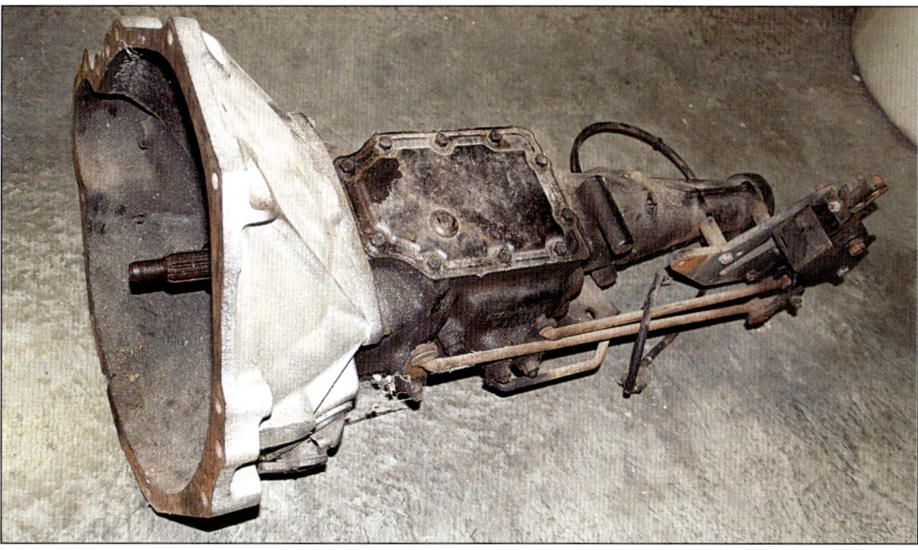

Ford's reliable Toploader received its name from the way that the gears are fitted into the case via the plate mounted on top. This differentiates it from many transmissions, such as the T-10, that load the gears on the side. In addition, the Toploader has an extra shift rod to differentiate it from the 3-speed.

Transmissions

Transmission selection is a little easier to sort out. Although several variations of each model were made to fit the different engine families, only a few families were used through the first generation.

Manuals

First-generation Mustangs with a manual transmission were offered with either a 3-speed or 4-speed.

3-Speeds

The first 3-speed was a carryover from the Falcon program. This small 3-speed was non-synchronized from first to second gear and was very weak (it is known as the "paper" transmission). This transmission was used until 1967, when the 3.03 fully synchronized transmission was used. The 3.03 was stout enough to put behind the 390. It was used until 1973.

4-Speeds

Three 4-speed transmissions were offered in the first-generation cars. In 1964, the German Dagenham 4-speed was originally installed behind some 6-cylinder applications. The BorgWarner T-10 was used in some early Shelby applications as well as some 1965 and 1966 cars. The T-10 can be identified by the gear cover being on the side rather than the top. The Ford Toploader was incorporated throughout the first-generation production run and is known for its durability. It was used in small and large input/output configurations, depending on the engine selection.

The 3.03 3-speed is a fully synchronized, heavy-duty transmission that became the real workhorse for the first-generation Mustang. It was installed behind 6-cylinders and big-blocks alike. It replaced the early Falcon 3-speed in 1967.

Automatics

First-generation Mustangs with an automatic transmission were offered with a C4, C6, or FMX.

C4

The small-block C4 transmission changed very little during its run in the Mustang line. The early 1964–1966 Mustangs had the "green dot" version, where if you wanted to begin in second gear, you put it in the

The C4 replaced the Ford-O-Matic transmission and was a simple, lightweight transmission with an aluminum case rather than cast iron. It was used throughout the entire first-generation run on small-block and 6-cylinder applications.

"white dot" position, and full shift was accomplished by putting it in the green dot position for 1-2-3 shifting. In 1967, Ford changed it and called it Select-Shift, and when you started in second gear, it stayed there.

C6

Introduced with the FE engine for the Mustang in 1967, the big C6 transmission could handle the torque and horsepower that was needed behind the big-block. The version that was installed behind the 428 Cobra Jet cars does not have ribs on the top of the bellhousing and incorporates a cast-iron tailshaft housing.

FMX

The FMX was used behind the midsize engines and was a 3-speed. In the original version, this transmission was simple but not very rugged. However, the FMX was the platform that Ford used to develop the automatic overdrive (AOD) transmissions in the 1980s.

Safety Issues

Obviously, a car built more than 50 years ago won't have some of the safety luxuries that are standard on modern vehicles. Although modified vehicles aren't covered in this book, if you intend to drive your Mustang on a regular basis, look into some of the following issues on your vehicle and consider a safety upgrade. Most of the issues are with the earlier cars,

The mighty C6 can handle 450 hp without breaking a sweat and was used behind all of the big-block applications. Starting in 1971, a small-block version was used behind 351s. Although they are much heavier than the C4, people seek out these transmissions for their durability and ease of rebuild. They do not require exotic parts to handle more horsepower.

The FMX transmission suffered some reliability problems and was used behind the midsize 351 engines. It was still a good platform and was eventually used to develop Ford's automatic overdrive (AOD) transmissions in the 1980s.

as Ford made refinements to the cars from year to year.

Single-Reservoir Master Cylinder (1964–1966)

Early Mustangs have a single reservoir to feed the front and rear braking systems. If a leak occurs anywhere in the system, the brakes will not work. On a dual-reservoir system, if the primary or secondary system fails, the other is not affected.

Several companies now make a conversion for early cars that uses a 1967–1970-style dual-reservoir master cylinder and proportioning valve. If you are using power brakes on 1965–1966 cars, the dual-reservoir master cylinder can conflict with the driver-side shock tower. Be careful when choosing a booster because smaller boosters will not operate disc brakes properly. I recommend the 9-inch booster conversion system from Mustang Steve's in Texas.

Long Steering-Column Shaft (1964–1967)

The long-style steering-column shaft, otherwise known as the "Spear-O-Matic," was a common design for all vehicles through the late 1960s. The shaft ran from the steering box, which was mounted to the frame rail, and up to the steering wheel. In a collision, this shaft is pointed right at the driver's chest. In 1967, Ford added a large crash pad to the steering wheel and began offering a two-piece shaft with the addition of the tilt steering column. In 1968, the shaft was redesigned with a collapsible tube in a tube to prevent spearing the driver.

Ididit offers universal collapsible columns and vehicle-specific tilt columns to solve the one-piece design issue. It also offers columns with Ford splines so that you can run your favorite (or original) steering wheel and a Ford-style turn-signal indicator, which makes installation much easier.

Fuel Tank as Part of the Trunk Floor (1964–1970)

With no barrier between the gas tank and rear seat, it is possible for fuel to get inside the passenger compartment after a hard collision. In a severe impact, a solid floor doesn't prevent the fuel tank from rupturing and fuel getting everywhere. Ford made the trunk a solid piece in 1971 and strapped the fuel tank underneath.

Several companies have tried to market solutions for the issue. A piece of aluminum with self-tapping screws won't help in a wreck that can crush the frame rails, and heavy tank covers may cause unwanted scenarios due to the fact that the car cannot absorb the impact of the collision as it was originally designed. The best

The company MustangSteve developed a power braking system for the 1965–1966 cars that has a 9-inch booster. This allows a dual-reservoir master cylinder to clear the driver-side shock tower. In addition, the 9-inch booster is compatible with disc brakes. (Most aftermarket systems use an 8- or 7-inch booster to help clear the tower, but the booster is not sufficient to run disc brakes.) MustangSteve also revised the pedal pin position for correct pedal function. I have removed many aftermarket systems and replaced them with this one. It works.

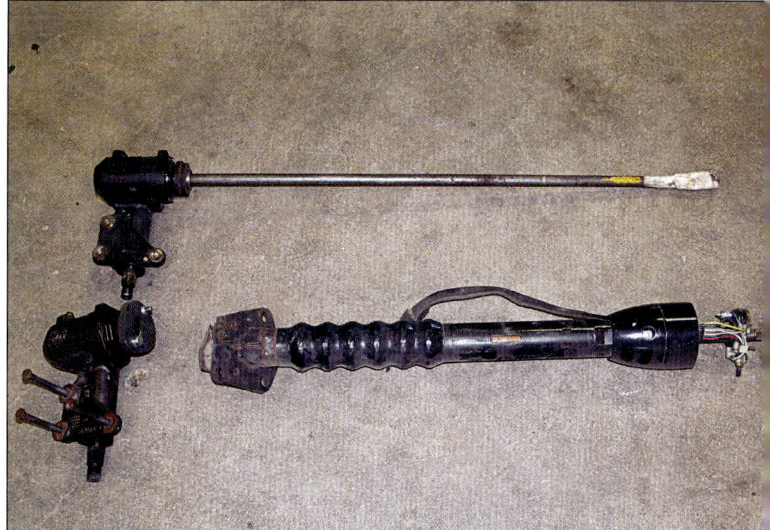

This comparison shows the long-shaft early steering gear versus the revised column that was used in 1968. In a front-end collision, the solid shaft is pointed right at your chest. On the bottom, the 1968 version has a tube-within-a-tube design that collapses on impact, and the accordion part of the steering column tube crushes on impact as well.

A racing fuel cell is expensive, but it's the only real way to provide safety during a very hard rear impact in any car. A racing cell has an internal rubber bladder that holds the fuel in place, and foam baffling in the bladder prevents the momentum of the fuel from splashing out all at once. This one is made by Fuel Safe for a 1970 Mustang and is a stock item.

Three-point-conversion seat belts are now available from Mustang vendors. They help to keep your upper torso from moving forward during an impact. They are available with or without retractors, and they come in colors to match your interior.

way to protect from this type of scenario is by using a racing fuel cell.

Fuel cells have an internal bladder that holds the fuel inside during an impact, and foam baffles prevent the fuel from sloshing out in a wave of momentum. Fuel Safe makes made-to-fit fuel cells for early Mustangs, and although they are much more expensive than a replacement tank, they are the safest option.

Seat Belts (1964–1968)

Seat belts were originally mandated by individual states, so requirements varied early. However, beginning on January 1, 1964 (before Mustang production), front lap belts became standard and rear seat belts were optional. In 1966, rear seat belts became standard. In mid-1968, Ford began installing optional shoulder seat belts, which became standard in 1969.

Three-point seat belts are now available for all the early Mustangs through most major parts suppliers. Most of them bolt to the rear door frame just above the shoulder.

Low-Back Seats (1964–1968)

Early seats do not provide sufficient head and neck support in a collision. In 1968, adjustable headrests became optional. In 1969, headrests became standard on low-back seats, and high-back seats were introduced in the Mach 1. Low-back seats were phased out in 1970.

TMI makes a headrest conversion to fit the early 1964–1967 low-back seats that matches the original fabric. Swapping out the low-backs for a set of high-back seats is fairly simple, and aftermarket sport seats to fit the first-generation cars are available.

Ford marketed a dealer-installed adjustable headrest to fit the low-back seats that were installed in the 1965–1967 Mustangs. These kits are extremely rare today, but aftermarket vendors now make a version that matches the original-style seat upholstery. Aftermarket high-back seats to fit the early cars are also available.

Carburetor Gaskets (All Years)

One of the most common culprits for an engine fire is the original-style paper gaskets that were used in Ford and Holley carburetors. If the engine sits too long, these gaskets dry out and crack, which results in fuel leaking all over the engine. This was a major problem with factory-installed Holley carburetors.

If you have a freshly rebuilt carburetor, run it once a month and bring the engine up to temperature to prevent the gaskets from drying out and cracking. This is especially important for cars that are stored during the winter. Holley and Edelbrock have new designs with modern gaskets that are reusable and won't dry out. If you plan to drive the car, use the newer gaskets.

This 1969 390 carburetor shows signs of the front bowl leaking on the manifold, which can become a fire hazard. The old-style gaskets dry out and crack, and when the engine is run again, the fuel seeps out. Newer-designed gaskets solve this problem. This one has one of the newer gaskets installed in the accelerator pump (the green gasket under the bowl).

Bias-Ply Tires and Alignment Specifications (All Years)

Mustangs were introduced with bias-ply tires, which had tall, stiff sidewalls and were very narrow. Bias-ply tires tend to track in an odd fashion, as I learned firsthand. In 1967, Ford began offering radial tires as an option, and the phasing out of bias-ply tires was complete by 1969. In addition, Ford had alignment specifications that were really designed for bias-ply tires, and when a restoration is completed with radial tires, the car doesn't track correctly. However, unless you are building a concours show car or the rules for the class of show judging doesn't allow them, use radial tires.

Bias-ply tires are awful. I have never enjoyed driving on them. Unless your judging category requires original-style bias-ply tires, run modern radial tires with a modern front-end alignment.

Vapor Lock (All Years)

Vapor lock occurs when the engine-mounted fuel pump or another part of the fuel system heats up enough to change the liquid fuel into a vapor. The fuel pump can't compress the vapor and push it through the carburetor, so the engine vapor locks. Once the engine and fuel cools, the car will restart.

Depending on where the condition occurs, several solutions are available. Most vapor lock occurs because the fuel pump is attached to a very hot engine, and that heat is transferred to the fuel and the diaphragm in the pump. An electric fuel pump mounted near the fuel tank solves most of these problems.

Running the fuel pump off of the camshaft is a simple and convenient way to do it, but it also means that the fuel pump is mounted to a major heat source. Fuel can vaporize at temperatures as low as 95°F, and with the engine running at around 200°F, it doesn't take long to transfer the heat to the device that is trying to pump fuel to the carburetor. Once the fuel turns to vapor, the pump can't compress it and push it to the carburetor. Modern cars use an electric pump that is mounted in the tank. Converting to an electric pump eliminates almost all vapor-lock conditions.

If vapor lock is caused by a fuel line that is too close to hot components, wraps and other heat-dissipation products are available. If the heat is coming through the carburetor, spacers are available to get between the carburetor and intake manifold to block some of the heat.

Rust and Corrosion (All Years)

Rust is a problem on all cars, but it is more of a safety issue on a unibody than a body-on-frame vehicle. As is stated in Chapter 4, a unibody gets its strength from thin sheet-metal panels being welded together, so when one gets rusted out, the structure is affected. Proper rust and corrosion removal and repair is the only solution.

This is typical corrosion behind the front-bumper mount in the frame rail. As you can see, the bracket failed and could not hold the bumper in place. The only way to fix this is to cut it out and replace that section of the rail.

Lighting and Wiring (All Years)

Halogen headlamps didn't come to the US until the 1980s, so all first-generation Mustangs suffer from poor interior and exterior lighting. After 50 years, several issues can occur: corroded wiring, cracked insulation, and the previous owners may have hacked into the wiring harnesses for a myriad of reasons.

Modern light-emitting diode (LED) lighting solutions are available to replace most of the original lighting. Some of these designs may require modifications of the original wiring, and new reproduction wiring harnesses in original and extra-circuit designs are available if the originals cannot be repaired.

The dim lights of the 1960s are being replaced with modern LED technology. These taillights are much brighter than the originals and should last a very long time. They are also available with sequential signals for most cars. LED technology is available for almost every bulb in the car.

PLANNING AND EVALUATION

So, you read the first chapter and decided to forge ahead. Good! The next step of the restoration process is to evaluate the car and yourself.

The most important advice is to build what you want. Don't let me, a potential buyer, a concours snob at the car show, or anyone else tell you how to build your car. Too many owners build a car to satisfy others and not themselves. Note that once you start personalizing or making decisions to save money, you limit the number of people who may be interested in purchasing the car once you are done with it. However, if you really want that pink and purple paisley finish, go right ahead. Please yourself first.

Restoration Levels

The next item to address is what you intend to do with the car once it is completed. Are you building a daily driver, a weekend driver, a show car, a concours car or thoroughbred, or for resale?

Daily Driver

A daily driver is a car that gets used, and while it may range from a minor cosmetic upgrade to a complete rotisserie restoration, the goal is to drive the vehicle. This also includes some upgrades to make the car safer or to give it some modern features. This also means that parts selection is different than with a concours car. Obviously, you don't want to buy a set of expensive original spark-plug wires when a set of new or reproduction wires is reasonable

Ford introduced the fastback bodystyle in August 1964 for the 1965 model year. Its sleek design was the choice for the Shelby Mustangs, and owners have modified them for performance ever since. This 1965 fastback has been upgraded with a 347 stroker small-block, modern suspension, and Shelby styling cues.

Most restorations are built for driving pleasure, and a well-maintained driver shows as well as it drives. This beautiful 1966 coupe is equipped with a 289 V-8, automatic transmission, spinner hubcaps, and original Poppy Red paint. (Photo Courtesy Bill Abrams)

for a car that will be driven. Even on a driver-level restoration, you need to make a decision on items such as fit and finish. For example, reproduction bumpers do not fit as well as the original bumpers, but you may be okay with the minor differences, as opposed to finding original (and expensive) parts.

Body repair needs to be done correctly. The biggest reason that cars do not show well or sell for less than what an owner anticipates is the quality of the bodywork. Daily drivers tend to become show cars when those pretty new parts get bolted onto the car. Even if you plan on driving the car, make sure that the body is done correctly. Swapping a bumper on a car is much easier than stripping down the car to correct improper bodywork.

Show Car

Cars that are built for show more than driving tend to receive a higher level of workmanship. Whether the cars are modified or all original, they are built to a higher standard than what is acceptable on a driven car. The more intense the build, the reliance on using Ford parts or top-of-the-line reproduction parts is increased. While reproduction parts are fine for a daily or weekend driver, judges reduce points in some classes of show cars. The fitment and finish are much more important on show cars, and this translates to higher costs. With cars that are modified, the judging is almost always based on workmanship because the modifications vary from car to car.

Concours and Thoroughbred

Concours cars are restored to the original Ford specifications, using correct reproduction parts or

Because of the high cost of concours and thoroughbred cars, they rarely get driven. Top cars are usually freshened up every few years from just sitting. Driving heats up paint on the engine, rock chips occur from driving, and relying on 50-year-old parts can make driving these cars detrimental. Trailers keep the cars fresh for the next show. This 1969 Mach 1 is one of the earliest Drag Pak Cobra Jet cars and is owned by Ron Dickerson.

Show cars require an additional measure of workmanship, regardless of the level of competition. If you are a novice to judged show cars, take the information that the judges give you and apply that knowledge to improving your car. If they are wrong (which they frequently are), don't get bent out of shape. Use the information to improve your car.

original Ford parts. Thoroughbred cars are built to a level that specifies only Ford original parts, and the top cars use only production-line parts, which can differ from Ford service replacement parts.

Sometimes, it isn't just having the "right" parts but the best "right" parts. I have a friend who had a thoroughbred with a correct original battery, but he kept getting silver-level awards because the battery wasn't that great. He had to spend thousands to upgrade to a nicer battery to get gold-level awards. Yes, it *is* that difficult. Building thoroughbreds is very difficult and in some cases impossible because the parts simply don't exist anymore.

Resale

Restoration for profit is possible with the right car. Typically, the less money that you have to invest in a car, the better. A friend of mine who makes a living reselling classic cars rarely, if ever, does any work on the cars before reselling them. As with other cars, if key parts are missing, it eats into the profit on the other end.

Consider whether a fresh paint job or a rare parts purchase will increase the value of the car by the amount that is spent and determine if it will help the car sell faster. For example, let's look at a 1965 K-Code fastback that is in decent condition but is missing the original 289 Hi-Po motor, which was replaced with a later-model 302 V-8. Not having the original vehicle identification number (VIN)–matching motor is a big strike for some potential buyers, and not having a Hi-Po motor at all drops the value. Hi-Po motors are rare and expensive, which is why the owner is selling it without one.

So, if you buy a Hi-Po motor, does it increase the value of the car to make it worthwhile, and does it help sell the car faster? A rare car with the right parts will usually sell faster, and not having the original engine will almost always affect the value of the car. Sometimes, a partial restoration and leaving the big-ticket items to the next owner is best.

It's red, the top goes down, and it has all the right powertrain parts that you could want. However, did the cost of restoration bring a return on investment? Restoring for profit is getting much tougher as labor and parts costs continue to rise.

Judging Standards

While many show circuits use the same judges and standards, there are differences between the major judging bodies and what each one wants to see. This is the key: if you want to score well in any show group, play by its rules. Sometimes, doing so requires a long process of changing your restoration to what that group wants to see.

The Mustang Club of America (MCA), Shelby American Automobile Club (SAAC), International Show Car Association (ISCA), and other governing bodies judge the cars differently, and a car that does well in one arena may not do as well in another. The person or people inspecting your car may not see things the same way that you do.

For example, an owner was showing his 1966 Shelby, which was a survivor in many ways, and the car had some of the original parts still installed that were showing their age. Rather than replace them with reproductions, he chose to leave the car as it was. One group docked him for the worn-out parts, but the other group commented, "We see what you are doing here," and he scored well. Some owners rant about judging bodies not seeing things their way. My advice is that if you want trophies with the name of a particular judging body, you better build it how that judging body wants.

Restoration Candidates

A good thing regarding the restoration of Ford Mustangs is that a vast majority of the parts are available, including complete rust-free bodies. In many cases, if you have a VIN, you can rebuild your car.

This trailer-find 1970 Mach 1 is disassembled, but further inspection shows that the body has been reworked with good original sheet metal, and the repairs were done correctly. This is a big cost savings on a project car. In addition, you can choose whether or not to keep the full roll cage.

The custom wheel flares on this car will be expensive to remove and repair, but the additional bubbling behind the wheel lip means that there will be major repairs to this car. Rust is rarely on just one spot on a Mustang, so inspect the body condition carefully.

This solid Texas car suffers from rusty floor pans. The pans rust from wet shoes on the carpet, not because of the weather. Other areas to look at are under the battery tray (battery acid eats the metal), the rear quarter panels (the drains clog and water sits in the trough), and the torque boxes (they catch all of the road debris).

Just because it can be done doesn't mean that it should be done. A rusty 6-cylinder base coupe and a rusty Boss 302 take the same amount of effort to bring back to life, and the Boss has more potential to reclaim the cost of body restoration. However, because the Boss Mustang is more desirable, the value of the parts will be at a premium. So, the coupe may be less expensive to restore overall, but it will bring less money than the Boss.

Rebodies

Generally, vehicles are rebodied for one of the following two reasons: 1) the car has enough damage or rusted panels that require major panel replacement or 2) the vehicle VIN tags have been placed on a better but similar body. Generally, the latter occurs on Mustangs of a higher value, and it is discouraged. Someone who wants a real Shelby wants a car that actually went through the Shelby assembly line.

There are many legal reasons to not rebody a vehicle. Once the switch is made, lawsuits can follow. Owners who have built well-done replicas may have up-front and honest intentions when they sell the vehicle as a "tribute" or "reproduction." However, someone who is less scrupulous may eventually sell it to someone as an original. When the buyer discovers that he or she has been deceived, the legal trail runs back to the original builder. Be careful and keep records of sales.

Several companies offer complete new bodies for first-generation Mustangs, and several states allow vintage cars to be rebodied legally. This is mostly due to the popularity of custom-built Mustangs. Buyers

With the resurgence of custom Mustangs, complete new bodies are available for many of the 1965–1970 bodystyles. Dynacorn sells this 1967 fastback body, and they are a great alternative for some builds instead of repairing a rusted-out hulk.

are much less concerned with having an original VIN when the car has a supercharged late-model drivetrain and custom interior. However, some people have attempted to use these new bodies to make a quick buck.

The reproduction bodies are different than the original bodies, and most top restorers know where to look. They are fine for certain builds, but just because it is legal in some areas doesn't mean that it is a good idea. Titling cars without an original VIN may be challenging in some areas. Contact the body manufacturer, and it should have the relevant information to help you get the car titled in your area.

Sometimes, the only option is to replace a majority of the sheet-metal panels. When it is done correctly, most prospective buyers don't have a problem. The higher the value of the vehicle when the project is complete, the more that builders lean on Ford parts versus using reproductions.

Car Selection

The following tips for selecting a Mustang to restore are guidelines and not steadfast rules.

- Any item is worth what someone is willing to pay for it. Many variables determine the value of a car, including the color, options, condition, and history. Don't get the wrong idea from the big car auctions and think that the value of your car just increased tenfold.
- Generally, parts for rare and desirable cars garner more money. Vehicle values rise and fall, but labor and parts never decrease.
- As the car's value increases, so does the level of restoration that is required to maintain the lofty value.
- In drag racing, each tenth of a second of improvement is expensive to gain. The same basic idea goes for show cars. The loftier the goal, the more likely the cost will increase dramatically.
- If you received the car as a family heirloom, reselling it becomes less of an issue because nostalgia takes over.

When most people look for a car to buy, they don't inspect the most important aspects of the vehicle. They look at the pretty red paint and their eyes glaze over, or they look at the ratty interior and are turned off.

If you want to know the real history of a car, look underneath. Sometimes repairs are left unfinished, heavy undercoating is hiding a poor repair, or repairs are simply missed. If you are investing large amounts of money in a car, borrow or rent a lift to look at the bottom of the car to discover the real condition of the vehicle.

The 1969–1970 Mustangs are notorious for rust around the rear taillight openings, and almost every one that goes through my shop gets a new one. A car with improper bodywork that has to be reworked is valued the same as a car that is rusty and ugly. Look past the shiny paint and look at the body condition as well as the fit and finish.

The reality is that the paint is usually hiding something bad, and the average person with patience can redo the interior more quickly than the body. Inspect the following items on the car. They are listed from most difficult to easiest.

Paint and Bodywork

For someone with no experience, paint and bodywork are the most challenging. They require expensive tools, such as welders and paint guns, and in some cases, regulations do not allow you to perform a paint job in a garage. Welding sheet metal takes practice to do properly without warping the panels. Most painters won't paint the car if they don't do the bodywork because the finish is dependent on the bodywork being done correctly.

Engine and Driveline

Wrenching on a motor is fun, and if you don't own some of the required tools, you can generally borrow items, such as a torque wrench, from the local auto parts store's loan-a-tool program. However, you likely don't have the machinery needed to machine the components prior to assembly, so you will need to hire a machine shop at some point during the assembly.

Paying a machine shop to assemble the motor may not be in the budget. However, if you install a part incorrectly, regardless of your level of expertise, the warranty issues are your responsibility. Most camshaft failures occur on start-up, and new camshaft manufacturers do not warranty your installation of their camshaft, regardless of whether you installed it correctly or not. Assembling your own motor is part of the whole restoration for some, and when it fires for the first time, it is satisfying.

Convertible Top

Convertible top installation is difficult. Many professionals install convertible tops, but few do so properly. Convertible top replacement involves new materials, old frames that have been beaten around for 50 years, and

Even the most experienced mechanic doesn't have all of the expensive machining equipment to prepare the drivetrain, so almost all engine restorations involve working with an engine machinist. Check with your machinist and decide what level of disassembly/assembly works best.

Fifty-plus years of going up and down and banging around is rough on a convertible top frame. The weatherstripping that is currently available does not work as well as the original, and to allow the top to open, the weatherstripping is in pieces, making even more places for air noise. Getting tops and weatherstripping to fit is a real challenge. If you do it yourself, be patient and work the task as a whole: top, frame, and weatherstripping.

reproduction seals that sometimes don't fit correctly. This can be frustrating even for professionals.

Interior

The interior can be refurbished with patience and common hand tools (mostly). The two exceptions are headliners and high-back bucket seats. Headliner installation can be done without the proper tools, but most headliners that I have seen installed without the steamers and experience are about 95-percent successful. There is always a crease somewhere.

Some of the high-back bucket seats can be difficult to re-cover. I have struggled with them. Low-back seats are much easier. Generally, carpeting can be a challenge, but it can be made to fit with some patience.

Wiring

Save money by researching and doing the wiring yourself. Fixing the wiring isn't difficult if you take the time to learn how to do so properly. This regularly includes fixing someone else's previous repair rather than diagnosing and fixing a new issue. Chopping the radio wires for a big stereo is a common problem.

Drivetrain Installation

Drivetrain installation involves large, heavy pieces; big tools; and fresh engine-compartment paint, but it is something that you can do. Generally, local rental yards have portable engine lifts, transmission jacks, engine stands, and other useful tools.

Everything is available to freshen up a first-generation Mustang interior, and with patience, anyone can make an interior look new again without professional help. This 1969 Mach 1 interior is just about ready for the new steering wheel and re-covered seats.

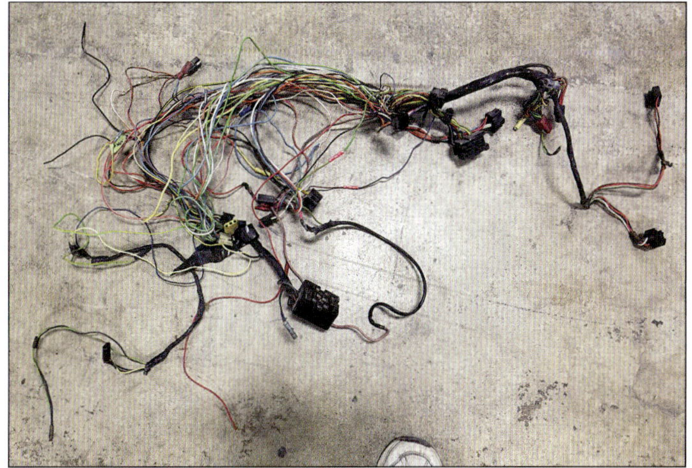

This 1968 under-dash wiring harness is a mess and was butchered by a previous owner during a stereo install (not me), and it has been robbed of some connectors (by me). Even so, with some patience, a voltmeter and some "borrowed" connector ends, it can be brought back to life.

With the proper tools, you can remove and install the drivetrain from the car. However, after everything is repainted and replated and that motor is going back in the car with headers, get some help to avoid scratching things.

Glass

Learning how to install glass saves you a lot of money. However, improper handling of the glass causes it to break. I went 20 years before I broke my first windshield. Adjusting the door glass is the hardest part of handling the glass. It is difficult and takes time to do correctly.

Selecting a Professional

The most important thing when working with a professional is to make sure that you are both on the same page for the project. When you walk in to see your car, it is important that what you see is what you were expecting.

Learn the proper way to remove and install glass and avoid mishaps like this. The owner went at this with gusto and a screwdriver—the glass usually doesn't survive. Removing and installing glass is a multi-person job.

From when I started in this business to today, half of my work has been fixing other people's blunders. Make sure that you both understand what you expect when the project is completed. Make sure that you set clear expectations and are not trying to get more than you bargained for.

Regarding the various restoration tasks, determine what type of professional is required to complete the build that you want. For example, a professional engine builder may not be the right person to paint the car.

When hiring a professional, remember that you pay for the level of expertise that he or she possesses. For example, Ford has not installed a pushrod V-8 engine in a Ford product since 2001 or produced a carbureted Mustang since 1985, and it is possible that the mechanic at your local shop has never worked on an old carbureted engine in his or her career. I have an engine analyzer and know how to use it, and modern engine computers do all of that work internally. A local shop may be good for a newer car, but it may not have the expertise to diagnose and repair a 50-year-old engine.

Make sure that the shop that you use has the expertise for your build. Restoration shops that restore all brands of old cars may or may not be a good choice. I have seen numerous Mustangs that were built by either street rod shops or shops with GM as their primary expertise, and the difference is obvious. Items on the car are detailed like a GM or street rod—not a proper Mustang. Having a car painted by a collision shop may turn out beautiful, but did it follow the specific sequence that you requested or just run it in and paint it like other cars? Most reputable professionals find out exactly what you want, but there are some aspects of the restoration process that I had to learn to do myself because finding someone to do it the way that I wanted was very difficult. Discovering that something was done wrong is expensive to fix.

A shop that specializes in Mustang restorations specifically should have the highest level of knowledge for your project. That doesn't mean that its work is better, but the expectation is that it will have a better idea of what you want. Some Mustang shops only restore to original condition, some only upgrade the car with new gadgets, and some are only interested in performance. In the end, make sure that you and the professional shop are on the same page regarding expectations.

Research as much as possible before you meet with a professional. Knowledge is king, and the more you know, the better. Never be afraid to ask questions if you are unsure, and if you are not comfortable with the answer, find out more information or move on to the next professional.

If possible, have a small project completed first to see how the shop works. For example, if you plan to find a shop to perform a major overhaul in the future, take the car to that shop for some routine maintenance beforehand. Evaluate how well the shop performs and determine if you are comfortable with hiring the shop for a major project.

Ask past customers about the last job that the shop performed. A colleague of mine once said, "You are only as good as the last job that you completed."

Don't be afraid to ask to see parts that did not survive the restoration process or needed to be replaced. Also, if you bought expensive parts, make sure that they are actually installed on the car. Switching out valuable parts for less valuable parts sometimes occurs. Ask about the shop's parts policy. Some shops want you to buy everything through them, but others may allow you to purchase the parts yourself and save some money.

What is the shop's warranty for their workmanship and the parts that it provides? Note that if you didn't purchase a part through the shop and a part fails, the shop likely won't warranty the parts that you provided. Also, some of the parts that a shop does provide may not be covered under warranty because some of the aftermarket parts are inferior. Understand up front what is under warranty and what is not.

Estimates on a 50-plus-year-old car are tricky. Some shops no longer provide general estimates because the larger the project, the further off the estimate will be. If you receive a shop estimate, it may not be accurate when restoring an old car. Parts that are intended for reuse may not survive the restoration process, and until the car is completely stripped, all of the damage may not be revealed. If you have the luxury, get several estimates just like you would with your new car.

I regularly hear people say, "I'll do the bodywork, and you paint it." It doesn't work that way. My paint is dependent on your bodywork to look nice, and if something goes wrong, I have to fix it. So, I'll be doing the bodywork too, thank you. Make sure that your professional will agree to allowing outside people (like you) or other professionals work on parts of the car.

Professional shops often farm out specialty items. Find out what is planned to be farmed out and make sure that it comes with the same warranty that the professional gives for his or her work. Think of the shop as the general contractor.

Photo documentation is important for insurance purposes and for future reassembly. Ask the shop what type of insurance is required while the vehicle is in the shop and what kind of insurance the shop has in case the building collapses or there is a natural disaster.

Ask about the payment structure that the shop requires for long-term projects and if a deposit is required. Also, ask if it is okay to stop by the shop and see the progress. Are you allowed in the shop area?

A common question is, "Do you know of anyone in my area who can do the restoration?" The answer is generally no. Restoration shops pop up and close down on a regular basis, and those that are well established may not do good work.

Begin your search by going to car shows in your area or attending local Mustang club meetings. Look at the cars and the workmanship and ask the owners who did the work. You may find a general pattern of which shops do good work and which shops don't. Ask the owners not only what they liked about working with a shop but also what they didn't like. Dependable data points will emerge regarding which shops are good to work with and which shops are not good. The quality may be good, but the relationship may not be.

Don't be afraid to ask questions. You are spending a lot of money and you deserve to know the answers. Here are two examples that reinforce how project expectations need to align between you and the shop.

Example 1

A customer brought me a 1968 convertible that had just been painted by another facility. The workmanship was not good. Aftermarket panels were used, and the fit and finish was horrible. The paint was certainly not what the customer was looking for. The customer chose a facility that changed out some panels that weren't necessary and bought parts without the customer knowing. In addition, the cost of the finished product was more than double the original estimate.

When the customer complained about the fit of the car, the shop representative said, "Hey, you didn't pay for the good stuff." The customer had the expectation that the car would be beautiful when done. Instead, he was handed the keys to a nightmare, and it took even more money to fix.

Example 2

A friend of mine who is an amazing painter was painting a 1967 Chevrolet Chevelle SS convertible for a customer who was "just going to drive it." I knew how much the customer paid for the paint job, and while it was not perfect, he certainly got his money's worth for what he paid. The owner of the car picked up the car on Friday, took it to a show on Saturday, didn't win a trophy, and was back at the shop on Monday screaming, "You ripped me off!" This customer did not actually want a "just going to drive it" paint job. Instead, he tried to get a show-quality paint job for a discount.

Even though this owner received far more than what he paid, both sides did not understand what the final product was going to be. Make sure that everyone who is involved with your project is on the same page.

Skill Set Evaluation

Just as important as evaluating the project is evaluating your skill set, garage, storage areas, and help network. Learning a new skill is great, just make sure that you are okay learning by working on your pride and joy. If you make a mistake, do you have help to make it right? Do you have a help network to help you pull the engine safely? Do you have storage to store a completely disassembled car? Will your back allow you to twist and contort to work under the dash? Do you have a help network that can show you how to use the welder that you just bought? If the answer is no, will your network of friends and car associates be able to help you find a solution? Is this restoration the place to learn to paint, or should you practice on something else beforehand? Evaluating your skill set helps you decide at what point to involve a professional.

Tools and Equipment

In addition to standard hand tools, consider the following special tools if you plan to restore a Mustang yourself: a digital camera, digital voltmeter, air compressor, glass-bead cabinet, parts-cleaning tank, a jack and jack stands, some specialty tools, and chemicals.

Digital photography has helped the restoration world in many ways. A modern cell phone with a quality camera works well. Use photos to document everything that you do. Photos help you document how parts were originally installed, such as the brakes and the position of the distributor rotor, which helps during reassembly. In addition, documentation is needed for insurance purposes. Whether you use a phone camera or something more exotic, take more pictures than you need.

A digital voltmeter is necessary to chase down shorts and for testing sensors and regulators.

The correct size of air compressor may be determined by power limits, the work area, and what tools you plan to use with it. Some air tools, such as power sanders, use a lot of air volume, which is measured in cubic feet per minute (CFM), and a smaller compressor will be cycling more than a higher-horsepower unit with a large reserve tank. For any project that you

Digital photography enhances restoration and maintenance work. It is easy to identify factory marks, document items such as the brakes for reinstallation, and in this case, take note of the routing of wires and lines before removal. Taking photos will help during reassembly.

will be doing most of the work yourself, I recommend using an air compressor with a minimum of 4 hp with as big of a tank as your area allows.

Inexpensive table-top glass-bead cabinet units are available, but a serious restoration requires a bigger unit for large pieces. It's almost impossible to complete a proper restoration without a way to remove paint, rust, and grime from parts, and a glass-bead cabinet is a great tool for these tasks.

A solvent cleaning tank is a much better way to clean greasy parts than relying on spray chem-

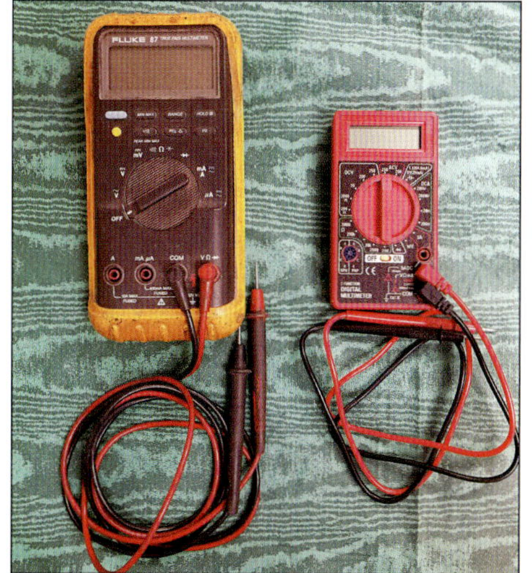

For a single restoration, the inexpensive digital voltmeter (DVM) on the right does everything that the professional-grade meter on the left does to find shorts, breaks, and voltage problems. If you plan to perform multiple restorations, a better meter makes more sense for reliability and accuracy.

Sand blasters, glass-bead cabinets, and paint guns can be air hogs, so use the largest-capacity air compressor that your work area allows. This 7.5-hp compressor is overkill for most hobby-level projects. However, the smaller the compressor and the smaller the air tank, the more work it has to do to keep up. Keep in mind that air compressors such as this one require a 220-volt outlet in your shop (just like most welders).

Parts-cleaning tanks are available in 5-gallon table-top versions as well as 20-gallon-and-larger stand-alone versions. It's a must to clean greasy parts before blasting or refinishing. Always use proper safety equipment when cleaning greasy parts.

Abrasive blast cabinets are like magic for removing rust and paint and for cleaning parts. They are available in small benchtop sizes all the way up to cabinets that hold a complete fender. Most small restoration jobs can use a Shop-Vac to pull the dust from the cabinet, but if you are using the cabinet a lot, consider a dedicated glass-bead cabinet vacuum.

Make sure that your jack stands are tall enough to allow you to get under the car and escape safely. Matching your jack to your jack stands is also important. If you are using wood blocks to make the jack lift higher or blocks under the jack stands to raise the vehicle higher, you need a bigger jack and stands.

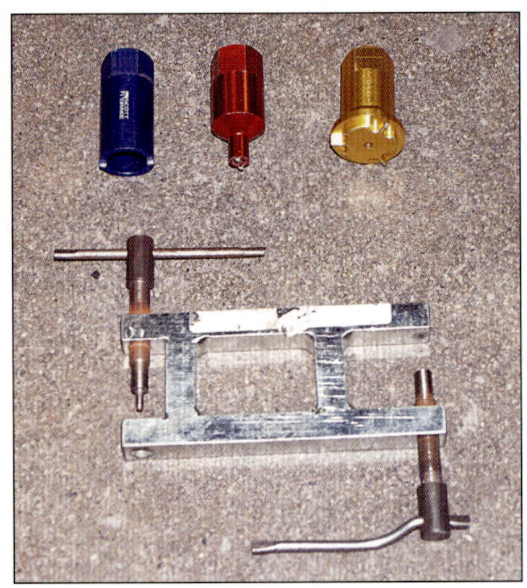

Specific-year specialty tools are available to keep paint scratches and chrome scratches out of your restoration. In the top row (left to right) is a tool to remove the bezel nuts on a 1965 Mustang wiper arm, a tool to remove the bezels from the headlight and wiper switches, and a tool to remove the ignition-key bezel on 1967–1968 applications. The bottom tool is used to remove and install the vent-seal rivets on 1965–1966 applications.

icals to degrease parts. Most standard tanks have a 20-gallon capacity, and 5-gallon table-top versions are available. Two types of cleaning solutions are available: flammable and non-flammable. Flammables (mineral spirits) tend to clean better, whereas non-flammable solvents don't explode and are detergent based. Check the local regulations in your area to determine which type of solvent to use.

Not everyone has access to a vehicle lift, so a quality jack and set of jack stands are a must.

Your Mustang parts vendor prob-

Check your local area regulations regarding what you can keep in your shop. Here are some of the chemicals that I keep handy at all times in my shop (left to right): weatherstrip adhesive in spray and liquid form (tube in front), weatherstrip adhesive remover (removes tar, bugs, and glues), Evapo-Rust (works great on rusty parts that you don't want to blast), Boeshield T-9 (displaces water and protects freshly plated and prepped metal parts), and PB B'laster (penetrating oil to break up rusted parts). Two items that are not shown are carburetor cleaner and paper towels. You need lots of paper towels.

Metal inert gas (MIG) and tungsten inert gas (TIG) welders work well when the voltage is properly maintained. That means having big transformers to maintain a good output like this older welder has. For the home shop, the new compact flux-core and gas MIG welders are fine for single restoration projects.

Modern paints demand a quality gun, and the guns are designed for use based on the tip opening. From left to right are a gun to spray body schutz and spray-on sound deadeners, a gun for spraying on polyester filler with a 2.5-mm tip, a primer gun with a 1.8-mm tip, and a gun for shooting actual paint with a 1.3-mm tip. Some high-solids clears are now requiring 1.1-mm-or-smaller tips.

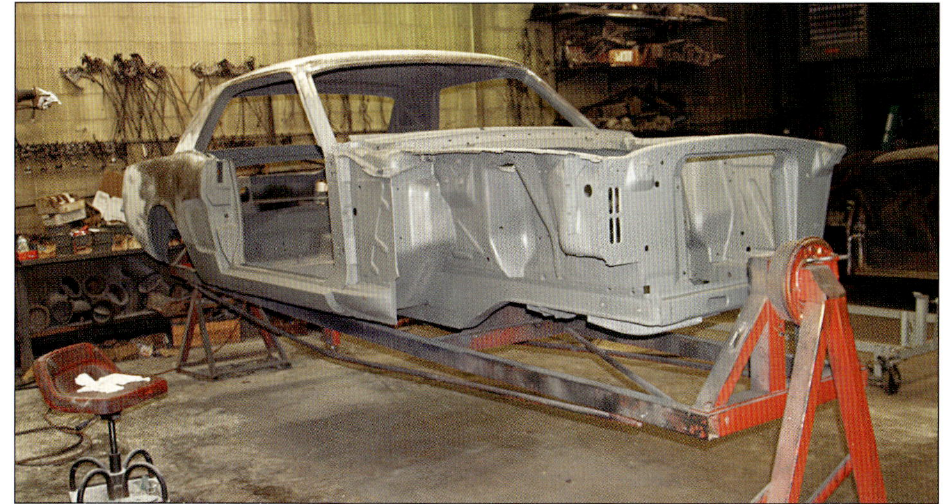

Although it is not a necessity, a body rotisserie helps when working on the underside of the body, especially with panel replacement. Most top restorations were performed on a rotisserie. Rotisseries are covered in Chapter 3. This car is owned by Triple R Mustang Ranch.

ably carries a line of tools designed to prevent damage to your car while removing and installing components. Ford also specified some specialty tools that may not be available from your local auto parts store. If you are a member of a Mustang club or group, you may be able to borrow these or build them for community use.

Chemicals for de-rusting, breaking loose rusted bolts, rust prevention, and removing or installing adhesives are must-have items.

If you plan to do a full restoration and do all of the restoration work yourself, consider purchasing a welder, paint gun, and rotisserie. A quality welder with good control is required if you do any bodywork. See Chapter 4 for more details. Paint gun selection is covered in Chapter 5. Consider purchasing a quality paint gun. Don't expect quality results with a cheap paint

Most rental yards have engine lifts available for when you need them. So, you can avoid the cost and storage of owning your own. Some new engine lifts fold up for easy storage. Consider investing in an engine leveler. They work well when you are trying not to scratch the paint when installing your motor.

Make sure that your engine stand is compatible with the engine you are using. The one on the right is 40 years old and made of heavy-gauge material, but it only has a single wheel in front. The stand in the middle has a front crossbeam to help with stability when rotating the engine. If you are dealing with big-blocks, stands up to a 2,000 pound capacity are available (left). The cradle (foreground) is great for storing small-blocks and for transporting to the machine shop.

Even on older cars, specialty tools abound. These are brake and suspension tools. Some are available on tool loan and others you may have to purchase or borrow. Always use the proper tool for the job (screwdrivers are not pry bars).

A transmission jack raises and lowers vertically and has a bigger pad than a floor jack, which raises in an arc. This is a must-have item for installing heavy Toploaders and automatic transmissions from the 1960s.

Some auto-parts chains offer free tool loans. You leave a deposit, which is returned to you when you return the tool. Specialty tools, such as this bearing race installer, are available as well as more common tools, such as torque wrenches. Consider taking advantage of the tools that are available by free rental.

gun because modern high-solids paint requires a quality gun. Rotisseries are covered in Chapter 3, and they are not required, but they are a tremendous tool for tasks such as welding in new floor pans. The big problem with purchasing a rotisserie is what to do with it after you have completed the project. They take up a large amount of storage space.

Depending on the level of restoration that you plan to attempt, some tools are generally available from rental places and automotive stores on a rental basis. Many auto-parts stores rent tools for free: you pay a deposit and get the deposit back when you return the tool. A nice thing about renting is if you don't plan on building several projects, you don't have to store or sell them after the project is completed.

Ford Parts Identification

Even if you are not doing a full concours restoration, it is important to understand the Ford parts numbering system, as some reproduction manufacturers use the same numbers to identify their parts. It is good to be familiar with the Ford parts system and have the information ready if you are heading to a swap meet to look for specific parts.

Ford uses a specific method to identify parts, but how they are identified on different types of parts can be confusing. The part number on the box may not match the number on the physical part, some castings only have a partial part number, some items use tags, and items such as glass and sheet metal use a different method of identification.

Ford date stamped many car parts, and for some builds, this means looking for parts that were produced before but near the assembly date of your car.

Ford Parts Numbering System

Basic Ford part numbers consist of a prefix, group number, and suffix. For example, part number C7ZZ-17A870-B is a bumper bracket for a 1967 Mustang.

Prefix	Group Number	Suffix
C7ZZ-	17A870	-B

Prefix

In the example above, the C7ZZ prefix identifies the year that the part was first introduced, the model of Ford/Lincoln/Mercury vehicle on which it was first used, and the engineering group that originated the part. Parts used on first-generation Mustangs, such as the door-hinge pins, have a 1950s part number on them, and Ford redesigned the pop-open gas caps and gave them a 1990s part number designation. Many parts were reassigned 1970s part numbers after 1972.

The first digit in the prefix stands for the decade in which the part was introduced, and the second digit is the individual year in that decade (0 to 9). So, the example part was first used in 1967, or "C7." The third digit is the vehicle line where the item was first used. The "Z" in the example denotes that it was designed for use on a Mustang. However, items that were designed for other vehicles frequently made their way onto Mustangs, and parts denoted for Mustangs were often replaced by parts that were used on other lines. The last letter in the prefix is the group that originally designed the part. Most parts end with the letter "Z," which is a Ford service part. The part inside the box may or may not be identical to the Ford production-line part.

Group Number

Ford groups all of its parts into specific sections, and this works directly with the Ford text and illustration books. The groups are four or five digits long with the exception of body and trim panels, which can be denoted by the bodystyle on which they were used. Within these groups, Ford may add a letter to the group, but they are still tied to the original group number.

Ford subdivides soft trim and exterior trim to help the Ford parts counter employees determine the correct trim, but the numbering system holds to the original Ford grouping. The automatic transmission group also follows the same pattern as the manual transmission group (7005 is a transmission case in both groups), but separating them from the manual transmission group makes finding the right parts quicker.

For the 17A780 example, the "A" denotes an expanded group number to accommodate more parts under the group, but it is still listed in the "17870" base number for bumper brackets.

Suffix

The suffix denotes the revision level of the part. Ford frequently made changes to parts, and when this happened, it changed the revision letter in the suffix. So, the "B" designation in the sample part means that the part was revised from the original design in some way. A "C" designation notes an additional change and so on through the alphabet (with the exception of "I"). A revision can also be denoted as double letters, such as "AA," "AB," etc.

When you begin seeking parts for the car, it is important to know the Ford parts numbering system so you can confirm that you are getting the correct parts. Even if you plan to use all reproduction parts, many vendors use the Ford system to identify their parts. This part is a bumper bracket that holds the bumper to the left-hand fender on a 1967–1968 Mustang.

Body Group Part Numbers

Body group part numbers differ from other part numbers, as they include the bodystyle designation for the part that was first released. For Mustangs, this is "63" for fastbacks, "65" for coupes, and "76" for convertibles. Common parts for all three bodies generally use the coupe designation. For example, a 1965–1966 outer rocker panel carries the part number C5ZZ-6510128-A (right-hand rocker panel). For quarter

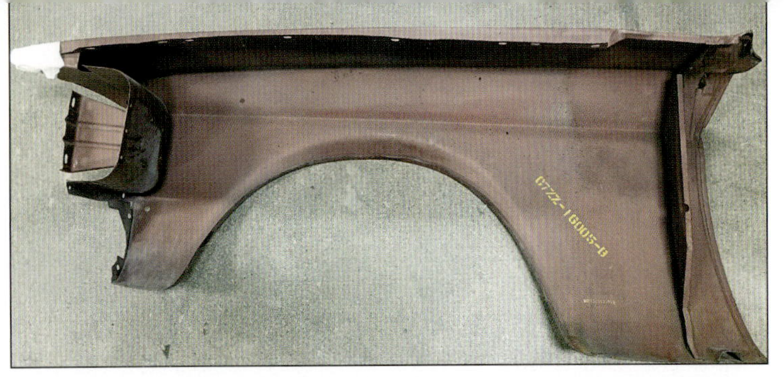

This NOS fender carries the part number C7ZZ-16005-B and is printed with the date code February 24, 1981. Early Ford sheet metal was painted in red-oxide primer, and later sheet metal was black EDP coated. Some sheet-metal dies wore out and lost some of their lines toward the end of the runs, so some restorers seek out the earlier parts.

Ford Parts Numbering System
(Sample Number C7ZZ-17A870-B)

Prefix: C7ZZ-	Base Number: 17A870	Suffix: -B
First Position = Decade of origin	Numbers range from 0000–99999	Revision level beginning with "A" preceeds A–Z, then AA, AB, etc.
Second Position = Year within decade	Letters in the base number denote an expanded base group	
Third Position = Model first used		
Fourth Position = Type of part		

First Digit = Decade
A = 1940s | B = 1950s | C = 1960s | D = 1970s | E = 1980s | F = 1990s

Second Digit = Year in Decade 0–9

Third Digit = Model First Used	Fourth Digit = Type of Part	Group Number Section (as defined in the Ford Text and Illustrations)
		1000–2999 = Paint/Wheel/Brakes
		4000–4999 = Rear axle/Driveshaft
	A = Light Truck	5000–5299 = Frame/Muffler
	B = Body and electrical	5300–5999 Front and Rear Spring/Rear Suspension
A = Full size Ford	C = Chassis	6000–6999 = Engine
B = Bronco/Maverick/Fairmont	D = Overseas	7000–7999 = Manual Transmission/Clutch
C = Remanufactured parts	E = Engine	A7000–A7999 = Automatic Transmission
D = Falcon/Maverick/Granada	F = General/Electrical	8000–8999 = Cooling/Grille
E = COE/Pinto/Escort	H = Climate control	9000–9399 = Fuel
F = Foreign/Racing	J = Autolite/Ford parts	9300A–9399B = Calibration
G = Comet/Montego/EXP	L = Industrial	9400–9999 = Carburetor/Accelerator
H = Heavy Truck/ Holmon-Moody	M = Performance/ Special vehicle	10000–12999 = Alternator/Starter/Distributor
J = Industrial/Marine	N = Tractor	13000–16999 = Lamps/Wiring/Fender/Hood
K = Edsel/Truck/Comet/Zephyr/ Marquis	P = Auto Transmission	17000–17999 = Speedometer/Bumper
L = Lincoln	R = Manual Transmission	18000–19999 = Heater/Air Conditioner
M = Mercury	S = Truck special order	**Body Parts Section: The number preceded by body-type designation: 63 (Fastback/ Sportroof), 65 (Coupe), or 76 (Convertible)**
N = Tractor	T = Heavy Truck	
O = Fairlane/Torino/LTD	U = Special Vehicle Operatons	
P = Autolite/Motorcraft	W = Axle and Driveshaft	00000–19999 = Body Front/Floor
R = Rotunda/Ford of Europe/Reman	X = Emissions/Muscle Car Parts	20000–39999 = Side Door/Pillar/Quarter Panel
S = Thunderbird	Y = Lincoln/Mercury Service Parts	40000–59999 = Back/Luggage Compartment
T = Truck/Bronco	Z = Ford Service Parts	60000–69999 = Seat
U = Econoline/Van		
V = Lincoln Continental		
W = Cougar		
X = Truck		
Y = Meteor/Bobcat/Lynx		
Z = Mustang		
2 = Pinto		
3 = Tempo		
4 = Comet/Monarch/ Cougar/Marquis		
5 = RV/ Continental		
6 = Pantera/Topaz		
7 = Courier/Ranger/Explorer		
8 = Capri (US)		
9 = Turbine		

This is a brief outline of the Ford parts numbering system. The better you learn the numbering system, the more informed you will be when seeking out parts at a swap meet.

panels, where all three bodystyles are different, the part number for a 1965 right-hand panel is C5ZZ-6327846-A for a fastback, C5ZZ-6527846-B for a coupe, and C5ZZ-7627846-B for a convertible.

Some trim may or may not have the body code that is used to designate the part. Trim parts that don't have a bodystyle designation are common to all bodystyles.

Service Parts

Items such as belts, hoses, filters, and batteries use a unique coding system. The service part in the box may or may not be the same production-line piece, and if you are restoring to a high level, you must know the difference when looking at parts. Parts with later part numbers may or may not be identical to the part that was originally installed on the car. For example, for voltage regulators, the early mechanical regulators were eventually replaced with solid-state units that function identically but look much different than the original part.

Labels and Logos

Through the first-generation production run, Ford used parts labeled "FoMoCo," "Rotunda," "Autolite,"

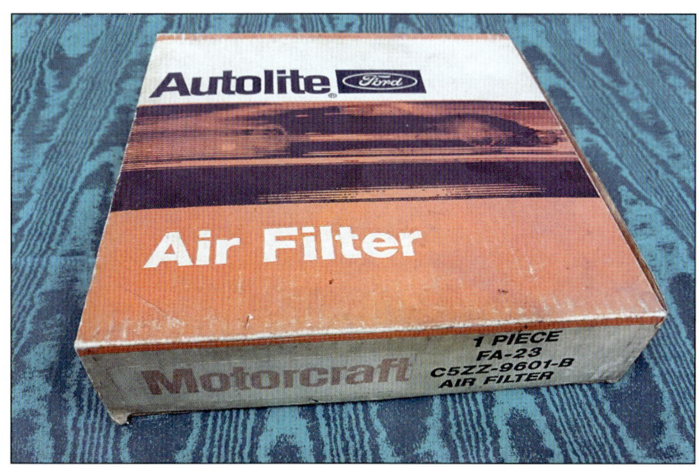

Air filters were designated with an "FA" part number. This original Autolite FA-23 was rebranded with a Motorcraft sticker probably around 1971–1972, but the filter inside was Autolite. This filter was used on 289-2V applications from 1965–1967.

Most production belts had the full part number embossed on the belt. Ford began labeling the service replacement belts with a "J" to denote V-belt, a letter "A" through "R" to denote the width of the belt, and a letter to denote the style of the belt: "L" for laminate (most Mustang belts) "C" for cog style, and "R" for racing. Later in the 1970s, Ford began to screen print the numbers on the belts. The top belt is a production belt for a 1967 289 engine with power steering (date coded March 1967 [367]), and the bottom belt is a service belt for the alternator on a 1969 250 6-cylinder engine (date coded January 1969 [169]).

Just because it is denoted with a service number on the box doesn't mean that it isn't a production-line part inside. This fuel filter is used for small-block applications and carries the FG-14 part designation, but the part inside carries the original C5UE part number, which means "Bronco line" and "Engineering group." There are several versions of this filter. The earlier version carries the "FoMoCo" script, and the later says "Motorcraft."

This distributor rotor for 6-cylinder applications says FoMoCo on the packaging but it is marked "Autolite" on the part. Only true purists care because it isn't seen after it is installed.

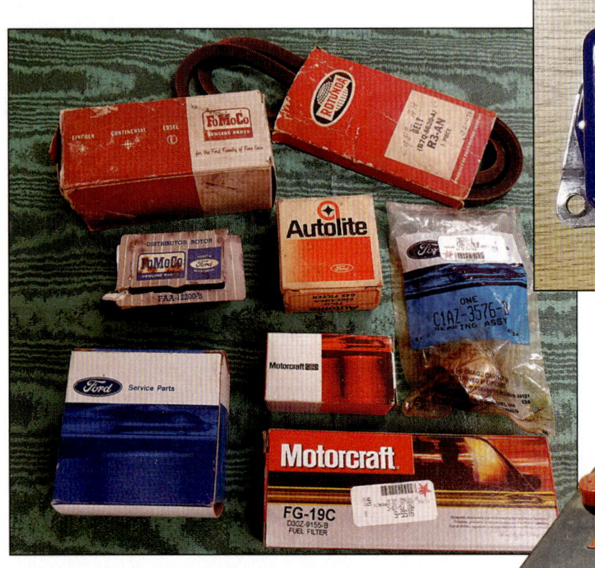

Ford packaging from over the years is shown (from old at the top to newer at the bottom). Learning the packaging may help in finding the right parts for your car, but the package doesn't always guarantee the correct part in the box. Ford made many running changes to parts through the years and changed vendors frequently.

A reproduction voltage regulator is on the left, and a new Motorcraft voltage regulator is on the right. The reproduction is an old mechanical style unit that looks like the original. The Motorcraft is a solid-state unit and will last longer but doesn't look original. Which one works best for your restoration?

Just because it looks correct doesn't mean it is good for your car. Reproduction battery manufacturers have come and gone, and this older battery split open and leaked all over a show car, causing extensive damage. Be careful when deciding which parts to install on your car.

"Motorcraft," etc. The parts that are correct for a certain year for high-end restorations depend on when the car was built. How "correct" you want to be is your choice. A 1968 Mustang with Motorcraft parts still has Ford service parts on it, but it doesn't have correct Autolite parts that match the era when it was built.

However, some reproduction parts that are marked with the correct Autolite logos may be inferior to Motorcraft replacement parts and could damage the car when they fail. Just because it looks right doesn't mean that it is good for the car.

Casting Numbers

All Ford castings have at least a partial part number and date code cast into the part. Engine blocks, heads, intakes, transmission casings, and rear-axle center carriers are all marked. High-performance parts

This 1967 cylinder head has the partial casting number "C6AE" cast into it. Performance cylinder heads usually had the full part number in the cast. The "289" denotes the small-block engine for which the head was designed.

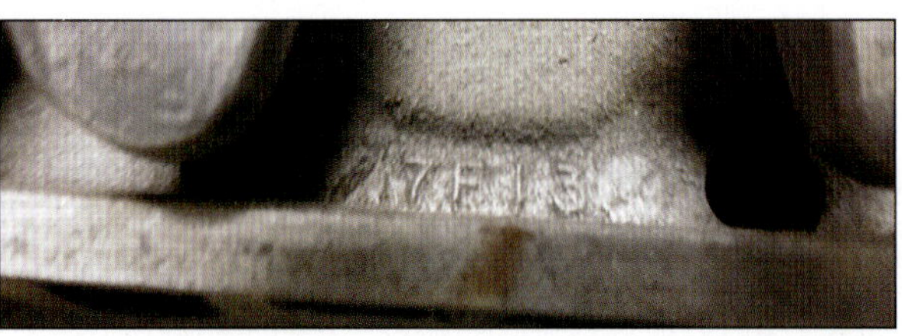

The "7F13" date code for when this cylinder head was cast denotes June 13, 1967. When trying to put together date-correct parts, make sure that the numbers fall within a month or so before your car was built. This was pulled from a July-built car.

The "C5AE-6015-E" block was used through 1967 and was also used in 289 Hi-Po applications with different main caps installed. This one is dated "5C15," which denotes March 15, 1965. The car was built on February 19, 1965, so this more than likely isn't the original motor.

generally have the entire part number cast on the part. For example, a 1968 390 GT cylinder head may only have "C8AE-H" cast into it, but a 428 Cobra Jet head has "C8OE-6090-N," which is the full part number. The date code usually consists of the year, month, and day.

Sheet-Metal Stamps

Ford sheet metal and some trim parts used a date-stamping method that did not include the year. The stamp consisted of the month, the day, the shift on which the part was made, and, in most cases, the plant where the part was made. Some panels carry the part number, but some don't. The important aspects to know are the month and day because they need to be within a month or two before the car's build date.

This trunk lid came from the same 1970 convertible, and it was made close to the same time as the apron. The "10 4 C3" code denotes October 4, third shift, Cleveland plant. Near this time, Ford also began adding the "ZB" stamp. The "Z" denotes Mustang, "B" denotes Body and Electrical, and "65" denotes coupe. Not all panels received this stamp.

Ford sheet metal uses a unique date-stamping system that doesn't specify a year, so sometimes panels made by Ford later will work on a "number's matching" body rebuild. This "LH" front apron in a 1970 convertible is stamped "10 6 D3," which denotes October 6, third shift from the Dearborn plant.

Original bumpers also received a date stamp on them, and this 1969 rear bumper is stamped "M9 69" with a date code of "4 15 1," which denotes April 15, first shift. They did not always include the plant information in the date code. Ford bumpers fit better than most reproductions, so if you are looking for an original bumper to re-chrome, look for a date code.

Glass

All factory glass came with the round CarLite logo and is identified as tinted glass with the addition of "SUN-X" below the CarLite logo. The date on the glass is in the lower right corner as a number and a letter. Windshields are marked "Laminate," and side and rear glass are marked "Tempered." Ford replacement glass carries the newer black-letter CarLite logo.

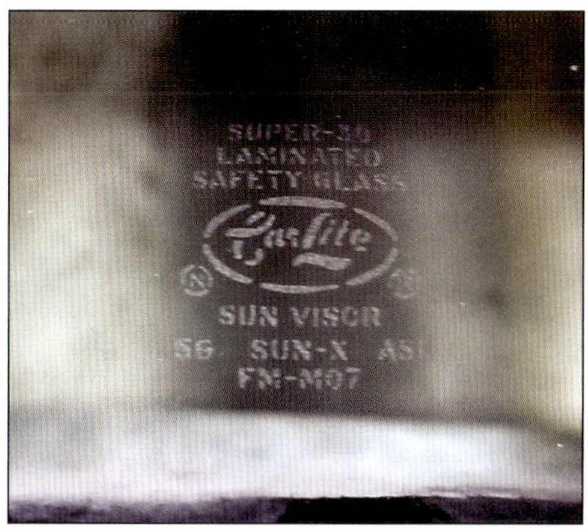

Factory tinted glass is marked "SUN-X" right under the CarLite logo, and the "LAMINATE" mark makes this a tinted windshield dated "5G" (July 1965).

All original Ford glass received the oval CarLite logo and was marked as either "LAMINATE" (windshields) or "TEMPERED" (side and rear glass). The date is in the lower left-hand corner, and "8H" stands for August 1968. This side window is from a 1969 Mustang SportsRoof.

This is a later Carlite windshield in a 1970 Mustang. The logo and style are different, and the "8B" date code is not correct for 1970. However, later Carlite glass works well in all but top show cars.

This aftermarket side glass fits just fine, but the markings are incorrect for a concours show car. Items such as incorrect glass can add up when potential buyers look at your car for restoration.

Tags

Ford used identification tags on items such as carburetors, engines, transmissions, radiators, power-steering pumps, and other parts to identify the parts and how they should be serviced. Kevin Marti's comprehensive book *The Mustang and Cougar Tagbook* covers all of these tags.

The engine tag was mounted with or near the ignition coil and helped assembly-line workers identify the engine for correct parts installation. From left to right, this tag decodes as the following: "351" denotes the engine size, "C" denotes the Cleveland factory, "73" denotes 1973, and "6" was the change level for this engine. On the lower line, "A29" denotes January 29, 1973, and the engine code, which gets tricky: "K" denotes EGR, non-Thermactor, non-California, "620" denotes a 351 Q-Code 4-barrel automatic, "A" denotes the first year of the cycle for 1973, and "G" denotes that this engine would have an A/C compressor mounted to it. So, this tag is for a January-built 1973 Q-Code 351 Cleveland automatic with air conditioning.

Build Sheets

If you a fortunate enough to find a build sheet in your vehicle, it provides a considerable amount of information that can help you restore your car. This sheet went down the assembly

This axle tag from a 1970 Shelby GT350 decodes as follows. Starting with the top line (left to right), the "WFB-D" denotes the axle code for the 351 with 3.00 locking gears (code "O" on the door tag), the date code "9DE" denotes the year (1969, which is "9"), the month (April, which is "D"), and the week (fifth, which is "E"). On the bottom line, "3L00" denotes a 3.00:1 gear ratio with a Traction-Lok differential, "9" denotes a 9-inch housing, and "986A" is the plant manufacturing code and revision level.

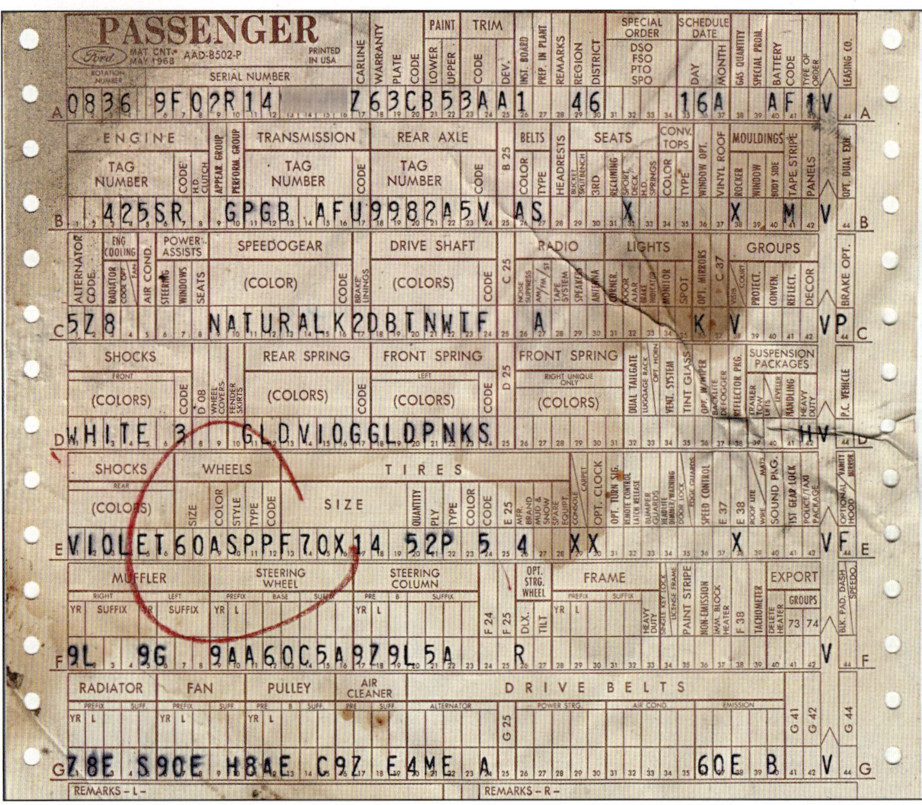

PASSENGER

Ford MAT CNT• MAY 1968 AAD-8502-P PRINTED IN USA

SERIAL NUMBER

A 0836 9F02R14 Z63CB53AA1 46 16A AF1V A

ENGINE — TRANSMISSION — REAR AXLE — BELTS — SEATS — MOULDINGS

B 425SR GPGB AFU9982A5V AS X X M V B

SPEEDOGEAR (COLOR) — DRIVE SHAFT (COLORS) — RADIO — LIGHTS — GROUPS

C 5Z8 NATURAL K2DB TNWIF A K V VP C

SHOCKS — REAR SPRING — FRONT SPRING — FRONT SPRING — SUSPENSION PACKAGES

D WHITE 3 GLD VIOG GLDPNKS HV D

SHOCKS — WHEELS — TIRES

E VIOLET 60ASPPF70X14 52P 5 4 XX X VF E

MUFFLER — STEERING WHEEL — STEERING COLUMN — FRAME — EXPORT

F 9L 9G 9AA60C5A979L5A R V F

RADIATOR — FAN — PULLEY — AIR CLEANER — DRIVE BELTS

G Z8E S90E H8AE C9Z E4ME A 60E B V G

REMARKS – L – REMARKS – R –

If you are lucky enough to find one, the factory build sheet tells you what it told the assembly line workers when building your car: the parts that were designated to be installed on the car. This one is actually in pretty good shape. It separated at some point, and the lower portion got wet, while the good part stayed dry. If you find one, it will most likely come out in pieces.

line with the car and indicated which specific parts were to be installed on the vehicle. Springs and other components are identified by color codes, and some items, such as deluxe wheels and upgrades, were noted as well as the base color and trim combinations.

Frequently, build sheets were left in the car, and they can usually be found under the seats, under the carpet and underlayment, under the dash area, or under the trunk underlayment. They are generally in poor shape, so take great care when retrieving a build sheet.

Distributors

Ford used the same distributor housing for many applications and simply changed the parts inside to suit the application. The base number for distributors, 12127, is cast into the housing, and the correct application is stamped into the housing during a secondary process. The date code is a three-digit date with the year, month, and week. Then, it was changed to the year, month, and day.

Carburetors

All Ford carburetors came with an identification tag. The tag contains the carburetor's basic information, and these tags frequently were lost or not reinstalled after the first rebuild. Every factory carburetor has the application stamped on the body of the carburetor. On FoMoCo, Autolite, and Motorcraft carburetors, it is stamped on the base of the carburetor. On Holley carburetors, it is stamped on the air horn. A three- or four-digit date code was also stamped on Holley carburetors along with the Ford part number.

The Ford factory carburetor tag usually didn't make it back onto the carburetor after the first rebuild. This one codes out for a 1969 Boss 302: "C" denotes the 1960s, "9" denotes the ninth year in the 1960s, "Z" denotes Mustang, "F" denotes General/Electrical, and "J" denotes a Boss 302 4V. On the lower line, "A" denotes the revision level, and "9DA" denotes the date code. The "9" denotes 1969, "D" denotes April, and "A" denotes the first week of the month.

The distributor housing was used for many different applications, so the base number "12127" was cast into the housing. The specific use was stamped on after the distributor was assembled. This C5AF-12127-N is a 289-2V distributor with a "6F10" date code, which denotes June 10, 1966.

These are four different small-block distributors with four different markings. From left to right is an early FoMoCo distributor for a 1964 with an external oiling port and round FoMoCo logo, a 1966 distributor with the square FoMoCo logo, a 1969 distributor with the Autolite logo, and a 1972-and-up distributor with a Motorcraft logo. The parts for a show car should reflect the era in which it was built.

Reference Books

As part of any Mustang restoration project, there are other helpful reference books to consider in addition to this book. They will answer 80 percent of the questions you may have when restoring your car. Most of the factory manuals are available on CD, and some may be available online with a subscription. Most of these references are available from Mustang parts vendors.

Each year, a set of factory shop manuals cover the chassis, engine, electrical system, body, and maintenance. These manuals are available

If a Ford carburetor is missing the data tag, Ford stamped some of the information on the housings at the base. This one is stamped "8ZG." The "8" denotes 1968, "Z" denotes Mustang, and "G" denotes the calibration, which is for a 289-2V automatic. With this information, you can get a replacement tag made.

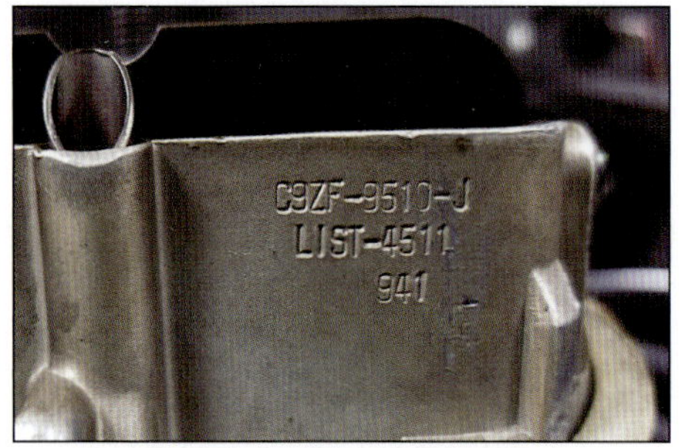

Factory Holley carburetors were stamped on the air horn with the Ford part number. For this carburetor, the part number is "C9ZF-9510-J" for a 1969 Boss 302. The date code that matches the tag, "941," is the first week of April 1969.

in reprint and on CD.

Factory assembly manuals are available as reprints from Osborn Reproductions, and they cover the assembly procedures for the shop manual groups. Although concours builders find them frustrating (Ford did not always follow the correct procedure or engineering recommendations, so some of the information is not valid), they are an invaluable tool to help with learning what parts go where and how to reassemble your Mustang.

AMK Products performed extensive research into the nuts and bolts that make up the Mustang and published the book *AMK Products: Guide to Ford Fasteners 1955–1973* about fasteners. Details include what type of fasteners were used, how the finish on the fasteners look, and a list of the part numbers. This book, in conjunction with the factory assembly manuals, helps you understand how to replace those hardware-store bolts that you found when disassembling your project.

Mustang & Ford Small Block V8: 1962–1969 by Bob Mannel is a well-done book that looks at unrestored original small-block engines and decodes everything that you need to put your engine back to its correct configuration. This is a valuable tool when you want to determine which parts will or will not work with your engine. It is the bible for small-block Fords.

Vacuum and electric system schematics and diagrams are available as aftermarket reprints. Large-print originals may also be found. These show all of the electric and vacuum circuits for your car. They also include component locations and where items should be mounted.

Although most of the decoding information is now online, I enjoy having the reference book *Mustang Decoder Book* handy in the shop or on the show field for quick reference.

The *Mustang and Cougar Tag Book* by Kevin Marti takes some of the information that I provide in this book and thoroughly explains tags and numbers in detail. It is a must-have item for a high-level restoration.

The *Mustang Recognition Guide* by Larry Dobbs, Donald Farr, Jerry Heasley, and Rick Kopec is an older book, but it is one of the most used books on my shelf. I highly recommend it.

The book *1964–1966 Convertible Top Repair Manual* is a must-have item for convertible owners and also provides excellent information for 1967–1973 Mustang owners.

If you plan to paint the car yourself, invest in the *Paintucation* series of how-to videos by Kevin Tetz or join his group online.

The once-huge *Ford Text and Illustration* books have now been put on CD, and they include all of the information subdivided into smaller reprints. They are available from Mustang vendors. These books include items not found in the abridged reprints. Note that most of the information reprinted is from the final version, which was printed in 1975. Some of the data reflects Fords part changes, and some of the information was not included in the final version, but they are still must-have items for a full restoration.

Although the book *Ford Performance* is oriented toward performance, author Pat Ganahl includes casting and part identification information for all Ford engines in first-generation Mustangs.

Finally, a visit to CarTech's website (cartechbooks.com) via the quick-response (QR) code below features complete step-by-step rebuild books for all of this era's engines, transmissions, and differentials. See Chapters 6 and 7 for recommendations of books on specific engines and transmissions.

Disassembly and Storage

By 1966, Ford had sold 1 million Mustangs, and to celebrate the milestone, it built 50 Mustangs in special Anniversary Gold paint. This replica is painted that color and has a 289 engine with a C4 automatic transmission, and a black deluxe Pony interior. (Photo Courtesy Mark Houlahan)

Bag and label your bolts. I denote the quantity, the Ford number for the bolt, and the finish. If I have a batch of bolts that need to go to the plater, I can put them right back in the bags and, if necessary, look up the exact style in my reference books.

Preparation in the early stages of a restoration project keeps you from frustration later. Make sure that your work area is ready to take on this project. From this point forward, your local Mustang "expert" may read what I have written and disagree. However, I will provide the reasons why I restore a specific way. There is a method to my madness.

Work Area and Parts Storage

A completely disassembled Mustang is comprised of thousands of parts from the hood to the smallest hardware, and disassembled parts require a tremendous amount of storage space. The area where you live may influence how you store the parts. In dry climates you may be able to use a public storage barn, but damper climates may require you to consider a different location. Stuffing parts in cubbyholes and forgetting where they are is a bad idea. Evaluate your storage area and plan where items will go. If possible, bundle items together (such as interior pieces) so that you don't have to search several areas when you go back to assemble the car.

Bolt storage and organization are critical. Many bolts look alike, so use a system to keep the small parts organized. Electrical parts cabinets, disposable food tubs, small parts trays, and sandwich bags work well for organization.

Totes, electrical-parts cabinets, and tackle boxes work well to store small items and group them together. Try to keep similar items, such as interior pieces or chassis pieces, together in totes so they can be easily found.

Digital photography is your friend when disassembling a car. Take pictures of where things are routed, any factory markings that you find, and how things such as brakes are assembled. The more photos the better.

A disassembled Mustang takes up a lot of space. Storing items in an outdoor shed is an option, but be careful. Just covering seats with bags may not keep critters out of the upholstery. Oil or paint on metal parts helps keep them from deteriorating while in storage.

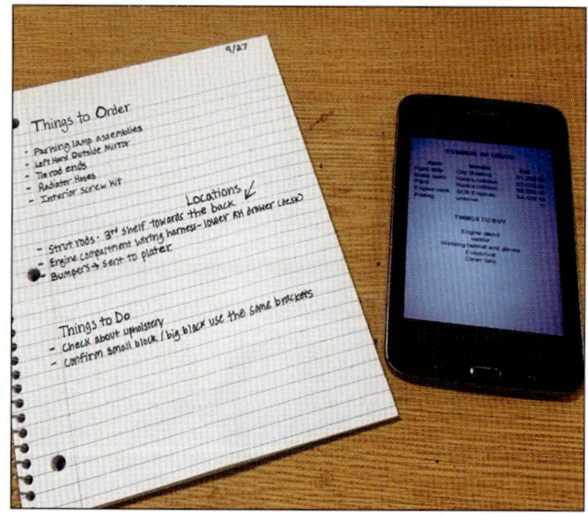

A journal helps you keep track of everything. You can also write down what needs to go where, important contact numbers, parts that you need to find or purchase, and anything else that is related to the project. Keeping a journal on your phone allows you to keep the photos with the journal entries, which is a nice advantage.

Documentation

Regardless of the level of restoration, document what you are doing. This includes labeling parts, using digital photography, and writing in a notebook. Documenting now increases your efficiency during reassembly.

Journals are great for keeping track of any questions, parts that need to be ordered, and where parts are located.

Start a journal. Assess the car and begin a journal with what needs to be done. Some items may be obvious (perhaps a paint job or a big dent pull), but others may not be. So, use a lift to inspect the car if you can. Depending on the level of restoration that you want, list the items that need attention.

Look for items that need to be replaced and start a "Purchase" list. If you are using only Ford original parts, start a "Hunt for" list. Rare parts show up for sale and then go away. If you are scanning the internet for parts and have your list handy, you may find parts over the course of the restoration—not just when you need it to finish the restoration. Determine which items must be refurbished (for example: chrome, upholstery, etc.) and get plans together. Some platers require a minimum weight or count for replating parts.

Paintless Dent Repair

Before tearing down the car, consider paintless dent repair. After 50 years, the car has received its share of dents, and now is the time to repair these before the paint is stripped from the car. Here's the rule of thumb: as long as the dent hasn't been creased (like a fold in a piece of paper), the dent most likely can be removed. This is a much cleaner way to remove dents than using body dolly work later, and it reduces the amount of filler that is needed. By doing paintless dent removal before the paint is stripped, the dents are much easier to see.

Align the body panels before the weight comes off of the car. This car is being aligned with the big-block and drivetrain intact and with the weight on all four tires.

Before the paint has been removed and teardown begins, my paintless dent guy fixes any dents that don't require body filler.

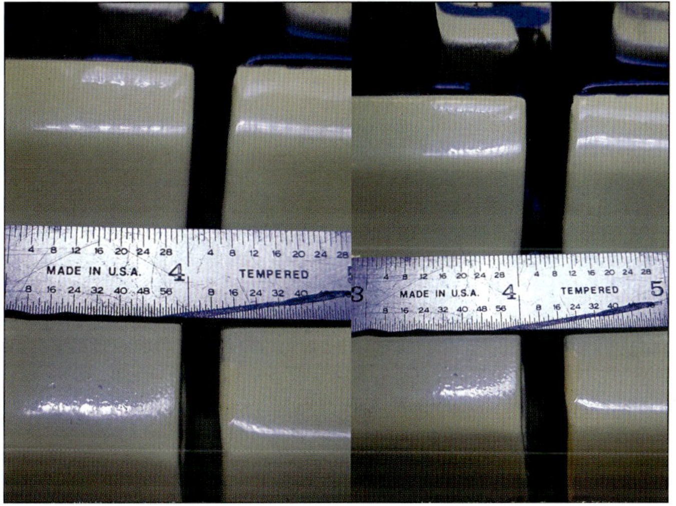

This shows how the size of a door gap changes before and after this convertible has been lifted into the air. The gap widens 3/16 inch, which means that the chassis is bending. This is why you align panels on the car with the weight on the chassis and tires.

Panel Alignment

Body panel alignment must occur before disassembly. The Mustang didn't get the nickname "the Hinge" for nothing. My second restoration project was a 1968 Shelby GT500, and the car came to me from the paint shop pretty and straight. I put a big FE engine in it, and I couldn't open the doors—they were hitting the fenders. When I lift a convertible on my two-post lift, I can watch the door line go away as it is raised into the air. For this reason, make sure that your body panels line up properly before you disassemble the car.

If you add aftermarket items, such as subframe connectors, make sure that they are installed before you remove the weight from the car. Otherwise, you may weld them into place and the car may not go back together correctly. Proper body panel alignment must be done with the weight of the car sitting on the wheels.

Disassembly

Where you start and how far you go is determined by how far you take the restoration. The Mustang is a unibody, which means that the sheet metal makes up the structural rigidity of the vehicle. So, structural metal, such as quarter panels and

Be careful when handling barn-fresh projects. Nature's critters tend to leave messes that can be hazardous to your health. A friend of mine once found a live racoon behind a door panel!

floor pans, can affect the straightness of the body when they are rusted out or removed. Whether you are planning to install the body on a rotisserie for repair or you plan to do the work on jack stands, secure and support the vehicle to minimize movement during disassembly. Before you remove the first part, document the car.

Cars that have been stored for a long time become home to unwanted guests, and those guests don't leave the car in a healthy state. Animal contamination is unhealthy and can make you sick. Use proper protection when removing nests and animal waste. Seats and upholstery that absorb urine and other matter need to be cleaned or replaced (if possible). Sanitize the vehicle before disassembly.

Hood

If you are only rebuilding the engine and not tearing down the body, mark the location of the hood and hood spring (if you remove them) with tape so that they can be reassembled in the correct position. This reduces the time to align the hood.

If you are doing repairs only and not replacing or painting, mark items with automotive tape to make reassembly much easier. Photos of gaps and approximate locations of hardware make reassembly easier.

Engine and Transmission

Removing the drivetrain can make a mess. You can't drain all of the coolant out of the block. So, when you twist and tilt the drivetrain, fluid will find its way out. Plan to do some cleanup.

Removing the exhaust pipes from the manifolds is one of the most difficult aspects of removing the engine. If you have time, spray penetrating oil onto the bolts for a few days before removal. It helps to allow several days for it to work.

If you plan to remove the engine and transmission together, consider using an engine-lift bar, which allows easy tilting of the engine. If you remove only the engine, mount a lift plate to the carburetor mounting pad on the intake to reduce potential damage from lifting from the ends. Make sure that your lifting device is capable of removing the engine. An FE engine weighs about 750 pounds, and moving a hoist with the arms all the way out drastically reduces the amount of weight that can be safely lifted.

If you own a big-block, you already know that there is very little room in the engine compartment. Generally, it is better to lift an FE engine out of the engine bay separately from the transmission. C6 and Toploader transmissions add a considerable amount of weight to the combination, and tilting something that already barely fits is not the best choice.

Removing the engine and transmission together depends on a few variables: the lift device, the ceiling height, and how high you can get the vehicle off the ground. Lifting the combination high enough to clear requires the boom on the engine lift to be extended to allow

Owners of 1967–1970 big-block cars know that there is not much room in the engine compartment, and extra care is required when removing and installing the drivetrain to prevent scratches and damage.

for its maximum height in the air. The farther out that the boom goes, the lower the lift's weight capability. The higher the lift that is required, the higher ceiling clearance is needed. The longer the engine/transmission combination, the higher in the air the vehicle needs to be so that the transmission can swing into position.

Air Conditioning

If your car is equipped with air conditioning and still has the R-12 refrigerant in it, safely recover the refrigerant for two reasons: 1) it's bad for the environment and 2) it is outrageously expensive to replace if you are not upgrading to a modern system.

Whether the air-conditioning system has original R-12 or an R-134 conversion refrigerant, evacuate any remaining refrigerant from the system. R-12 is expensive, so don't just unhook the lines and release it into the atmosphere. Also, make sure that you don't pay for your own refrigerant when they put it back in.

Interior

The front seats come out by removing the four plugs under the car and using a long 1/2-inch socket and extension. The nuts are unique for the seats in a Mustang. Removing the seats first provides space for crawling under the dash.

Depending on the year of your Mustang, the steering column has either a long shaft from the steering box or a coupler that is mounted in the engine compartment. All columns are attached to the dash via a mounting bracket. Mark the location of the bracket with tape, and when you remove the column from the car, measure the tape from one end and remove it if you are refinishing the steering column. Once you have completed refinishing the column, reapply the tape, and installation will be easier.

Remove the seats from the underside of the floor pan with a deep-well 1/2-inch socket and extension. The bolts are located under four rubber plugs. The nuts are a special design with a captive washer.

Removing the carpet usually reveals some history of the car. Look carefully after removal for items that may damage the carpet (metal objects may find their way under the carpet) and look for the build sheet.

Removal of the dash pad and instrument cluster helps you access nearly everything else under the dash. As the cars evolved, the dash area became more complex and crowded. Early Mustangs were simple with simple heaters and wiring. Then, in 1967, they had in-dash air conditioning and a tilt steering wheel, and it continued to get more crowded from there. In early Mustangs, the dash metal was welded to the car, but starting in 1969, it was bolted to the car. This allows you to remove the dash with the wiring intact to the dash. Take photos of wiring-harness and connector locations and mark the wires and

Another location for tape is on the steering column. There is a slot on the early columns to allow for adjustment. Mark the location of the column with tape or a scribe mark. Then, measure to one end and photograph if you are going to repaint the column to note the location.

The 1964–1968 lower-dash metal is welded into the interior, and the lower dash is removable from 1969 onward. This allows you to remove and install most of the wiring harness in place, which is a great time saver and also means spending less time upside down on your back when reinstalling dash components.

where they connect before removal.

Most window and door cranks are attached with Phillips screws. If you plan to reuse the door panels, invest in panel-clip pliers to help remove the panels. The panels are made of pressboard and bend easily if you try to pry them off with a screwdriver or other tool. In addition, be careful that the spring clips don't pull through the mounting slots on the panel. When pulling off the water shields, pull slowly because they are attached with a bead of non-hardening sealer. If you plan to strip and repaint the doors, take a photo of how the sealer was laid on the door to replicate it later.

If you plan to replace the headliner, the headliner tucks up under the front and rear glass, so removal and installation occurs with the glass out of the car. The headliner bows are color coded and need to be put back in the correct holes, so mark the holes in which the headliner bows were installed. I generally remove the headliner, mark the front and back, and roll it up with the bows in the sleeves so that they don't get out of

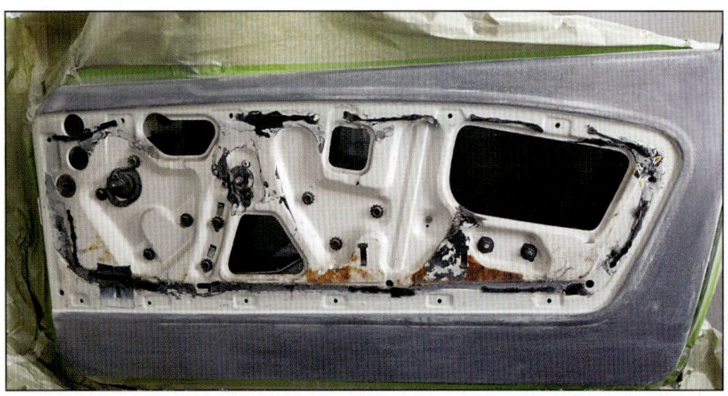
If you don't have a set of the factory assembly manuals, take a photo of items such as the inner door panels where the water-shield sealant was applied. After you paint the door, it is easy to reproduce the strip caulk to hold the shield.

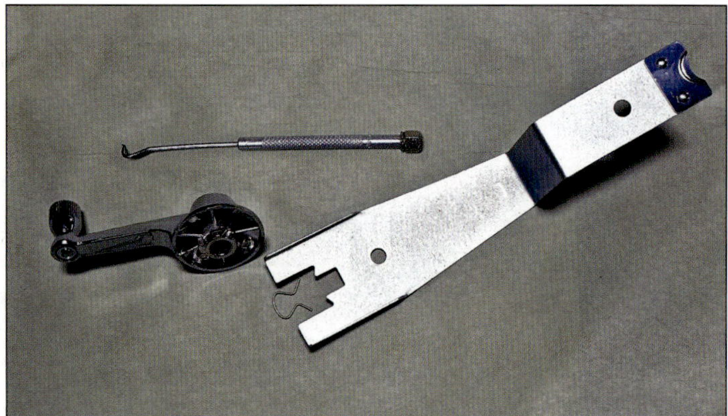
Early 1964–1965 cars used a clip to hold the door handles and window-regulator handles in place. Use this fancy tool to remove and install them or use a dental pick and blunt bar. There is less chance of damage with the correct tool.

The headliner bow location may have two holes for the bow to install in the roof. Scribe or mark which hole the bow was installed in for easier reassembly.

One of the more frustrating items to remove from the car is the strut-rod bushings. The longer they have been on the car, the harder it is to remove them. The inner sleeve rusts to the strut rod, and the rubber welds itself to the inner sleeve. I have had to drill them out.

Take out the old headliner and headliner bows as an assembly. Then, keep the bows in place for storage. This keeps them in order for reassembly. Bag the rear springs and wires if used and keep them with the headliner.

This little tool allows you to remove the lower control arms on the front suspension with the springs and upper control arm in place. Instructions for making one and using it are found in the shop manual. It's a nice tool to have. If you are in a club or group, make one for everyone to borrow when needed.

order. Then, when you are ready to install the new headliner, just transfer the bows in order.

Convertible Top

Carefully inspect the convertible top and framing for damage before removal. The whole frame is attached by six bolts that mount behind the quarter side covers as well as the tack strips along the back row. If you are only replacing the top, you can leave the frame in place. However, document where items such as the side cables and tack strip go as you remove the top. Inspect the tack strips for damage because they tend to crumble. If you intend to tear the convertible top frame down to refinish it, note and document where all of the pieces attach to each other. Be careful when removing the plastic fluid lines from the convertible top's side pistons. The piston housings are aluminum, and the fittings are brass, so it is very easy to strip the piston threads.

Front Suspension and Springs

Take caution and safety into account when removing the suspension. The front coil springs are under a great amount of kinetic energy when they are compressed to remove, so improper removal creates a dangerous situation. Make sure that

Get rid of the old pickle fork, especially if you plan to reuse your tie-rod ends and ball joints. Ball-joint separators minimize damage and are usually available through auto-parts store loan-a-tool programs.

Be very careful when using a front coil-spring compressor. There is a lot of kinetic energy when you compress the spring, and it can be dangerous. Most inside compressors look like this one with hooks. Plate-style compressors tend to be a little safer.

your removal tools are in excellent condition. I have seen one break, and the coil spring shot out and stuck in the wall.

In addition, note that the suspension is big, heavy and has lived under the car all of this time. It is the most difficult part (as far as loosening bolts goes) that you will likely encounter.

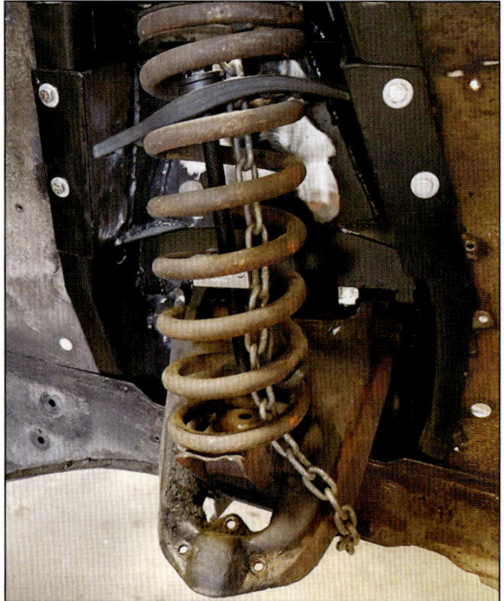

When disassembling, I run a safety chain through the spring to contain the spring if something slips or breaks while removing the spring. It's better for the car to take the hit than you.

Original strut-rod bushings tend to weld themselves to the inner sleeve and to the strut mount, so spray them with penetrating oil for several days in preparation. The older the rubber bushings, the harder they are to remove. Document the bushing stack, nuts, washers, and sleeves for correct reassembly.

If you are only removing the lower control arms, there is a tool that sits between the upper control arm and the frame rail and removes the tension from the lower spindle and control arm so that they can be removed. Dimensions to make this tool are contained in the factory chassis shop manual.

Whether the components are originals or recent replacements, inspect the tie-rods and ball joints for torn dust seals and for wear. If the stud is difficult and tight to move, they are okay. If they move fairly easily, replace them.

As previously stated, there is a lot of energy in a compressed front coil spring, so use extreme caution. Don't use an impact wrench when tightening the compressor tool. This will damage the tool. Once the springs have been removed, immediately loosen the compressor and release the energy in the spring.

Power Steering

Mark the power-steering lines and photograph the direction in which they are laid to replicate the lines

These two hex holes are on the driver-side frame rail, and Ford used a hex insert rivet to mount the power-steering bracket to this frame rail. The hex rivet crushed and held against this hole, but rust and the power-steering piston pulling against the bracket will strip this hole. Then, the rivet will just spin, and you can't remove the bracket. If this happens, you may have to weld a nut or rivet in place to reinstall the bracket.

during assembly. Inspect the lines for cracking and damage, and unless they are in good shape and only to be used on a full show car, replace them. Never trust 50-plus-year-old hoses for regular use.

Carefully remove the driver-side piston mounting bracket from the frame. This bracket uses hexagonal thread inserts on the bottom of the frame, and they regularly strip the frame upon removal.

The rear spring-shackle bushings can be extremely difficult to remove from the frame rail, and it is difficult to get tools in place to remove them. Channellocks, spray lubricant, time, and contortioning are usually required.

Rear Suspension and Axle

Remove the axle and springs as an assembly or one at a time. The key in each case is to remove the weight and compression from the leaf springs before removal. Raise the rear of the car and place safety stands on the rear frame to allow the axle to hang. Place a support under the axle. At this point, remove the rear axle from the springs or remove the springs from the axle.

If the shocks start to spin during removal, use a strap wrench on the shock body to hold the shock while your partner removes the shock nut from the interior.

Rear shock absorbers that have been in place for a long time can be difficult to remove and require a second person inside the vehicle and one person holding the shock from underneath.

Some owners pull the rear axle with the springs attached, and some do each part separately. The key is to get the tension off of the rear springs. Support the body in front of the rear springs to allow the springs to relax. Then, separate the axle from the springs. Support the axle and then remove the springs.

Fuel Tank

The fuel tank from 1965–1970 is removed through the trunk and is attached with screws from the top side. Fuel tanks had a drain plug installed until the middle of May 1969. Then, Ford stopped using a drain plug. Drain or siphon the fuel out of the tank prior to removing the tank. If you plan to reuse the fuel tank, empty it and use compressed air to dry it out completely. A small amount of fuel left in the tank can crystallize and clog a new fuel system after it is installed. Be cautious when

This cutaway view shows what happens to a fuel tank when a vehicle sits for long periods of time. Ethanol fuels release water vapor into the tank, which rusts the tank from the inside out. Old gas can also varnish up the fuel system. The entire fuel system of this car had to be replaced.

If you are planning to purchase new window seals, the best way to avoid breaking the glass is to just cut through the seal and peel off the top to remove the glass. The seal just pulls out after the glass has been removed.

If you are planning to reuse the seal, slowly work the seal up and over the lip using a soft tool and gently push the glass out with the seal. Freeing the top and sides is usually all that is required.

In 1971, Ford stopped making the fuel tank part of the trunk floor and mounted the tank underneath with straps. These straps can be difficult to remove due to rust and debris buildup.

using cleaners to clean the tank because they are usually highly flammable. Remove the sending unit and inspect it for corrosion and damage.

Glass

Until 1969, Ford used a gasket on the windshield. Then, it changed to a butyl bedding for the glass. If you remove the glass and do not reuse the gasket, it is less risky to cut the glass out of the gasket than try to pull the gasket out with the glass.

If you want to save the gasket, the Ford shop manual says to loosen the gasket and push it out of the car. The way to do this is the same way to install glass. Insert a draw string (see Chapter 12) or a soft tool through one of the corners, peel the inner lip, and tuck it under the body lip as you go. Then, carefully push the glass up and out of the car.

For cars with butyl front sealant, use a draw line (it looks like a small piece of cable) to cut through the butyl all the way around and gently push out the window. Never pry on the windows. If you do, they will shatter.

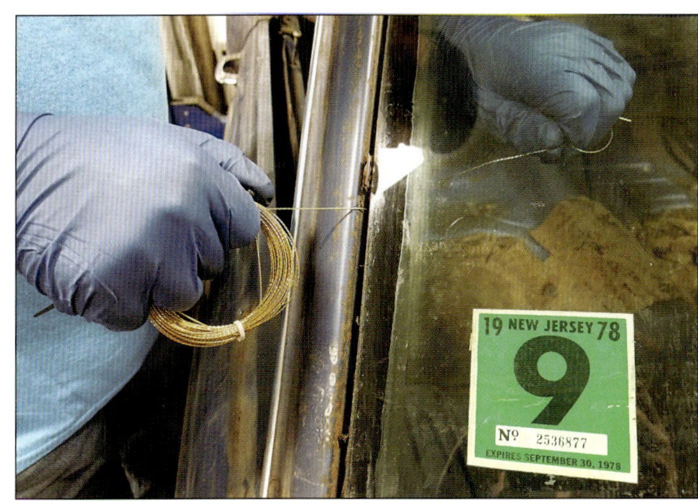

The 1969-and-up cars used a butyl adhesive to hold the windshield in place. Automotive stores sell wire specifically for cutting through the butyl. Use soft wedge tools to hold up the glass and not allow it the to re-fuse back together.

Rotisseries

A rotisserie is a wonderful tool for making repairs on areas that are difficult to reach. Most rotisseries attach to the front and back of the body and allow you to rotate the vehicle 360 degrees. Unlike some rotisseries that are made for a generic application, using a rotisserie on a Mustang requires different rules.

Because the Mustang chassis is a unibody, there is no heavy frame that holds it together. Early coupes and fastbacks did not come with torque boxes to tie the inner frames to the outer frame rails, so the Mustang unibody can be very flimsy.

One of the most basic designs for a rotisserie features two tall engine stands, but this design has problems. Holding the Mustang unibody at both ends (typically the bumper mounts) allows the body to flex. When you start cutting out body panels for rust repair, the body loses even more rigidity and may not go back together the same way. The unibody must be secured along the entire length of the vehicle as much as possible.

Build a Body Buck

After the car has been disassembled, you need a way to move it around. One of the simplest ways to do so is to build a body buck, dolly, or cart. These can be as simple as a four-sided square on which to place the body or something that converts from a dolly to a rotisserie (like professionals use). Keep the following things in mind when building a dolly:

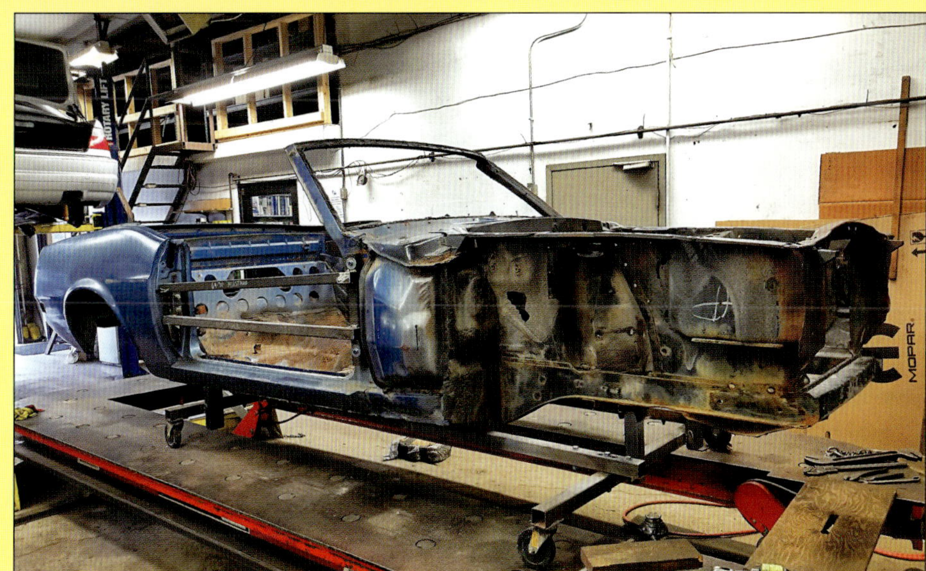

Simple body dollies can be welded together from 2-inch square tubing and general-purpose hardware-store wheels. After teardown, this convertible needed a trip to the frame shop to fix a twist, and the dolly rolled up onto our trailer and worked with the frame machine.

1. The Mustang unibody weighs between 750 and 1,000 pounds (or more), depending on the year, so design the dolly to handle that much weight.
2. When selecting casters, use heavy-duty casters that can handle the weight. Also, the larger the caster, the easier it rolls on uneven surfaces.
3. While you do not have to make it bolt down for rolling around your shop area, if you need to transport it somewhere (for example, the paint shop or blaster), it is better if the body is bolted to the dolly.
4. After 50 years, your unibody will probably not match the dimensions that Ford listed for your vehicle, so build the dolly to the dimensions of your car. You may have to straighten it after the frame has been tweaked. ■

First, make sure that the front and rear mounts are tied together with a brace so that the two ends move together. If you pull one end and they are not tied together, you are relying on the flimsy unibody to keep everything together, and that does not work well and something will probably bend.

Since a unibody vehicle can flex more than a body-on-frame vehicle, the unibody must be secured in more places than just the front and rear bumper mounts. This setup may work with heavy frame cars, but for the same reason that the ends are tied together, a system to secure the front and rear rotation points together is needed. Spinning the car on a rotisserie without the rotation points tied together twists the body. The more you can bolt to the frame, the less movement will occur when cutting off panels for repair. Lock down the Mustang unibody so that it stays put when you start installing new panels.

The bigger the wheel size, the better. Large wheels roll easier than small wheels on gravel, and if you are taking the body to be stripped, you may have to roll on uneven surfaces. Select a unit with large wheels for easier transport.

A proper rotisserie for bodywork holds the body at multiple points—not just the front and rear bumper mounts. The bases are held together with a central rod, and the front and rear mounts are held by two long side rails. Everything moves in sync; nothing is getting twisted.

This photo shows why the central rails are a good idea. Note the plate that ties the transmission-tunnel brace to the rotisserie. The more connection points you have, the less the body will move while installing replacement panels. Additional mounting points can be along the entire length of the unibody.

This rotisserie converts to a body dolly for fitting quarter panels and doors. After the quarter panels were mounted, the car went right back up on the rotisserie for underside work.

Width

The wider the wheel on the rotisserie, the more stable the unit is when it is rotated. Unfortunately, if you plan to transport the body for any reason, such as media blasting, it needs to be able to ride safely on a trailer. Most open car trailers use an 8- or 8½-foot-wide platform. Some are as narrow as 77 inches, and some are as wide as 102 inches. Make sure that your unit fits properly and safely on the transport platform.

If you are looking to purchase a rotisserie, the Roller Hoop is a great unit. The hoop ensures that the car can't tip over, and the car can be braced like this one to keep the body from flexing when making repairs. It is great for shops that don't have much space because it isn't wide and the car center is much lower to the ground. (Photo courtesy Roller Hoop)

Balance

The mounting points for the bumpers on a Mustang chassis are not on the same plane. One resides below the center of rotation, and one is above. Most rotisserie manufacturers note this and can make these adjustments, but if you are building your own rotisserie, note that you can't use the same straight mount on both ends. Coupes and fastbacks are more top heavy and have a different rotational center than convertibles, which use a second inner rocker to compensate for the missing roof.

I designed my rotisserie originally for a convertible, and my setup allows for one-man rotation on a convertible because of where I placed the center rotation axis. When I install cars with roofs, they tend to be top heavy, and it requires two people to stabilize the car for rotation. Search for a unit that allows a neutral rotation axis for the chassis.

Height

Because the vehicle must be able to rotate 360 degrees, the height of the unit is important. You don't want the roof to contact the center post or ground. The problem with going too high is that the higher you go,

The balance of the car is important on the rotisserie. The centerline for coupes and fastbacks is different than convertibles due to weight distribution. This one was designed for convertibles, and one-handed operation rotates the chassis. Coupes and fastbacks tend to be top heavy and require a little more effort to hold the car.

the wider the base wheels need to be, and that can restrict transporting the unit. Also, when transporting a well-balanced rotisserie with the ability to swing completely on its back, you can transport the unit without it sticking up in an enclosed trailer.

Helpful Brackets

If you are doing a partial restoration and are working only in specific areas, the following three photos show ideas to keep your car mobile and in place while you work on it.

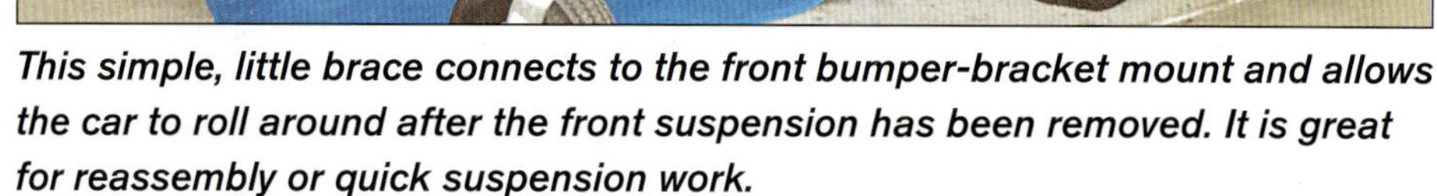

This simple, little brace connects to the front bumper-bracket mount and allows the car to roll around after the front suspension has been removed. It is great for reassembly or quick suspension work.

This rear brace aids in moving the car after the rear suspension has been removed. Note that the bracket uses the spring-mount positions.

This fixture was custom built to allow the fenders and hood to be painted as an assembly in the booth. Blending paint with this type of fixture works great.

CHAPTER 4

Body Preparation and Bodywork

The year 1967 saw the first major redesign of the Mustang, which was mainly to accommodate the new big-block 390 V-8 engine. This 1967 GT fastback is owned by Thomas Bruening of Germany. The car was originally from Atlanta, Georgia, so it is not a T5. It is powered by the 320-hp 390 with a 4-speed Top-loader. (Photo Courtesy Manuel Wiemann)

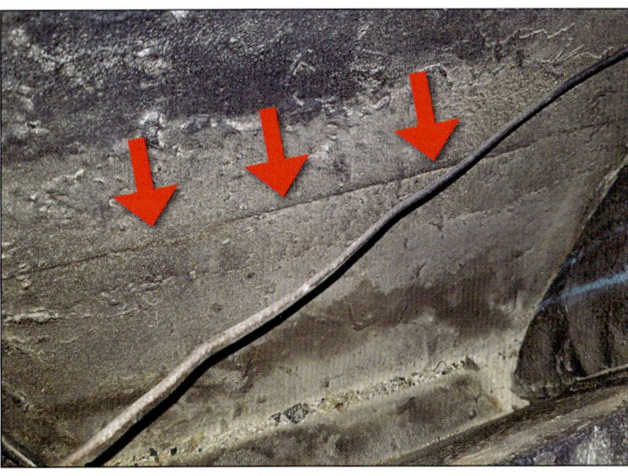

This 1967 Mustang was restored back in the early 1980s, when flange-welding patch panels was common practice. This type of restoration is generally not acceptable by today's standards, and the weld line sticks out like a sore thumb to judges and potential buyers.

I have a saying for bodywork, "If they can't tell that you did anything, you did it correctly."

Bodywork on a classic Mustang is much different than collision work. "Can't tell" means doing the bodywork correctly—not cleverly covering it up. A correctly performed repair lasts longer and is less likely to cause problems during the restoration process.

It is also true that some body restoration techniques from 30 to 40 years ago do not pass in today's top restorations. Flange welds, heavy undercoating, and aluminum-flashing floor pans are no longer acceptable. (I have actually pulled a street sign out of a floor-pan repair). I have had potential employees tell me that they "just don't want to do it to that level." Take the time to do the bodywork correctly.

Preparation and Evaluation

Opting for a full body restoration requires the body and body panels to be stripped of current paint and rust. This can be done several ways, including sanding, using chemical strippers, media blasting, and more.

A sander and several boxes of 80-grit sandpaper allow you to strip the car in a shop or garage. Coarse sanding with a power tool can build heat and warp panels, and a big sander won't reach the hard-to-get-at areas. Wire strippers and fiber paint-stripper tools can be used in those areas. If you are too aggressive with sanding, you can thin out the metal and cause problems down the road. Sanding removes rust and some heavy undercoats.

Aircraft-grade chemical strippers are good for taking off the top coat but have a problem with baked enamel substrates and may take several applications. While they allow you to strip the car in a shop, they can be dangerous to use, so follow the manufacturer's directions. The panels must be completely flushed to remove the chemicals from the panels. Chemical strippers do not remove rust or heavy undercoats.

When using a sander to strip paint, use a large wheel, such as like this 8-inch disc, and soft backing. The larger the disc, the wider the swath. Wider discs also prevent digging into the metal like smaller discs do.

Chemical paint removers work well on secondary paints and top coats but tend to require longer times to get through the original baked-on base primers. Work in a well-ventilated area and use gloves because the stripper is very caustic.

Media Blasting

The results from media blasting (stripping with media) depend on what type of media is being used. All of them make a mess, and if you want to buy a blaster to do it yourself, they all require a lot of cleaning of the residual mess because the little particles fly everywhere.

Silica sand is generally not recommended on anything other than the underside. Sand builds heat, and if the person applying the sand has the pressure too high, the body panels become warped. Sand digs into the metal and leaves a coarse finish for primers to grab onto, but it also digs out the zinc in the panels, and things rust faster.

Black beauty is ground-up coal slag, and like sand, it leaves a slightly

Small siphon-feed blasters are great for small jobs, and by using the right abrasive, you can clean up small areas without warping the metal. Pressure blasters are also available, but be careful: the more pressure, the greater chance for heat and warping the metal.

Dustless blasting generally uses glass bead, which works okay on outer paint but does not work well on sound deadeners or seam sealers. The tendency is to crank up the pressure to speed up the job, but that leads to warping the metal. Be careful.

There are only a handful of places left in the US that can chemical-dip the entire car. Pro-Strip in Indianapolis did this 1968 fastback. Remember the dip removes everything, so be prepared to seal the inside of frame rails and other areas to prevent rusting from the inside out.

coarse finish on the metal for paint adhesion. However, unlike sand, coal slag doesn't build heat, so, at the proper pressures, it can be used to clean sheet-metal parts. It is less effective than sand at removing heavy sound deadeners, and it removes rust from the panels. Like sand, it goes everywhere, and cleanup is a long process. If a particle gets in the paint, it will generally not react with the paint.

Baking soda removes most of the paint and does not gouge into the metal like sand or coal slag. It is not very good for removing heavy sound deadeners. Baking soda reacts very badly with paint products, so if you have the car soda blasted, clean every surface with the recommended chemical cleaners to prevent a reaction when the car is painted.

Plastic media removes paint, and the plastic will not react with the new paint if it comes in contact. Plastic does not remove rust and is poor at removing sealants and undercoats. It requires a high-horsepower compressor and may be more expensive than other media. It does not gouge the metal, so the zinc is not removed, and parts don't rust as fast as with other media.

Dustless stripping adds water to the media to reduce the mess that is normally associated with blast stripping. Most dustless media is glass bead, but other media can be substituted. Dustless blasting may also reduce the amount of material that gets into the car, so cleanup may be easier (or harder, if you let it dry into a clump of mud).

Carbon-dioxide blasting doesn't remove paint or rust. It is used for an original car and paint finish. It removes the undercoating, grease, and sealants, and it is safe to use on rubber parts. It turns rust from an orange-red to a gray color.

Companies that can chemically dip the entire car to remove everything inside and out are getting difficult to find. The process removes everything: rust, paint, sealers, and heavy sound deadeners. The finish is bare metal. The problem is that it removes sealers and coatings in places that you can't access, and this bare surface quickly rusts if it is not properly recoated.

Baking is a method to remove heavy sound deadeners inside of the doors. A part can be baked at 800°F, which burns off the undercoating, but it doesn't affect the body panels (if they are cooled properly). This is usually used in conjunction with other methods, such as plastic stripping, which doesn't work well with heavy sealers.

Should you repair or replace a body part? In general, most body-repair experts would rather repair a damaged or rusty panel than replace it. However, in many cases, doing so is not cost effective or the panel may be too far beyond repair. As previously mentioned, some aftermarket panels require a lot of time to make them fit properly, and the cost savings of making the panel fit evaporates versus using an NOS panel.

Panel Alignment

Body panel alignment is about getting the panels to fit flush in relation to each other and to make the style lines match up from top to bottom. How far you want to go depends on your goals. The gaps from the factory were not perfect, and perfect gaps indicate to some enthusiasts that the car has been tampered with. While the original gaps were not perfect, the gaps on some of the aftermarket panels are even worse. Before tearing down a car, align the body panels to make sure there are no glaring bodywork problems. After the panels are aligned, work the panels and make gap and style-line fixes.

The first aspect regarding alignment deals with the body bolts. There is a liberal amount of slop in a Mustang chassis, so use this to align the gaps on your car by first lining up the style lines (body creases). The quarter panels are fixed, so alignment generally starts from the edge of the quarter panels. When aligning the body sides, start from the quarter panel-to-door gap and then attach the fenders and install the hood. Installing the hood with the fenders helps establish the in-and-out gaps on the fenders. Then, go back to the doors. Help may be needed for door alignment. They are heavy when you are trying to move them ever so slightly. Also, when tightening bolts, do them in small increments and in a pattern. Items such as the hinges can move as the bolt tightens, and if they do, you have to start over.

People refer to "paint-paddle-perfect" gaps, which means that you can slide a paint paddle between the gaps, and they will all have the same spacing. A paint paddle runs between 0.125 and 0.175 inch thick. Find one that suits you and make it your permanent measuring stick: If you don't use the same paint paddle each time, you may come out with an ununiform result. In addition, the flat paint paddle doesn't fit in some of the curved gaps on a body contour. Measure the thickness of the paint paddle and then purchase a drill bit

Paint paddles can vary in thickness, so if you want to use one to measure the body lines, find one and designate it for all of your measuring so that the gaps stay consistent. Soft plastic bars can also be used and may be more uniform than paint paddles.

Where a paint paddle won't fit between curved panels, use a drill bit that matches the thickness of your panel, measuring flat. Round plastic stock can also be used.

Sometimes, you need to weld up and build down edges to fit panels. This rear edge on a reproduction valance panel was pulled out. Then, additional material was added and shaped to allow it to fit to the quarter panel.

that is approximately the same size to measure gaps on curves.

So, you adjusted the panels so that the gaps are mostly uniform, but some gap issues still exist. Here is how you fix the issue. First, some people use body filler to build up the edges of the gaps. Don't do this! In the words of Kevin Tetz, "Reconstruct with metal; enhance with fillers." As good as the fillers are now, they are not to be used for a long-lasting repair on a gap. Gaps get beat around and slammed, and thick fillers shrink and crack. If there is any real reshaping to be done, do it in metal first. Then, use fillers to finish the repair, not *be* the repair.

Dents where you can reach the back side can be worked with a hammer and dolly or with old-fashioned spoons. Gaps can be reworked by adding or removing metal. Grinding and welding can be tricky because removing too much or adding can weaken the metal around the repair. A tiny bead row of welds ground down and shaped removes warbles in reproduction panels. Once you have the metal where you want it, use a short-strand fiberglass-reinforced filler to fill in the tiniest imperfections. After that is shaped, go over it again with a polyester filler to fill in the roughed fiber filler. The filler work should be as minimal as possible, especially on the edges, which can chip easily.

Rust, Pinholes, and Dents

Light surface rust on sheet metal and slightly heavier scale on some items, such as the strut rod mounts, can be removed with little effect on the panel. Carefully get all of the rust out of the dimples that were made by the rust patch. Leaving traces of corrosion in the panel can affect the paint adhesion and cause reactions.

Rust-through in any panel needs to be removed and replaced with new metal or replacement of the entire panel or part. Covering up the problem only provides a short-term solution. The problem will continue to grow. I have pulled apart many cars that were patched only to see the problem continue to get worse behind the cover up. Rust needs to be completely removed and replaced.

Pinholes are similar to rust, with the addition of small holes in the surrounding metal, which has thinned out and caused a weak area in the panel. If at all possible, cut back the hole to thick metal and weld in a patch piece. Some websites recommend to weld up the pinhole, and I have done this myself. However, half of the time the patch works and half of the time the metal is too thin, the weld blows through, and you have to make a patch piece anyway. If the weld does hold, you may still have thinned-out metal in that area, which causes flexing and paint problems in the future. The same goes for brazing or simply filling pinholes with filler, which likely will result in future issues. The best solution is to replace the thin metal with correct-thickness metal.

Reputable repair shops would rather fix an original dented panel than try to make a poor-fitting aftermarket panel fit. It can take longer to adjust a poorly fitting panel than to straighten an original panel.

Previous Repairs

First-generation Mustangs that have never had any repairs are rare, so you will most likely discover previous repairs during the evaluation. The saying, "If they can't tell that you did anything, you did it correctly," is also true of previous repairs after the repair has been exposed.

Previous repair work that needs to be redone is often found after the stripping process. This quarter panel was repaired back when these cars were less scarce—lots of body filler was used, and the problem went away. This needs to be cut out and replaced properly.

Did the person who made the previous repair simply use filler or fix it correctly? Did the previous repair change the contour of the body that wasn't noticeable before? Was the reason for the teardown due to an improper repair?

In general, some items, such as old filler, should be dug out to see the extent of the damage, even if the repair was done correctly. I once purchased a set of doors from the rust-free area, and when I stripped them down, I found evidence of a big hit on one of the doors. Rather than buy another set of doors, I just went with the previous repair, as the next set of doors likely has the same probability of being repaired.

A hammer and dolly can be used to bring up dents that can be accessed from the front and back. This half-doughnut dolly is slightly curved to allow shaping of the panel as it is being worked.

Using slap files is an old-school way to remove dents from sheet metal. They work great on older metal (and replacement panels), but newer cars have a much harder metal, and they don't work as well.

Repair Techniques

Dented metal is stretched metal, which generally means that it does not go back into place after it has been stretched. When attempting to repair it, it will act like a water ripple—push on the middle, and the sides pop up. Work both sides of the dent if possible. Several methods can be used to remove dents from panels, including using a hammer and dolly, slap files, shrinking, and pulling.

Choose a dolly that fits the contour of the panel. If you are removing a dent from a place that cannot be accessed with a hammer, two dollies working together will also work. There are two methods of using a hammer and dolly: hammer on and hammer off. "Hammer on" means that the dolly is placed directly under where the hammer is going to strike, which provides a base of resistance for the impact. "Hammer off" puts the dolly off to the side so that the metal can be bent by being leveraged against the dolly.

Most hammers have a rounded face to prevent crescent marks when you hit the metal. Shrinking hammers are ridged and slightly fold the metal on each strike to shrink the area that has been stretched.

Slapping files are an older way to work older steel panels. Slap files look like a bent rasp file. The ridges on the slap file act similar to a shrinking hammer in that they may shrink the metal very slightly on impact. Slapping files are used on the edge of the dent to raise the dent to the surface, rather than force the dent up from the center.

Shrinking with heat is usually used on metal that is "oil canned." That is, if you push the metal down, it pops, and when you release it, the metal pops back. Shrinking with heat is usually performed with an acetylene torch, a stud puller, or a propane torch (in some cases). Propane torches are difficult to use because it is hard to get the heat in a small area. The trick is to find the center of where the oil can is occurring and then heat up a dime-sized area to glowing red. After a few blows with a shrinking (or regular) hammer, quench the area with a cool, wet rag. The hammer helps get the metal molecules in place (and shrinks it if using a shrinking hammer or dolly), and the cold rag shrinks the metal.

Large dents are generally pulled by a hydraulic puller or a slide hammer. In the old days, you had to drill holes in the panel to make the stud work for the slide hammer. Today, stud pullers weld a small stud to the panel, which then attaches to the slide hammer. Once the dent is pulled, simply grind off the stud.

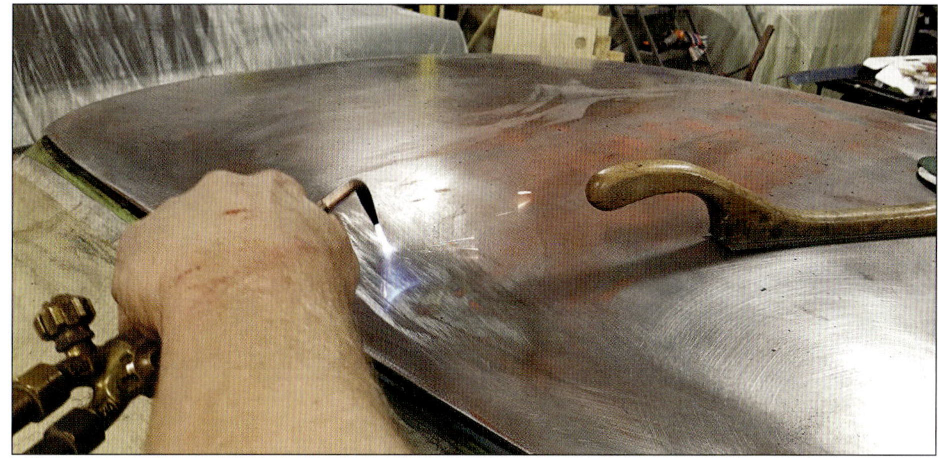

When you can push on the metal and it "gives" and then pops back, it has been stretched and needs to be shrunk. Shrinking metal involves heating the metal in a small area with either a torch (shown) or with a stud puller gun. The metal does not have to be superheated.

Once the metal is heated, a hammer with a serrated face is used to align the molecules in the metal. Light raps are usually all that it takes. Apply a wet cloth to the spot to cool the metal and draw the metal back in, removing the "oil canning." Once the metal is tight, the paint is going to stay put.

For dents in areas where you cannot get to the backside with a dolly, a stud puller works great to pull the dent back into place. The stud gun spot welds a pin to the panel. Then, use a puller to pull the dent back into place. You can then grind off the pins and work your way to the middle of the dent. Be careful not to overheat, as you can pull the metal up and out of the panel.

The factory used lead to seal items such as quarter panels to the roof section, and with the improvement of epoxy adhesives, very few shops still use lead. I still use lead because the strength is still superior to some fillers. Lead work is hazardous, even with today's lead-free body solders.

Lead work is soldering, which uses heat, a flux, and the solder (lead). Use an acetylene torch to heat the area, melt the lead flux (tallow), and spread the tallow on the area to be filled. Once the lead is in place, shave it with body shapers or coarse files.

Four kinds of welders can be used to restore the body. The most popular is metal inert gas (MIG) welding, which uses a gas (carbon/argon) or a flux-core wire. MIG welders are relatively inexpensive, and learning to make welds that hold well is quick. Tungsten inert gas (TIG) welding makes much cleaner welds (for experienced welders) but takes a little more experience learning to control the current. I haven't done arc welding/stick welding, but I would not recommend it on sheet metal. Spot welding was used by Ford to put the car together. Adapters are available for some MIG welders, but home-use spot welders generally don't have the power to spot weld like factory spot welds, and units that are big enough to properly weld the panels are expensive. Spot welds with a MIG welder followed by "messaging" the look afterward may be the best bet.

Brazing was also used to tack on items such as quarter panels. A few spots on the car had small brazed welds. These occur mostly on the quarter-panel areas. They are all painted, and to get the paint to stick to the brass, the braze must be properly fluxed so that it flows out.

Because of the safety issues and the fact that epoxies are getting much better, using lead in seams is getting more difficult to do. Tallow is used as a flux to help lay down the lead in the seam. Once the lead is in, it is easily worked with a body file.

The unibodies were brazed in many places (like this rear trunk divider), and you can duplicate the brazing with the correct torch, or you can use a MIG welder to simulate the braze.

Spot welders such as this one work fine for welding panels together, but they don't duplicate the much larger spot welds applied at the factory. To replace the factory spot welds requires a much bigger (and more expensive) spot welder as well as custom tips and arms.

Brazing is done with a propane torch. Be careful about heating the metal and warping the panels.

I do most of the welds with a MIG welder, but how do you replicate the factory spot welds once you have welded in the panels? The absence of spot welds tells the judge or the next buyer that repairs have been made.

Panel Repair

I have a rule about sheet-metal panel replacement: remove as little as possible to get the job done. There are many pictures on the internet of cars with the back half removed because a restorer cut off anything that had rust on it. The massive problem with removing entire sections is that there are no more reference points from the original car. The new reproduction panels do not fit the same as the originals, and now you are at the mercy of the fitment of the new panels to each other, which doubles your frustration. By leaving as many of the original panels in place (even if they are rusty), I now have three-dimensional references, and I shape the new panel to the original panels.

For example, if a car needs a taillight panel and a quarter panel, I work on the taillight panel first. This way, I align the taillight panel to the original quarter panel and trunk lid. Next, I remove the quarter panel and have the new taillight panel in the original position to make the new quarter panel fit. I also leave the door and trunk lid in place to align the style lines and peaks in the sheet metal. So, I know that the panels are aligned to the original specifications and not to the aftermarket fitment.

There are several different ways to remove panels, including saws, cutoff wheels, nibblers, and plasma cutters. Be careful with plasma cutters. They work well but can build heat and warp panels. Remove as little as possible to complete the task. Cleco clamps or self-drilling sheet-metal screws can be used to hold panels in place where you can't get a clamp. The

Types of Welds

These are various types of welds that will be used when restoring your car.

The most common type of welding is metal inert gas (MIG) welding, using either gas or flux-cored wires. Flux-core MIG welders are just fine for home shops. Proper welds such as this need a minimum amount of grinding (or none at all).

Tungsten inert gas (TIG) welding typically lays down a cleaner weld, but proper TIG welding takes some practice and experience to know how to adjust the current to the welder. Top welders have worked a long time to master this technique. Inexpensive TIG welders are generally not very good if they don't have good (or any) electric current control.

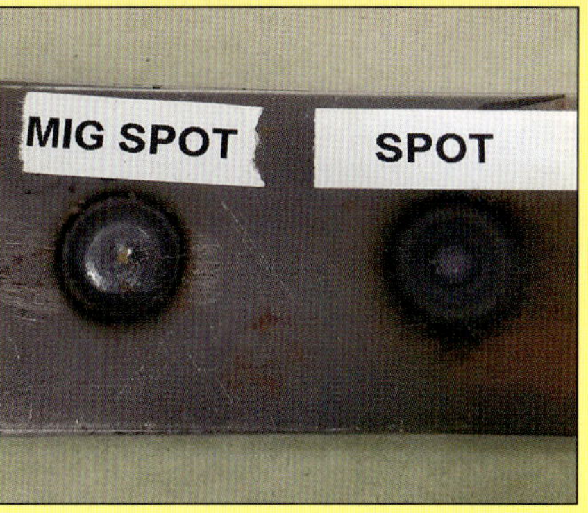

Most of your Mustang was spot welded together. On the left is a spot weld done with a MIG welder and a spot-weld adapter. The one on the right was done with an actual spot welder. The MIG spot weld does add a little wire to the area and needs to be cleaned up to look like a factory spot weld.

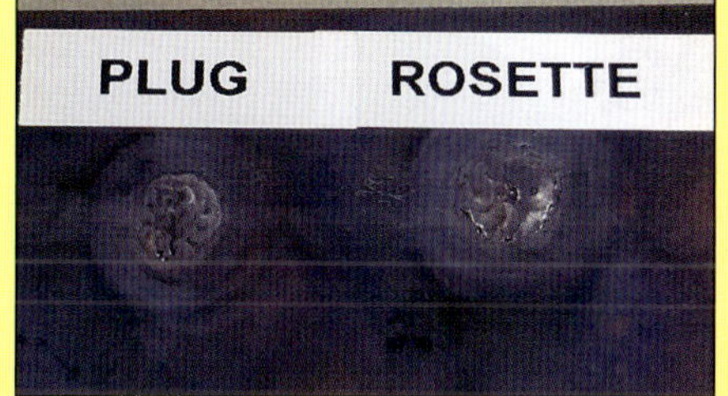

Plug welds are typically the most-used welds today when replacing panels that were originally spot welded. The plug weld has a small hole in the top panel and a solid bottom panel. Rosette welds are similar and are used to fill in holes. The plug started from the inside out, and the rosette started from the outside in.

Flange welds allow for the option of welding on the inside and outside if desired. Some repair panels come pre-flanged, where the metal has been bent to allow a lip to go behind the mating panel for a flush fit. As noted earlier, hiding the flange can be difficult, so be careful if you choose to flange weld panels.

Butt welds allow you to replace panels without the telltale flange to show that a repair has been made. These clamps allow two panels to be welded with the proper gap between them for butt welding. Be careful using them on curved surfaces: they can flatten the metal and take the contour out of the panel.

These fancy reusable rivets are called Clecos, and they help hold panels in place while they are being plug welded. If you don't need to be fancy, self-tapping screws work well too. Either way, you will be welding up the holes for the Clecos or the screws.

Plasma cutters are a great choice for cutting out metal for replacement, and inexpensive ones are fine for home use. Two things to think about when shopping for a plasma cutter are the duty cycle (longer times of cutting) and consumables. You go through a lot of tips, so buy a cutter where the consumables are stocked locally.

screws require drilling a hole that you can easily weld up and grind smooth when you are done.

Specialty spot-weld cutters are available to cut the factory spot welds for removing panels. You can drill all the way through them if you wish, but you have to fill in the holes with this method.

Lower Quarter-Panel Repair

The lower quarter panels are common rust areas. While the replacement full quarter panels are pretty good, the patch panels and "skins" are less than ideal. Keeping as much of the original body lines in place will help when reshaping the repair piece.

Spot weld cutters cut through the top layer of metal and leave the bottom layer intact. These work fine but remember, as with high-speed cutters, they don't last long, and when drilling out 200 spot welds, you will go through a lot of cutter blades.

We left the lip of the outer quarter panel on the inner quarter panel to act as a template for trimming the outer panel to the original body line. Once the outer was trimmed, we could then cut off the inner panel and fit the new inner to the original body line.

This customer purchased skins, which are not as well defined as full quarter panels and are really designed to be welded over the old metal. Considerable reworking of the panel is needed to get it to fit, and the labor cost to get a poor panel to fit may outweigh its inexpensive price. Note that it sticks out about 1/4 inch in the very back.

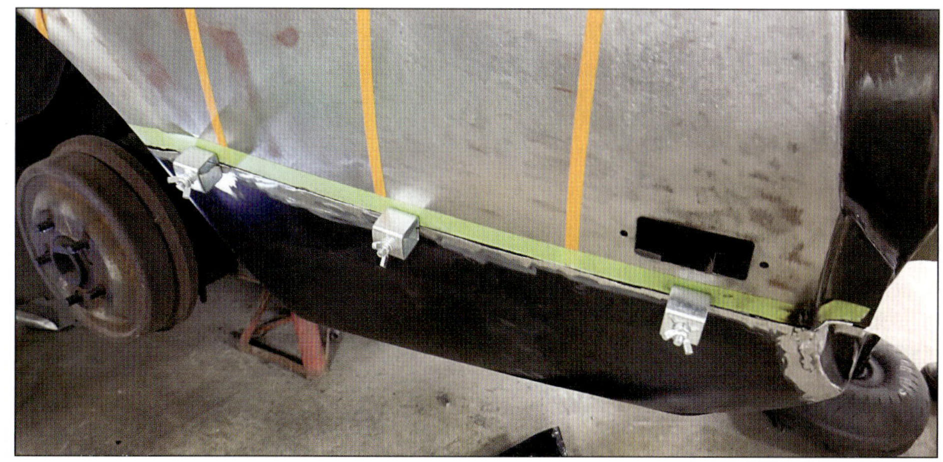

The butt-weld clamps are in place, but remember that they can flatten out curved panels. I made cardboard templates of the original quarter body line and used these templates to correct the contour while welding in the panel. Note the 1/8 inch taken out of the rear panel to get it to fit the original body line.

Battery Tray Repair

The battery tray area is notorious for rusting out, even in dry climates. This occurs because of the battery acid bubbling out of the old batteries and onto the metal. The replacement panel has a slightly different pattern on the top of the apron, so many restorers buy the new panel and patch the bottom tray area as needed to retain the original upper contours.

The battery tray area not only rusted from salt but also battery acid bubbling out of overcharged batteries. This battery tray had been fiberglassed over, and the problem just worsened.

A new battery tray has been tacked into place. Check the placement of the tray with tram lines (if you have the body dimensions) or to reinstall the fender before making the final welds.

Use a spot-weld cutter to remove the old panel. Before welding in the new panel, use weld-through primer on all welding surfaces to protect the seam after installation.

Apron Spot Welds

Another problem area is the weld joint between the shock tower and the apron assembly. This area was spot welded with four or five spot welds. Water gets between the panels, and they rust from the inside out. Since it is flat steel, the area can be easily repaired, and you can spot weld or MIG spot weld the welds back into place (note they are not perfect and placed randomly on the panel). Be very careful: the VIN stamp sometimes crept into this area, making repairs difficult.

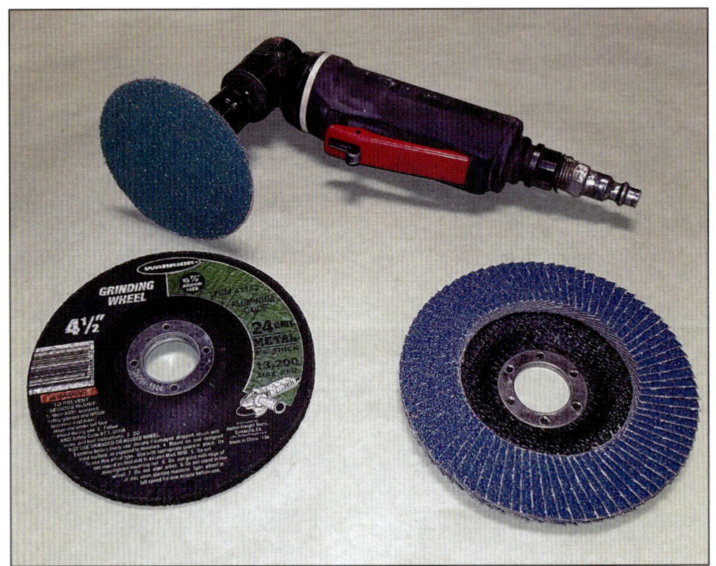

These are the typical tools for grinding welds smooth. The grinding disc on the left is the most aggressive. The flap disc on the right works well and runs cooler than the grinding disc, which means there is less chance of warping. A Roloc disc mounted on a right-angle grinder (top) helps get into the smaller areas.

Floor Pan Repair

Floor pan repair has become much easier with the introduction of the replacement one-piece floor pan. Floors rust out from wet shoes soaking into the carpet, so rust can be a problem even in dry climates. Butt welding patch pieces in a rusty floor can be time consuming.

The full floor is a much quicker job if you have rust on all four seating areas. With the full floor, once the old floor is out, begin the installation from the center out. These floor pans can be short side to side, and they need to be stretched out from the middle to fit. Some of the older patch panels have the side flange pointing down rather than up like the originals. If you want it to look like the original, bend the flange the other way. Use Cleco clamps or self-drilling sheet metal screws to hold panels in place where you can't get a clamp.

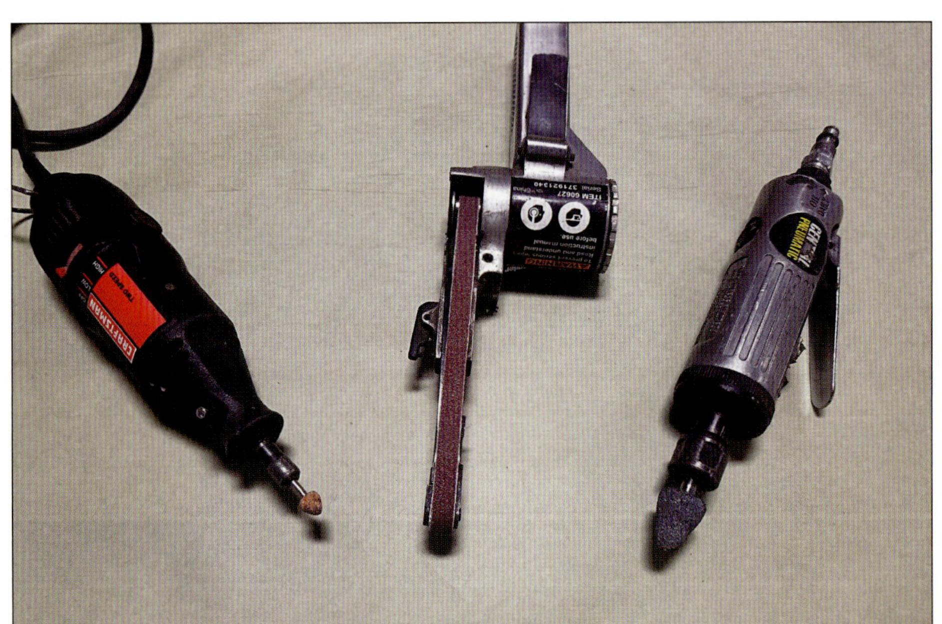

For grinding in tight spaces, stones mounted in your rotary tool work well. In the middle is a 3/8-inch belt sander that works well in corners and is relatively inexpensive. Various-shaped stones are also available for 1/4-inch-shaft die grinders (left and right).

Grinding and Sanding

Grinding produces heat and removes metal, both of which can be bad if done improperly. Grinding items, such as flap discs and Roloc-style discs, run cooler than hard grinding wheels. Take your time and allow things to cool to avoid warping the panels. Grinding stones for a die grinder or rotary tool can be used to get into hard-to-reach areas.

Hinge Repair

Door hinges are a common problem, as the bronze bushings wear out and cause the door to hang improperly. Inspect the hinge part for wear to the metal. If the hinges are damaged, replace them. If the hinge

Most original and aftermarket fiberglass requires a lot of rework to get it to fit. The fiberglass bumper on this Eleanor *car stuck out from the sides a 1/4 inch, and it required considerable building up and sanding down surfaces to get it to fit the body lines of the car.*

metal is not damaged, knock out the bushings and pin and install new ones from a parts vendor.

Fiberglass Repair

With the exception of Shelbys, very little fiberglass was used on Mustangs, with the exception of hood scoops. Some early 1969 SportsRoofs had fiberglass endcaps. Don't try to use Bondo filler on fiberglass; stick with proper fiberglass repairs. The key to a lasting fiberglass repair is getting all of the air bubbles out of the repair. Delaminating of the fiberglass occurs when air gets trapped in the repair and can happen several years after the repair has been made.

Rust-Preventative Paint

During the restoration, you may open up areas that you won't be able to access after the car is together. While you have the opportunity, apply an encapsulating rust preventative coating to the inside of these surfaces to prevent future problems.

Recheck Alignment

Once all of the major bodywork has been completed, reassemble and align the body again to make sure that nothing major has changed. Even though the weight is not on the car, you can recheck items such as body lines to make sure that they all fit.

Installing a One-Piece Floor Pan

The introduction of the one-piece floor pan improved the restoration process. One-piece floor pans are better defined, and since there is usually rust in all four corners, it reduces the amount of welding that is needed to install the pan correctly (no flange or butt welding the floor pans).

While one-piece floor pans work well for 1965–1968 Mustang coupes and fastbacks, there are a few things to know before getting started on convertibles and 1969–1970 cars. For this, I used a 1970 convertible as a guinea pig.

Convertible Owners

While I recommend the one-piece floor even in a convertible, you will need to modify the floor pan. The convertible has inner rocker panels, and the floor pan welds to the underside of the inner rocker panel. It is not flanged and welded to the outer rocker like it is on a coupe or fastback. This means that you need to trim the flanges off the outer edges and trim some in the back seat area to make it fit.

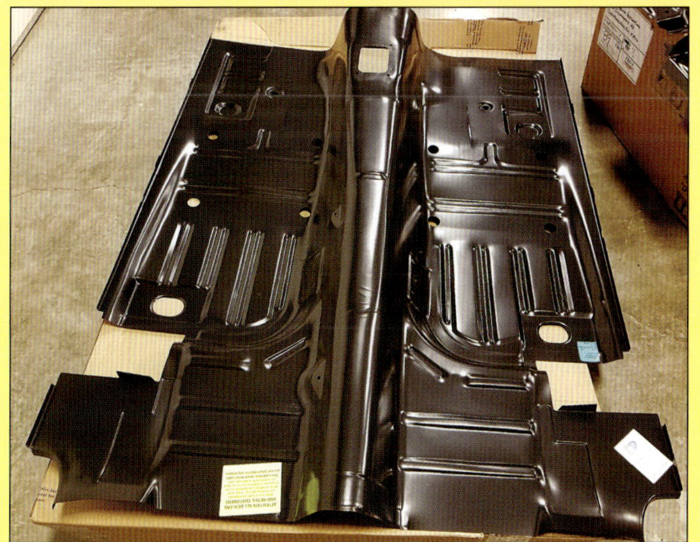

The one-piece floor pan is better defined than some of the patch pieces. It allows you to replace all of the bad rust in the car without having to stitch or flange weld, and it makes for a much cleaner repair.

Installing a One-Piece Floor Pan *continued*

The big problem lies within the inner rockers. If yours are solid and you are not changing them, the one-piece floor won't bend 5 inches to slide underneath the inner rockers. I ended up cutting the panel down the middle and welding it back together. This is not something that you have to do on a roof car, and it is not needed if you are cutting out the inner frame rails. The seat platforms are also different, so either reuse your old ones or modify the new ones to fit the inner rails.

We chose a 1970 Mustang convertible because it has rust in all four corners and is very solid with good inner rockers and torque boxes. The 1970 convertible is also the perfect storm for problems with the one-piece floors, as it requires the most modifications. The one-piece floor was designed for 1965–1968 coupes and fastbacks.

The frame structure is solid, so I left it in place, but here is what you have with the floor removed. The toe boards also had some rust on them, and they will be patched at a later date. Note the door braces that keep the body from moving.

1969–1970 Owners

While the contours on the 1969–1970 floor are better than the patch pieces that we are used to, they are still not correct for a show car. For some reason, they put a drain plug in the front (which the 1969–1970 did not have), and the ribbing is incorrect. This is a dead giveaway to most judges and casual buyers who know the difference. If you require the floors to have the correct ribbing, patch in some of the ribbing borrowed from the inexpensive patch pieces for the earlier 1965–1968 floors.

In 1970, Ford added a "hump" on the driver's side of the transmission tunnel to clear the factory Hurst shifter. This feature is not included in the new one-piece floor pan. It is extremely difficult to see this feature under the car, but if you feel you need the clearance (and you have the Hurst shifter), graft the hump from your original into the new floor. ■

Before you start cutting out pans, mark the location for the emergency-brake brackets that are welded to the underside of the pan.

For convertibles only, the floor pans weld to the underside of the inner rockers, so trim off the outer flanges of the floor before installing them in a convertible.

Any time an inner panel is exposed, take advantage and paint some rust-preventative coating on the inside of the panels. The brush on the end of the paint stick allows you to get far into the frame rails and coat them.

For 1970 Mustangs only, if you want the clearance for the Hurst shifter, you can cut it out of your original (or from another car) and graft it into the new pan.

This is a side-by-side floor-pan comparison of the ribbing differences for 1969–1970 Mustangs. I'm not sure why the manufacturer put a fake drain plug in there, but if you need to have your floors look original, this needs to be modified.

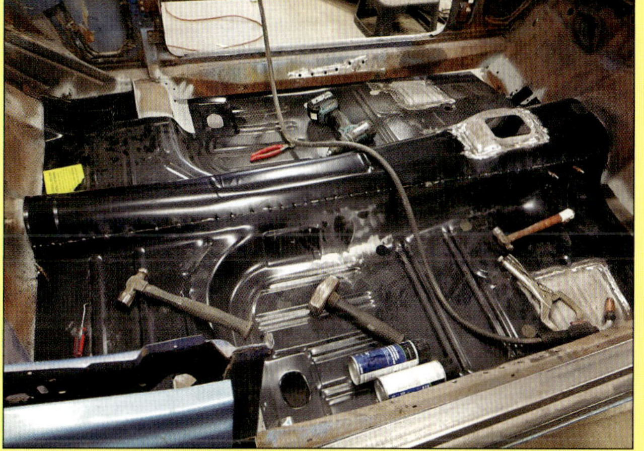

If you have a coupe or a fastback, you can lay the floor in and start welding. Weld from the center of the tunnel out. I have found that the floors tend to draw in short, and this stretches the pan properly. For convertibles only, the floor fits under the inner rails, and it isn't going to bend 5 inches to clear the rails. I ended up splitting it down the middle on the passenger's side and then stitch welding it back into place. This may be a lot of added work, but the better body lines of the one-piece floor are worth it.

With the original seat platforms in place, I am ready to go underneath and install the convertible reinforcement pans and weld to the underside of the inner rockers. Coupes and fastbacks can be welded entirely from the inside of the car.

CHAPTER 5

Paint

Painting a car takes time and experience, but you have to start somewhere, and perhaps now is the time. In this chapter, I focus on the specifics of painting a Mustang to its original condition, some situations to avoid, and how to get out of those situations.

Before starting the painting process, check your local laws. Some areas do not allow you to paint your car at all, and the body shops are regulated to the point that every piece of sandpaper must be accounted for as hazardous waste. Other areas have certain city regulations, but in the country, you may be able to do whatever you like.

It is possible to get the results you are looking for by doing the work yourself. Remember these two things: 1) it takes time, and 2) cleanliness is everything. Unlike collision work, people look at the back sides of panels on a restored Mustang. They get down close and look at the finish. Because of this, a good paint job takes long hours to prep the panels to get the desired finish. This is why collision shops want to work on your car in their spare time. It takes a lot of labor to get the finish just right. Cleanliness is everything because no matter how smooth you lay down the paint, dirt and contaminants in the paint can ruin an otherwise-beautiful paint job. When prepping for paint clean everything—and then clean it again.

Nothing says summer fun quite like a Mustang convertible. With only a few styling and safety changes, the 1968 Mustang changed little from the 1967 model. This 1968 GT convertible is owned by Billy Carrol of Nashville, Tennessee, and is finished in Acapulco Blue with standard blue interior, a 302-4V engine, and an automatic transmission. (Photo Courtesy Billy Carrol)

Home Paint Booth

Remembering that time and cleanliness are big concerns, let's cover setting up a home paint booth. Make sure that where you are going to paint is free from debris that can get into your paint. The dirt floor in a barn is not a good place to paint your car. Also, taking your time with the paint means that your two-car garage will be out of commission for a while. Make sure that you have the time allotment for a proper job. Also, make sure that your neighbors won't mind. Just because it is legal doesn't make it a good idea to exhaust paint fumes into your neighbor's yard.

Never use anything other than an explosion-proof exhaust fan in a temporary paint booth. One spark in that environment is dangerous. Either use an explosion-proof fan or have the motor outside of the flow of the exhaust running the fan blades from a belt.

Static electricity can cause problems when you are painting your car, so design your paint area with that in mind. Paint vapors can become charged particles in the airflow of the painting area, and they are also flammable. Sparks can cause explosions and ruin your day. Plastic used to build a painting area can also become charged and draw dust. The body of the vehicle can also become charged and attract dust to it like a magnet. Exhaust fans that are not explosion-proof can create sparks and ignite your work area.

Your work area should include the following:

1. An area large enough to move freely around the car.
2. A way to keep the paint fumes contained and the dirt out.
3. An explosion-proof exhaust fan to remove the paint fumes
4. A compressor to power the paint gun
5. Sufficient lighting to see your work

Make sure that your painting area is sufficient in size to paint your car without things getting in your way. As opposed to a basement pool table that has the pole in the way of a trick shot, you must have sufficient room to maneuver and get to hard-to-reach areas. Most commercial paint booths are approximately 14 feet by 25 feet, which provides enough space to paint most vehicles intact but not enough space if you paint each panel individually. Make sure that the area where you plan to paint can be sufficiently cleaned, unlike the aforementioned dirt-floor barn. A clean, dry area with access to running water is best.

Paint fumes can go everywhere and stick to everything, so most one-time paint job sites usually use a form of plastic sheeting to keep the paint fumes contained. Use clear plastic to allow light to transmit from outside of the painting area. How the sheeting is hung is up to you. A framework of polyvinyl chloride (PVC) pipe can be made to hang around the car, but that amount of pipe can be expensive. Otherwise, the plastic sheeting can be fastened directly to walls with duct tape or staples—just be careful where you are attaching it.

Remember, plastic sheeting can build up a static charge, so prep it before painting. A dish soap and water coating over the plastic works well. The plastic must be sealed so that you don't draw in dust and dirt from between the seams or under the door. Also, design the entrance to the paint booth so that it can be sealed to prevent dirt from getting into the paint area. Make sure that most items, such as the air compressor and lighting, are outside of the paint area. These items can cause electrical sparks that can ignite the paint fumes.

Do not use box fans to exhaust paint fumes! This is very important. Standard home box fans have an open motor design, and sparks can be generated that are exposed to the flammable area around the fan. I have a friend who painted cars in his garage for years, and then an explosion blew out his garage door. Even though your buddy may have been painting with a box fan for years, don't use one.

The only safe way to exhaust the paint fumes from your site is with an explosion-proof motor, and they are expensive. They can be purchased from industrial supply houses, and a matching fan blade is required. How the fan is mounted is up to you: in a box on the floor or mounted in the wall. Keep the design to the size of paint booth filters (20 x 20 inches in most cases) and know that there are different types for intake and exhaust. Sizing the intake and exhaust depends on the CFM that your fan can push. Have enough filters on the air intake so that the side plastic sheeting doesn't get sucked inward when the fan is turned on.

Most modern paint guns are high-volume, low-pressure (HVLP)

guns. Find a compressor that has a large reserve of air, not just high horsepower. For example, my paint gun uses 15.9 cfm, or 118 gallons a minute uncompressed. The volume of the compressor tank and the amount of air that the compressor can compress in a minute determines how often the compressor runs to keep up with the paint gun. Waiting for the compressor to catch up is not good for the paint job's overall finish.

Because a modern paint gun uses more air, the size of the air lines is also important. A 1/4-inch hose does not deliver enough air to properly run one of these guns because it can't flow enough volume. A 3/8-inch line is enough if you use the correct type of fittings to allow more air into the gun. Make sure that there is enough air line to reach around the entire vehicle. Secure around the air line so that air and dust aren't allowed to enter the booth at the point of entry.

My paint booth has 10 inexpensive lights mounted to the sides of the booth. If possible, your lighting should allow you to see the entire car without having any shadows. Inexpensive lights can be used, just make sure that they are mounted on the outside of the painting area because the electrical starters and tubes can cause sparks. Shine them through the clear plastic or install Plexiglas to shine the light through and attach it to the plastic. The more light, the better.

Ford Painting Sequence

How you paint your car is determined by what makes you comfortable and what your space allows. Generally, items such as the doorjambs and the underside of the hood and decklid are painted first, which is usually when the rest of the car is painted.

Although Ford had running changes to the way that it painted cars, here is the sequence that it followed to paint Mustangs if you want to duplicate the factory way:

The doors and the trunk lid were painted after they were installed on the car. The front doghouse (hood, fenders, front valance, and stone guard) was painted before being installed on the car. The rear valance was painted after being installed on the car and was held by a few screws and allowed to hang to allow paint to reach between the panels. The end caps were either spaced off the body or painted off the car to allow overspray to get between the panels. The body was primed with red-oxide primer (or slop gray in Dearborn 1969–onward).

Then, seam sealers and some sound deadeners were applied inside the quarter panels and trunk areas. A primer coat was applied, and then the body color was applied. After body color, the engine compartment and pinch welds were painted. How far and how much they were painted depended on the line worker at the time. Outside sealers on the firewall and wheelhouses were applied after the painting process. The interiors were painted after the body was painted.

Proper Color Myth

I regularly hear the following from someone who got penalized by the concours police: "They said that the shade of color of my car is incorrect." Well, it's time for me to get in trouble with the concours police. In fact, you can take a car from each month and each plant from the year that your car was made, line them up fresh from the factory, and none of them would be exactly the same color. I have a friend who has been painting since the 1960s. He received the "factory pack" paint from the Ford suppliers, and it never matched perfectly.

The truth is that the supply and blending from the 1960s was not precise, and the color varied. So, unless your shade is *way* off, you are fine, and the judges don't know what they are talking about. Taking the color computer from the paint supply company to a part of your car only provides the closest match—not an exact blend of color. The paint has changed so much from the original tints that it is impossible to exactly match what was on the car.

Being able to match the engine-compartment black color is another myth. The truth is that the gloss and shade of the black that was used in the engine compartment was generally a semigloss black, but I have seen it almost full glossy on a 6,000-mile car, and the shade varies from gray-black to black. The process used by Ford recycled some of the paint, and the suppliers used different formulas. There is no such thing as "correct" chassis black. However, if you are building a car for judging, you may be required to use the formulas for chassis black that are preferred by that judging body.

Epoxy primer is yet another color that varied considerably over the course of the first-generation production run. An unsubstantiated rumor is that leftover paints were dumped into the chassis black and primer vats and reshot onto the underside of the car. I can confirm that I have seen original red-oxide primer that varied from a near-salmon color to a dark-blackish red-oxide color. Most builders find an example of the original from the car and blend to this color.

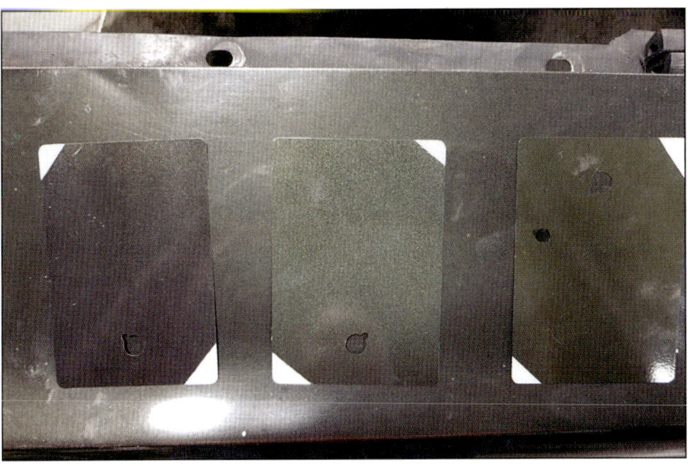

Three different results were produced from three different paint suppliers of 1969 C-Code Black Jade. The fender that the test panels are laying on has been faded from sunlight as well. Sometimes, you have to search several companies to get the closest match.

Most paint suppliers have a computer to try and match your original paint. It only shows the closest match—not the exact match. You need a credit-card-sized area of paint for the computer to get a reading.

Most epoxy primers cannot be tinted to match your color, but some manufacturers sell their epoxy primers in various shades that can be blended together to match your original shade from the factory. My rule of thumb is this: I have seen shades of red oxide all over the place but never straight-out-of-the-can red oxide. Blending it somewhat allows for a more original look than straight red oxide.

Paint Runs and Orange Peel

There are a few reasons to consider paint runs and orange peel in your paint job. First, if you are going for authenticity, the MCA wants to see paint runs somewhere in the engine compartment. This is not because Ford wanted to run the paint, but the method used to apply the paint caused runs in most of the cars. Therefore, the MCA looks for this in some of its judged classes. This doesn't mean that some cars didn't come through with nice engine-compartment paint, but their standard is to what it sees as common, rather than the exception.

Paint runs and drips were also found on the floor-pan runners, and besides the MCA rules, I actually recommend that you do this if you are applying primer to the floor pans. The reason is this: if I crawl under a car that I am looking to buy and I don't see these drips on the floors, I know the floors have been changed. I have seen some paint runs on the underside of the car that look like Niagara Falls. The paint was laid on very thick.

In 1969, Mustangs built at the Dearborn plant began using Slop Gray on the underside of the car instead of the red-oxide primer. This paint varied as well, but if you are going for authenticity, check your Dearborn car for the type of primer that was used. For a short time in 1970, Dearborn painted the underside of the cars with leftover body paint from the previous day. The

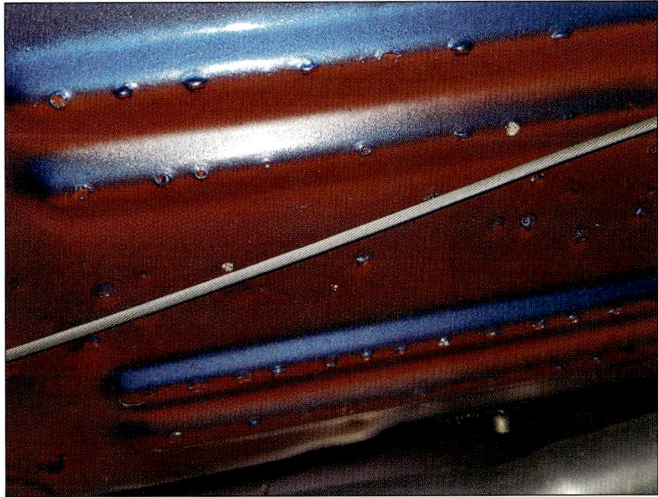

The underside epoxy paint was also laid on very heavy, which resulted in paint drips coming off of the reinforcement ridges on the floors. One sure way to tell if a floor has been replaced is if it has perfectly smooth floors or is heavily undercoated.

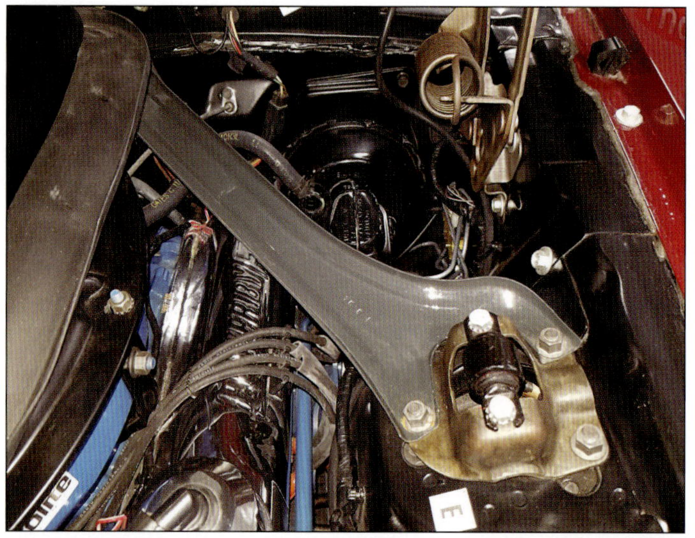

In 1969, the Dearborn plant began using a color called Slop Gray, which replaced the red oxide underneath. Some detail parts were painted this color, and it varied in color. Metuchen and San Jose stayed with the older formulas.

Orange peel was the result of baking the enamel onto the car and gave the finish of the paint a slight bumpy texture like an orange peel. Original cars for high-end judging need to have some peel in the paint. Other cars can be buffed out to the shine that you desire.

exterior paint is actually more robust than the primers, but it made for some weird combinations. I had a Medium Metallic Blue car with Lime Green Metallic floors. Yuck, but it was restored to those colors.

Orange peel trips up many show car owners, and if you plan to show your car in stock classes, some orange peel is needed in the paint. Orange peel makes the surface of the paint look like that of the surface of an orange: bumpy. This is from the process of baking the enamel to cure it on the body and was not intentional. The good news is that with HVLP spray guns, you get some of the same effect. How much orange peel you leave in the paint is up to you.

Paint Types

There are two types of top coats to consider: single stage and multistage. With single stage (what the car was sprayed with originally), the color and clear are combined together. Single-stage paints are difficult to find due to the regular use of base-coat clear-coat systems. Some suppliers do not carry them anymore, and the mixing-bank colors are getting old just sitting there, which can cause problems with the finish. Only consider single-stage paint for concours cars.

Today, most cars are painted with a base coat and clear coat. The color is a soft paint, and the protection is in the clear top coat. Base and clear paint can tend to be shinier than single-stage paints.

When selecting a paint system, stay within the same family line of products. Reactions and contaminants can be a problem, and mixing products from manufacturers may result in having to pay to respray.

Interior paint was a high-hiding, low-build (thin) urethane enamel. The low build allowed the paint to lay in areas such as the moonskin contour on the doors. Most Mustang suppliers sell lacquer paints for the interior because it works the same way, but it is not as durable. You can shoot enamel in the interior if you shoot it lightly.

For the blackout hood on Mach 1s and Bosses, a black enamel was used (textured in 1970). The only time that Ford used lacquer paint on a Mustang was on the hood scoop for the Boss 429.

Supplies

Although most restorers don't do a complete paint job, I am frequently asked if I can paint a car for an

Ford's original production-line paint procedure was a coating of epoxy primer, followed by a coat of gray build primer and finally the single-stage top coat. It was not terribly thick paint. Most factory paint is in the 6- to 8-mil range.

inexpensive price, such as $1,000. You can't even buy the materials for that price. I compiled a list of supplies that are needed to repaint an entire Mustang from inside out. Depending on which system you use, you may use more or less, but the purpose of this information is to get you thinking about what you will need to paint the car.

You may not use two gallons of color, but you want to have some paint leftover for future touch-ups. You get what you pay for with paint. Less-expensive paints generally use old technology, and if you have a problem, economy-line paint manufacturers may not provide assistance if you have problems. Also, optional items may not be included, such as spraying polyester fillers, as opposed to guide coating and blocking. Take a deep breath, use this information when going to a paint supplier, and use it to form a paint budget.

Here's a checklist of most of the items you need to consider when doing a complete respray of your car. As you can see, the cost of doing a complete paint job adds up.

- Surface cleaner and wax removal (1 gallon)
- Rust-encapsulating paint (optional, 1 quart to 1 gallon, depending on need)
- Epoxy primer (2 gallons)
- Epoxy primer hardener
- Epoxy primer reducer (if required)
- Primer surfacer (2 gallons)
- Primer surfacer hardener
- Primer surfacer reducer (if required)
- Guide coat (amount determined by how many blocking passes are required, usually 8 spray cans or a few quarts)
- Body filler (amount depends on condition of the body, 2 or more quarts)
- Lightweight body filler (amount depends on the condition of the body, 1 quart)
- Body-filler spreaders
- Primer/sealer (1 gallon)
- Primer/sealer hardener
- Primer/sealer reducer
- Seam sealer (spray on or brush on, 4 tubes or 2 quarts)
- Sound deadener (3 to 4 quarts, more for Mach 1 and Grande)
- Engine-compartment black (also used on pinch welds, 2 quarts)
- Engine compartment black hardener
- Engine compartment black reducer
- Interior lacquer or enamel (1 quart)
- Interior paint-quality lacquer thinner (lacquer) or reducers/hardeners (enamel)
- Base coat color or single-stage paint (2 gallons)
- Reducers for base coat/single stage
- Hardeners for base coat/single stage
- Clear coat (if used, 2 gallons)
- Reducer for clear (if used)
- Hardener for clear (if used)
- Automotive masking tape (10 rolls)
- Roll of masking paper (1 or 2)
- Sandpaper (180, 230, 400, 600, 1,200, 2,000, and 3,000 grit)
- Strip caulk (1 package)
- Cleanup lacquer thinner (1 gallon)
- Measuring cups
- Paint sticks
- Paint strainers
- Lint-free paper towels
- Regular paper towels (several rolls)
- Tack cloths (1 box)
- Disposable gloves (1 or 2 boxes—no powder)
- Cutting, polishing, and glazing compounds
- Polishing cloths (many)
- Dust masks for sanding the body (1 box)

Priming

There are three priming steps for a modern car: 1) a base paint to allow good gripping to the metal, 2) a build primer (also called primer surfacer) that allows you to fill in small imperfections, and 3) a seal primer that locks in the bodywork and buildup from the color levels. Ford didn't use a seal primer, but with new technology and after 50 years of road abuse, you should.

Priming begins with either an epoxy primer or a self-etching primer. Both of these primers provide a firm point for the paint to mount. Which one you use depends on how authentic you are going to go as well as the budget.

Build primers are used where you block and sand the panels along with guide coating to find high and low points in the paint. This usually involves several applications before all of the small imperfections are removed from the surface.

A final seal primer coat is applied right before the color coat is applied to the finished bodywork. This acts as a barrier between the fillers and primers and the body color. Body color is pretty aggressive and can reactivate the primers underneath, causing problems with the paint.

Primer is generally thicker and more abrasive than color and clear, so I recommend that you have a primer gun specifically for shooting primer. These guns have a larger nozzle than guns that are intended for color and clear, and the abrasive nature of primer can eventually distort the smaller nozzle on the primary paint guns.

Application

At the beginning of this chapter, I wrote that the primer on the underside was applied very thick, causing runs. Build primers are also laid on very thick because most of it will be sanded off. However, the seal coat should be laid down as smoothly as possible, so investing in a good primer gun is a must.

Do exactly as the manufacturer says regarding application. Today's paints are precise in their mixing, so carefully follow the technical data sheet.

After applying two coats of epoxy or self-etching primer, spray the first coat of build primer fairly soon after the base primer coat. I usually do this within an hour. This helps to slightly intermingle the two primers. Most epoxy coats have a window of time (72 hours or so) in which you can spray over the epoxy before it needs to be sanded. The build primer is intended to be sanded but the epoxy is not. Apply the build primer per the manufacturer's instructions and let the paint dry completely.

Guide Coating and Block Sanding

Block sanding the fill primer allows you to use small amounts of primer to fill in small areas of the body that don't require reworking the metal, such as small sanding scratches from the bodywork. This can be done by using a guide coat or using spray polyester. The guide coat comes in aerosol form, and you can lightly dust the paint over the surfaced to be blocked.

During block sanding, the high points get sanded down, the guide coat is removed, and the low spots still have the guide paint on them. Avoid breaking through the build primer to the base primer. If you get a

Guide coating is a method that helps you find small imperfections in the blocking process. An inexpensive paint is used to contrast to the primer, and then sanding the guide coat paint off reveals low spots in the bodywork. Apply the guide coat with a good spray nozzle for best results.

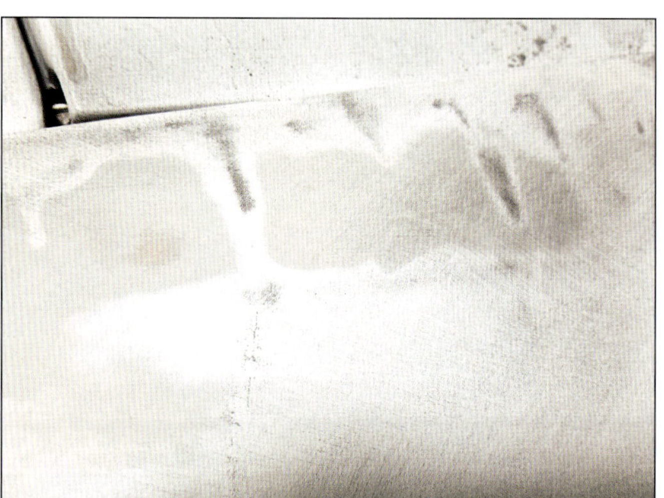

After the area has been sanded with a long file, you can see two patterns. The guide coat can still be seen in the deep gouges in the fiberglass, and the darker areas around the gouges show where there is a high point and we cut down to the primer below.

One option to several rounds of block sanding is spray polyester surfacer. It sprays like a thin coat of filler and reduces the amount of blocking to get the panels straight. It requires a special gun with a large 2.5-mm opening, but it can be a time saver.

spot that is high enough to where it breaks through to the metal, you may need to dolly out the high and low points before moving forward. Small valleys can be filled with a layer of polyester filler and sanded smooth. Depending on how wavy the body is (and they get wavy after 50 years), it may take four or five rounds of primers and block sanding to get the body straight.

A method to reduce the number of rounds of block sanding is to apply a layer of polyester filler to the panel. This is a spray body filler that acts like a thin layer of filler over the entire surface. When it is sanded, it acts like the build primer layers that were mentioned previously. In general, the cost of spray polyester may run the equivalent of several layers of build primer, but it saves time. I prefer to do a guide coat first to see any large imperfections that I may have missed during the bodywork phase. This allows me to keep the polyester as thin as possible.

A technique that you may or may not master is feeling for imperfections—even those that don't show up after block sanding. I use a thin cloth or even a cotton glove to help me find small imperfections. Gently work your hand over the surface to find these small warbles and mark them for flexible filler repair.

Sound Deadeners and Sealants

Some sealers and sound deadeners were applied before paint, and some were applied after paint. As a general rule, the areas such as the inside of the interior and the inside of the trunk area were coated before color was applied. Areas such as the engine compartment and wheel

The sound deadener shot inside the rear quarter panels was applied before the car was painted. It can seep through the paint like it did on this 1970 Mach 1.

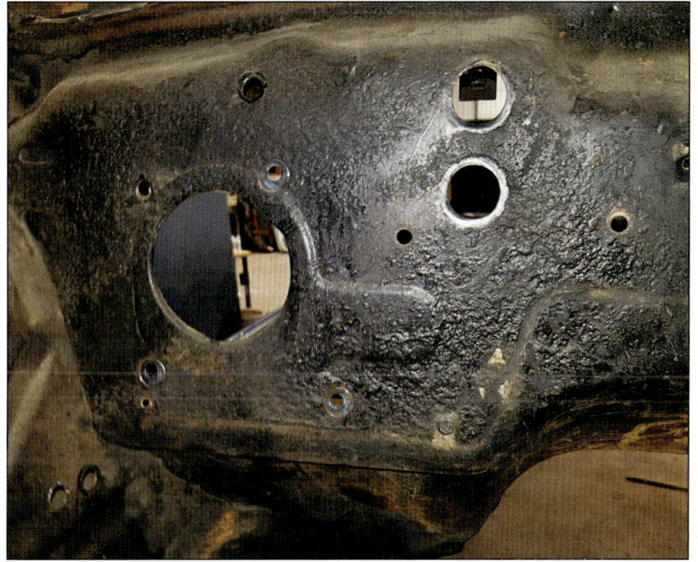

The sound deadener used on the firewall was applied after the engine compartment was painted. You can see blue body color under the heater-box-attaching holes, which indicates that the body color was painted before the engine compartment was painted.

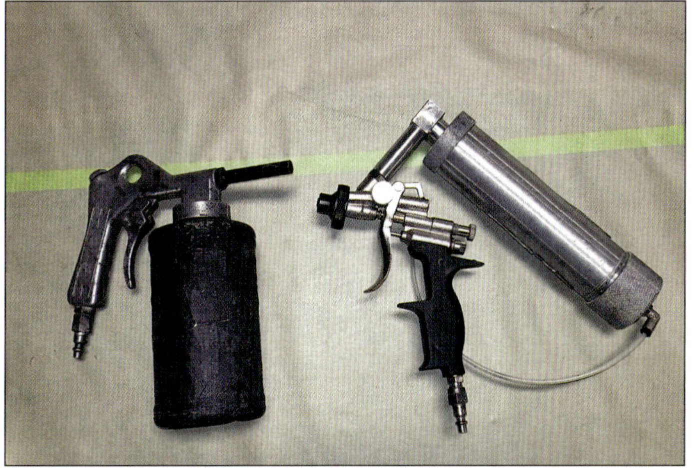

Two gun choices for spraying on the sound deadeners are shown. The spray gun on the left is an old siphon-feed body schutz gun, and it works well for all but the high-end restorations. The gun on the right is a pressurized cartridge gun, and you can adjust the air pressure and spray pattern to get the different application finishes just like it was at the factory. Remember that some of the sealers were brushed or troweled on.

wells were coated after paint.

The Mach 1 and Grande platforms received additional sound deadener in the doors and under the bottom of the car. Various cars may be different from plant to plant and from month to month. The best way to replicate this is to document the car before stripping down the car. Did you do that? If not, in general the inside was done before paint and the outside was done after paint.

To make things even more confusing, the *Weld and Sealant* manual that is available for some years is more incorrect than correct for most cars built. If you are building a car for show, follow the guidelines of that group's judging standards, and replicate what you found during teardown.

Ford used several methods for applying various sealers. Some appear to be applied by tube (around door hinges), brushed or troweled on (around the rear bumper-mount brackets and the front firewall seam), or sprayed on (inside the trunk and interior areas). These methods appeared to change, so the best way to apply the sealer is to duplicate what you documented. The line assembler and the way that the sealers were applied varied. Some assemblers would coat the entire area, and others would make a few thin passes.

Most sealers and sound deadeners hardened, with the exception of the caulking used under the fenders and the bedding compound that was used on the front and back window. Which brand of sealer to use has changed over the years. At first everyone was using 3M Body Schutz for undercoating and sound deadener. Then, that was not acceptable. My advice is that it isn't so much what you use, it's how it is applied. The body schutz gun has a very big nozzle, and it sprays one way—very coarse. It's good for some areas but not good for others. A pressurized applicator allows you to set the coarseness level and aid in applying the sealers. In general, the body schutz gun works just fine. For concours cars, a pressurized gun makes the judges a little happier.

Masking

Eventually, you will mask off areas that won't receive paint, and buying the right tape can prevent headaches. Automotive-grade masking tape is designed to not leave

You can use regular masking tape for things that are not going to touch a painted surface, as it uses a different adhesive than automotive tapes. Automotive tapes are more expensive, but they won't leave the residue that cheap tapes leave. The difference in color in the automotive tapes denotes how much heat the tape can endure, specifically in heated baking paint booths. Either works fine in an air-dry application.

Vinyl tapes are used to get sharp edges and to curve for stripes and fine lines. When laying down sharp-contrast areas, use the small tape first. Then, come back with masking tape before masking the area with paper or plastic.

Soft-line tape is a round tape that is great for sealing off doorjambs. The round nature of the tape prevents the spray pattern from laying down a hard line that is difficult to sand down. Instead, it leaves a soft line like what you need when painting the blackout on the rocker panels. You can make your own soft-line tape by rolling regular tape into a tube with the sticky side out.

residue like regular masking tape does. So, use the correct tape where the tape touches a painted surface.

When laying down stripes or custom designs, use vinyl or plastic tape that bends and curves to your design. These types of tape are generally 1/4 or 1/8 inch wide. Once the design is down, add wider tape and paper to finish the masking work.

Soft-line tapes are generally not tapes at all. They are foam rolls with an adhesive on one side. A soft-line tape works to eliminate hard tape lines and overspray in body gaps. As you spray, the angle of the spray doesn't get all the way under the rolled surface and acts to feather out the paint spray and eliminate the hard tape line. It can be placed in areas such as door gaps to keep overspray down after you have painted all the door gaps.

If you don't want to use the foam tape, you can roll masking tape sticky-side out and use it, but the foam tape works better in areas such as the doorjambs, as it is more flexible. When using soft-line tape, keep the adhesive away from the paint area. The adhesive can cause a hard line and is difficult to remove.

This is the reason to use automotive-grade plastic sheeting and masking paper: automotive plastic sheeting has a static charge in it, so when a piece of dust or other contaminant sticks to it, it stays there and doesn't get in your paint. Automotive masking paper is designed to not let the paint seep through, and it doesn't have ink on it like newspapers that can react to paint.

Paper or Plastic

The days of grabbing a stack of old newspapers to cover a car before painting are gone. There are three reasons why you should not do this: 1) The paint can seep through newspapers and get stuck to something it shouldn't. 2) The ink on the paper may react to the paint or the surface, and you may not notice until it ruins the paint job. 3) Newspapers gather dirt while they are waiting to be used, which can get into the paint. The cost savings of using newspaper or non-automotive painting paper and having a problem can far exceed the cost of the roll of masking paper.

Plastic sheeting is available in rolls that allow you to cover the entire car quickly to prevent overspray. It quickly allows you to perform spot repairs as you can cover the whole car and trim out the area that you are repairing or painting.

Back Masking

Back masking prevents hard lines that need to be sanded later. Back masking leaves a soft edge or no edge. Rather than taping directly to the edge of a part, start by taping the back of the panel with wide tape to expose excess masking tape. The masking paper then attaches to the exposed tape rather than the panel surface. You can also run tape across the back side to provide support to the masking paper when covering large openings, such as doors and trunk areas. This prevents the paper from flapping when painting, preventing contaminants from getting in the paint.

When laying down masking

The trunk area on this 1967 Mustang was painted before the outside panels (edging the inside panels). Back masking this trunk area begins with wide tape applied under the lip of the trunk area to form a base for the paper to adhere to.

A frame is taped together to provide a base for the paper to lay on so that it doesn't fluctuate like a speaker when painting. The more support the better.

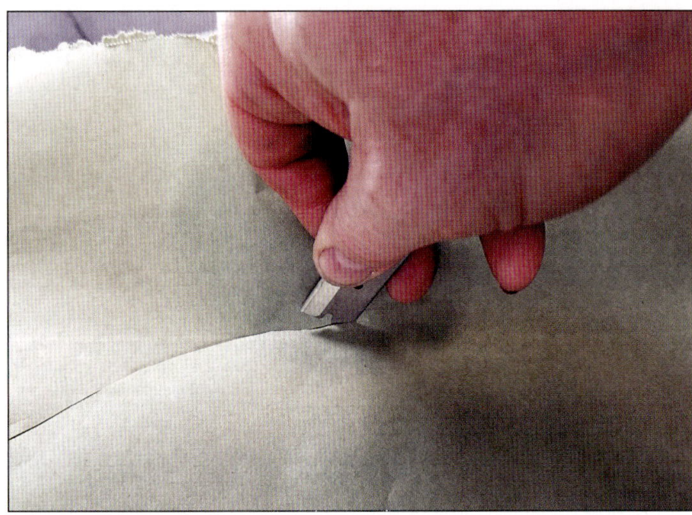

Lay the masking paper in and carefully trim the paper around the opening without cutting through to the tape.

The trunk area is ready for paint. With the framing, the paper won't come loose under the pressure of the paint-gun spray.

paper or plastic, keep the covering as smooth as possible. Dirt and overspray can get into folds of the paper and the plastic and eventually get into your paint. If you encounter folds, tape them down to prevent any kind of hiding place for contaminants.

When masking for repairs, don't lay down hard tape lines. The typical squared-off repair may look fine after the hard line is sanded off, but these paints activate under layers, and the square repair area shows up in the finished painted product. Take the time to sand back from the repair and feather out the paint to avoid hard lines.

Painting

Cleanliness and time are the most important things when painting. You got to this point with care, and by rushing at this point, you may ruin an otherwise-good paint job.

Before the car rolls into the paint area, clean it thoroughly with air and wipe it down completely so that you are not bringing problems in from the outside. Likewise, completely clean the paint area before introducing your car so that dust isn't falling on what you are intending to paint. Then, clean everything again.

One of my painter friends told me that 90 percent of the contaminants that end up in the paint come off of you. Hair, dry skin, sweat from reaching across the car and dirt from your clothes end up in the paint. I regularly see videos with painters not wearing long sleeves or head coverings. That works okay if you have a full downdraft booth but not in anything else. Tyvek suits are available for painting, and they not only keep overspray off of you, they keep you out of the paint.

Speaking of personal protective equipment (PPE), make sure that your mask is approved for spraying automotive paint. Dust masks or a bandana will not protect you from the rough stuff in the paint. Find disposable gloves that don't have powder (when you see the fingerprint under the clear coat, you will know why).

Safety equipment protects you and keeps debris out of the paint. Most trash that ends up in the paint job comes from you, so wear a full painting suit to reduce the amount of contaminants. Gloves prevent the oils on your fingers from touching any body surface and reacting to the paint. Always use a respirator that has been designed to be used in a paint environment, such as the one on the bottom left. For maximum protection, you can get an oilless compressor and hood to feed you fresh air from outside the paint booth (right).

Cleaning is everything. Regular paper towels can leave fibers and particles on the surface you are cleaning, so use lint-free towels when doing the final cleaning. Surface cleaners remove any remaining dust, oils, and trash that you may have missed. Follow this with a tack cloth to catch any remaining debris.

If your paint suit does not have a hood, wear a head covering to keep your hair from falling into the paint. Some locales may require the painter to have a supply of fresh air from outside of the paint area. This involves using an oil-less air compressor to feed the painter fresh air through a hose. Check your local laws to see if this is required.

Static charges can build up in the paint area, so grounding the body to the floor helps keep charged overspray from sticking where you don't want it. I usually run a chain from the body to the floor to ground the body.

Final preparation involves cleaning the car one more time. This is done with compressed air, surface-prep solvent, and tack cloths. First, put on your suit and gloves, turn on the exhaust fan, and blow off the entire car or panels to be painted with compressed air. Next, use lint-free towels and a surface-cleaning solvent to wipe clean the entire surface. Use a dry towel to remove any solvent residue before proceeding to the next area. Blow off the paint surfaces again and then use a tack cloth lightly to remove any remaining contaminants in the paint areas. Use the tack cloths lightly because you don't want to leave any of the tack cloth residue on the surface.

Mix modern paints exactly as the data sheet says. This must be done as is recorded on the data sheet.

The purpose of the primer/sealer coat is to lock down all of the bodywork, primers, fillers, and other items that can be reactivated when the color is applied to the paint. The primer-sealer coat is like epoxy/etch primer in that it is not intended to be sanded after it is applied (although, you can remove contaminants if you wish).

Apply the sealer coat right before color goes onto the car, whether you are painting the jams first or everything at once. There is a time frame to begin applying color. Don't start too early, and don't wait too long. Not waiting long enough traps solvents in the sealer coat, and waiting too long won't allow the color to adhere to the seal coat. I generally give the seal coat an hour to cure. Then, I go over it and "nib" out any dirt with 600- to 800-grit sandpaper before applying color.

Some painting techniques come from the paint that you select and some come from the equipment that is used. Spray pressure, distance from the object being sprayed, and patterns are determined by the paint gun. Paint overlap, viscosity, and the number of coats are determined by the paint manufacturer. The key is to remain consistent when painting.

Viscosity

In addition to mixing the paint as the manufacturer states, viscosity is also important. Viscosity, or the thickness of the paint, is affected by the temperature and the paint mixture. If it is too thin, the coverage can vary. If it is too thick, it can trap solvents under the paint.

Check the paint viscosity by using a viscosity cup. A viscosity cup has a small hole, and you time how long it takes to empty. This information is found on the data sheet and is usually marked with the time (in seconds), the size of the hole in the cup, and the temperature of the room. For example, viscosity measurements may be 16 to 18 seconds/DIN 4 cup/ 68°F (20°C). This means that it takes 16 to 18 seconds to drain a 4-mm DIN cup at 68°F. You can thin the paint with the recommended reducer to get the best coat coverage.

Coats and Overlap

The number of coats is determined by the manufacturer, not by the fact that you want it really shiny. In the old days, I'd put extra coats of clear on the paint to give it a deeper look. Today, manufacturers do not recommend this because it won't allow the solvents to draw out of the paint. Then, when you are wet sanding, you start smelling solvents, and in the hot sun, it causes problems. Use the recommended coverage by the paint manufacturer.

For years, I was told that the overlap between passes was one third (meaning that each new pass covers the previous pass by 1/3). However, in my most recent paint class, I was told that overlap is now 3/4 of a pass with the new paints and guns. Talk with your paint representative regarding the recommended overlap on your products.

Gun Setup

Your paint gun manufacturer should provide all of the information that is necessary to shoot a specific paint. The distance to the panels, pressure at the gun, pressure at the cap, and pattern width should be provided. If it is not provided, the general pattern is 8 to 12 inches from the item being painted and a 6- to 8-inch oval football-shaped pattern on the gun. Most professionals recommend opening the gun's fluid flow at fan width, running the paint gun full out. If you have good pressure at the gun, that is where it is designed to work.

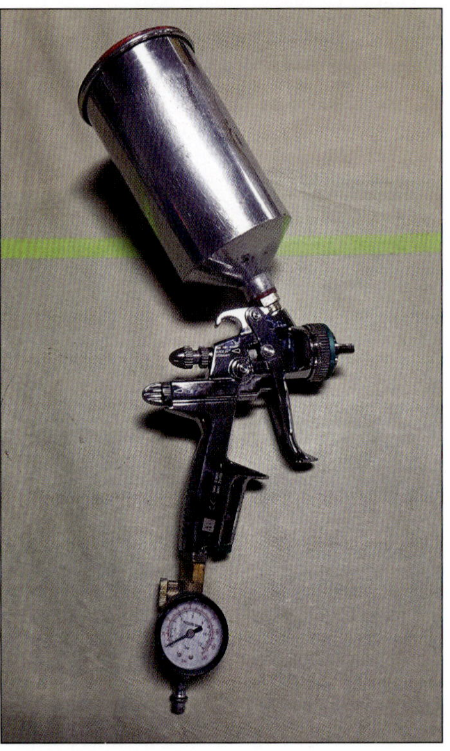

Newer paint guns have a built-in pressure gauge in the gun. It is important to know the pressure at the gun (not the pressure at the wall regulator). With 25 feet or more of flexible hose, the air expands and can surge so that the pressure on the wall regulator may not be the same as what you read at the gun. So, consider adding a regulator at your gun if you don't have one.

Set the air pressure of the paint gun properly, and read it at the gun (not on the regulator on the wall). The 25 feet of hose can cause a tremendous pressure spike when the trigger is pulled, causing a pressure drop as the compressor tries to catch up with the loss of air volume. Regulating the pressure at the gun eliminates this problem.

Jambs

Most color begins with painting doorjambs and the underside of parts. This allows the car to be assembled for consistent paint on the body. Paint overspray on the outside panels should be scuffed before the final paint is applied to the outer panels. After the jambs are dry, mask off the gaps with soft foam tape to prevent overspray in those areas. Mask off the back of painted hoods, trunk areas, etc. to avoid dry spray and overspray.

Tips

At last! When painting the car, keep the following in mind:

1. Always keep the paint gun perpendicular to the surface being painted. Angling the paint gun, especially when shooting metallic paints, can cause tiger striping and puddling of the paint.

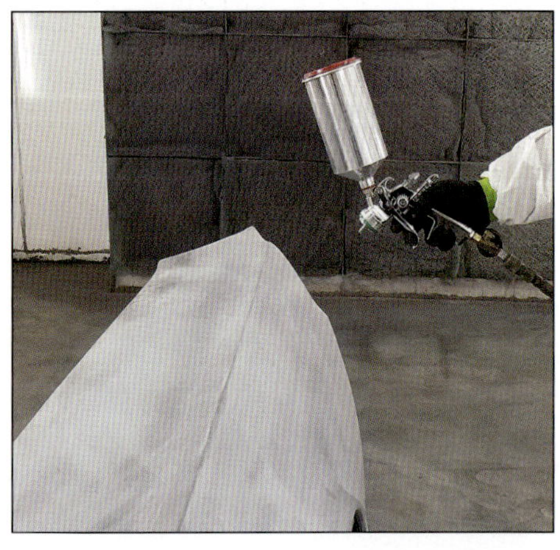

Always keep the gun parallel to the surface you are painting. This is difficult, especially when painting the middle of the roof panel. Don't swing your arm out at the end of each pass—keep it at a constant distance to the panel.

2. Stand the farthest away from the exhaust fan and begin at the roof and work your way down. If you do not have a fully heated down-draft booth, there will be some overspray in the air. Starting at the top means that the over-spray will fall down (gravity), and working toward the exhaust fan means that less overspray is flowing over the car.
3. Always run the paint pattern past the item you are painting. Stopping at the end rather than past the panel lays additional paint at that point. Always paint toward a wet edge. So, don't paint the roof from the inside out. Paint one side outside in. Then, come around and start at the inside and paint out to the outside on that side. This avoids dry areas and keeps the flow continuous.
4. Vary the pattern, especially when using metallic paint. For example, if you are painting a hood, run one pattern horizontal and the next one vertical. This may help reduce tiger stripes in the paint.
5. Be aware of the air hose! Drape it over your shoulder and hold it with your non-gun hand to keep it out of the paint. When painting, you may forget that the hose is there. It can touch the paint and ruin the paint job. If I am painting a full car, I have someone in there with me to keep the hose clear and yell at me if I get too close.
6. Going in and out of the paint booth between coats brings new contaminants into the booth. Have a clock in the booth (or visible from outside) and allow the coats to flash completely before adding the next coat. Rushing traps solvents and causes problems. Use good time management and minimize the number of trips in and out of the booth. Mix plenty of paint if you can and have it ready so that you don't have to step outside until it is necessary.

Here is a quick tip from a mistake that I have made: I keep the flexible hose draped over my shoulder and control it with the other hand to avoid slapping the freshly painted panels. A helper to make sure that the hoses don't get bound up is also a plus.

Overspray

On a concours paint job, proper overspray must be applied to the floorboards, onto the cowl area, and into the inside of the rear wheels. This was originally done with high-pressure paint guns, so it takes a little more effort to accomplish with modern HVLP guns. The overspray should protrude about 1/3 of the way into the floor pans on the underside of the car, being heavier out toward the pinch welds. In the wheel wells, the overspray should extend to the frame-rail area and under the lips. In the engine compartment, it can feather out to about the shock towers.

Don't have a baking paint booth? After the car completely dries, let the sun's ultraviolet rays do the job for you. This may draw out any last solvents in the paint and cure the paint faster. It's good to do before wet sanding and polishing.

The amount of overspray under the floorboards varied depending on who was doing the painting on the assembly line. Generally, 1/3 of the way in is a good point. It should taper to primer color as it moves to the middle.

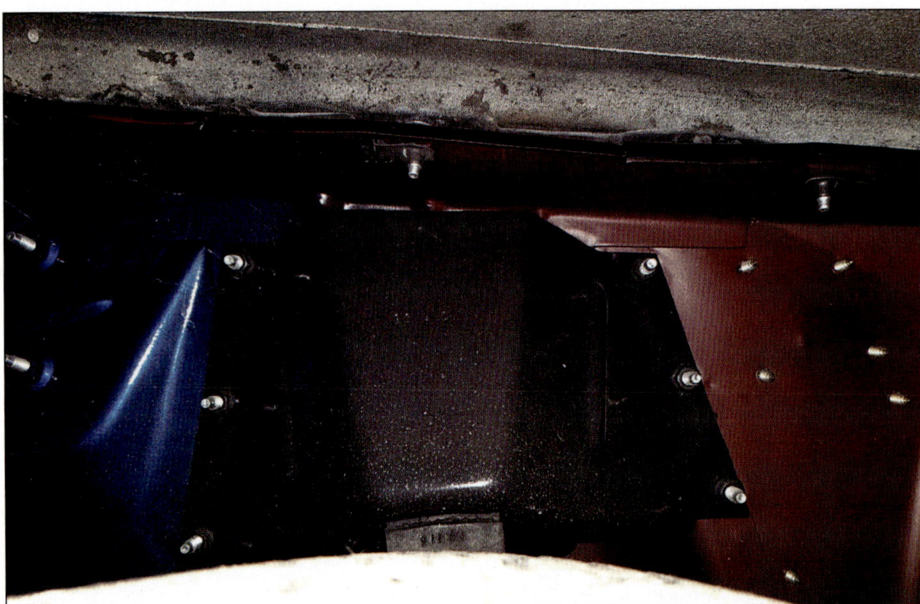

This overspray in the wheel well extends about halfway, but I have seen originals painted up to the battery area, and I have seen the chassis painted black in this area as well. Document where yours was if you can or find out what the judges like to see before painting the overspray.

Issues

Paint issues are inevitable. Generally, small runs in the paint can be sanded out, or you can use a razor block to cut them off and then finish them during the color-sanding process. Very small dust specs can usually be removed during the color-sanding process. Contaminants in some metallics cause the base coat to mottle around the contaminant, which will require the area or panel to be repaired.

Color Sanding and Buffing

The original paint had a small amount of orange-peel texture to it, so if you are building a stock show car, keep some orange peel in the paint. The HVLP process today now leaves a small amount, and if you want to remove it, sand out the finished paint. The process begins with 1,000- or 1,200-grit sandpaper and then moves to 1,500, 2,000, and 3,000 grit. Soak the paper or pads thoroughly to soften the paper before wet sanding. Unsoftened paper can

Very tiny dust particles can generally be sanded out of the paint. Once the little ring around the paint is gone, you are good to go. Make sure you spread out the sanding so that you don't develop a low spot when sanding out small dust particles.

This breakthrough to the primer occurred because the primer built up on the edge of the panel and it wasn't prepped properly. This was a quick fix, but cutting through to the primer can ruin the paint job.

Wet sanding the clear coat on modern paint results in a milky white residue that gets thinner with progressive finer sanding. If you start seeing body color in the residue, stop! That means you have broken through to the base coat.

There are many different buffing and polishing systems available. Consult with your local supply house to see what it recommends. I start with a cutting compound and then use a polishing compound. New systems are developed regularly.

Keep the panels clean during the polishing process and don't allow compounds to build up on the panels or the buffer. Use medium pressure and allow the compounds (not the pad) do the work.

cause deeper cuts than the abrasive surface. Each finer level of paper is intended to remove the scratches from the previous level. Work in alternating patterns if working by hand and change from cross patterns to round patterns and back.

The next step is using compound and polishing. As with the paint, find a system and stick with it. Various compounds are intended to be used with various machine pads, so use what is recommended.

The compounds and polish are intended to do the work—not the buffer. Use light to medium pressure on the paint and keep moving. It is easy to heat up and melt the paint with the buffing machine, and, like sanding, it is easy to break through on peaks of panels, so be careful in these areas.

CHAPTER 6

Engine

Many different engines were used during the 10-year run of the first-generation Mustang. I provide information about motors in this chapter by focusing on techniques rather than a step-by-step walk-through of a rebuild. This small-block V-8 rebuild may not directly help you rebuild a 6-cylinder or an FE, but some of the techniques will.

The Ford shop manual is an excellent place to begin an engine rebuild. If you don't have one, purchase one from a Mustang parts vendor. Some of the aftermarket repair manuals leave out some details that are needed to do the job correctly. However, rebuild books from CarTech that are specific to your engine are available and are higher quality than the auto-parts store generic repair manuals.

If you are doing a full restoration, don't just assume that the motor is okay just because it ran when it was

Some consider 1969 to be the high point of the American muscle-car wars, and the Mustang led the way with GTs, Shelbys, and the new Mach 1 and Boss cars. This 1969 Mach 1 is fitted with a 428 Cobra Jet engine, ram air, and a 4-speed transmission. It is finished in "Give me a Ticket" Candy Apple Red.

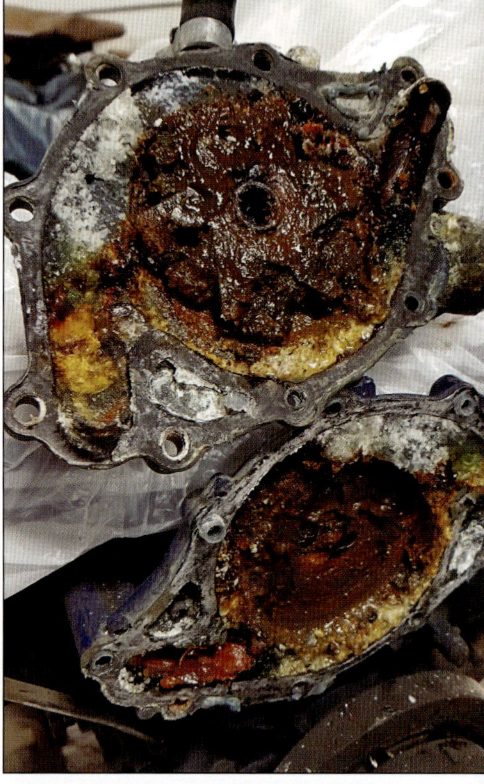

This small-block V-8 water pump came from a "ran when parked" engine, according to the owner. If you are going to store your motors long-term, prep them properly to avoid damage like this. The engine required a complete rebuild.

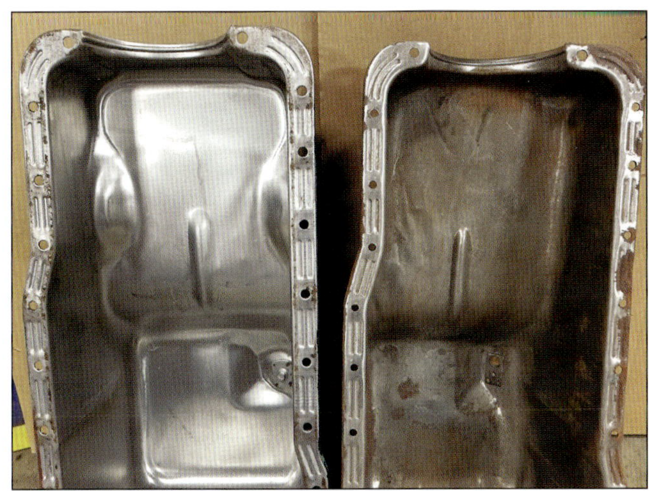

Be wary when purchasing parts at a swap meet: not all parts fit Mustangs. The oil pan on the left has the indentations for the Mustang engine-compartment crossmember. The truck pan on the right does not.

When buying engine parts at swap meets or online, get a seller contact and a guarantee against cracks and unseen damage. This crack (the bright yellow line through the bolt hole) could be fixed, but it is costly to do. You can't guarantee against normal wear, such as valve wear, but the parts have to be usable.

parked. Motors degrade just sitting there from corrosion in the coolant system and oil leaks.

If you purchase a motor at a swap meet, be wary. Customers regularly bring me motors that are "fresh rebuilds," but they are often assembled incorrectly. One even had bad rod knock when I fired it. Plan on at least a gasket set and have an engine builder inspect it before trusting someone else's work. Finding that vendor at next year's swap and getting reimbursement can be difficult.

When I sell engines or parts and when I buy engines or parts at swap meets, it is agreed by both parties that the parts will pass a Magnaflux check. Magnafluxing detects tiny metal cracks in the cast-iron components, and in general, if it passes a Magnaflux check, it is a usable part. On high-performance motors and parts, seek out someone who has experience and knows what to look for.

Engine History

Let's talk briefly about the engine history, as it also sheds some light on some of the issues you may encounter with your particular engine restoration.

6-Cylinder (170, 200, and 250)

First introduced in 1960 and built in Lima, Ohio, the three versions of the straight-6 engine are all part of the "Thriftpower Six" line of inline sixes. This engine was a low-cost workhorse that produced much-needed low-end torque for street vehicles. It wasn't fancy, but it was very reliable and dependable. Although it was mainly installed in economy-minded cars, options such as power steering and air conditioning were available, and they are sought after by collectors for these reliable drivers.

The 170 engine was borrowed directly from the Falcon line at its introduction and sported 101 hp, four main bearings, and a 1-barrel carburetor. The 200 engine didn't see installation until the conversion to alternators in August of 1964. The 200 sported seven main bearings, which improved harmonic vibration and provided much stronger bottom-end capabilities. Early 170s and 200s had three freeze plugs, and later 200s and 250s received five. In 1966, Ford went to a six-bolt bellhousing design.

The 250 was introduced in 1969 and was a punched-out version of the 200. It became the sole inline economy motor in 1971 through the 1973 model year.

The inline-6 bottom ends are actually quite good and reliable. The big problems with the inline-6 were the integral intake manifold and the poorly designed fuel/air path. This caused hesitations during acceleration and prevented serious time and development into any kind of performance enhancements. In addition, the cylinder heads could crack if they were not properly torqued. The oiling system is fine on the 6-cylinder. As Ford designed it, it is a good, reliable engine, but it is not flashy.

Small-Block V-8 (260, 289, 289 HP, 302, and 351 Windsor)

Although Ford built more 6-cylinder cars at first, the Ford small-block V-8 was the engine that established the Mustang's reputation and propelled it into the performance wars of the 1960s. The small-block V-8 is the most successful V-8 ever produced by Ford, having served over 39 years (1962–2001).

The good thing about the Ford small-block V-8 is that aside from some machining techniques from 50-plus years ago, there are no real issues with the basic design of the motor.

335-Series V-8 (351 Cleveland)

First introduced in the Mustang in the 1970 model year, the Cleveland V-8 shares technology from the small-block Windsor and the 385-series big-blocks. Big intake ports and huge valves reveal Ford's thinking during the horsepower wars, and these motors made good horsepower but lacked low-end torque.

When building a Cleveland, pay attention to the oiling system, as it can use some help, and the piston shift seemed to be a little more of a problem than on other motors. Piston shift is how centered the piston hole is in relation to the sleeve around it. Visualize the hole off center where the piston sleeve would be. When boring out the block, the cylinder wall can get thin on one side.

Boss 302

The Boss 302 is a small-block 302-style engine with canted-valve heads. The original Boss engine was noted for the original pistons cracking at the skirt, but this was redesigned in all replacement pistons. The pushrods could flex at high RPM, so if you plan to exercise the motor, upgrade them. Other than that, you have four-bolt mains and heavy-duty everything, which results in very few issues.

FE Big-Block (390, 428, and 427)

FE engines, while powerful and available to Ford until 1976, were 1950s technology. They seemed to build a ridge in the block very quickly, and rebuilds are more common on the FE than other motors. Since there were high-performance versions of the FE, they could suffer some of the same issues as the 427 race engines: cracks at the back of the block on the head-bolt threads and cracks on the outside of the head down the inside of the bolt holes near the water jacket.

The Drag Pak cars began getting oil coolers in 1969 to help reduce the oil temperature and reduce the number of engines that Ford had to replace under warranty—it was not there for drag racing! Stock engines suffered from a small port on the right-angle oil filter adapter, and many engines got the 427 version with bigger passages when they were rebuilt. Drag racers noted that the FE's bottom-end oiling needed help, but it is good for a street motor.

385-Series Big-Block (429 and Boss 429)

Since the 429 didn't rev like a Cleveland, it didn't really suffer from any of the Cleveland-like oiling issues. Being newer technology, the ridge problems of the FE were also not as prevalent on the 385-series engines.

The Boss 429 suffered from the O-ring design on the heads, which is one of the reasons that there are so many low-mileage Boss 429s around today. They blew up frequently, and most top engine builders weld up the heads and install a standard-style head gasket. The valvetrain also had some issues, but this motor was all power, and things will break. Drag Pak Cobra Jet versions, Super Cobra Jet versions, and Bosses also got the oil cooler to help with warranty issues.

Machine Shop

Most automotive enthusiasts do not have a full complement of mills and lathes to do the machining required to rebuild a motor. Even if you plan to assemble the engine yourself, here are some items that the engine builder should do to prepare the motor for reassembly:

- Hot tank and/or shot peen and clean the parts.
- Bore and hone the parts, valve jobs, etc. (all the "machining" stuff).
- Install the pistons on the rods. FE piston pins are held on the piston with retaining clips, but most engines use a press-on piston pin that needs to be heated to get it on the connecting rod. Most engine builders have an inductance heater to easily install the pins. Don't use a torch.
- Install the cam bearings. Again, machine shops have a nice tool to do this and make sure that it goes in with the correct orientation.
- Install hardened valve seats. These engines were not made to run on unleaded fuels, so have the machine shop install hardened valve seats to keep the valves wearing properly.
- Install freeze plugs and pipe

plugs. The machine shop can do this not because it is difficult but because I have left one out in the past, and it made a terrible mess.

Engine Considerations

Remember, these engines are now 50-plus years old. There are some items to consider when building older motors. In addition to the engine quirks that were previously mentioned, here are some other things to remember when dealing with the older motors.

Ford made 1 million Mustangs by the middle of 1966, which means that there were 1 million motors too. When Ford was mass producing engines, it probably wasn't taking the amount of time that your engine builder is taking to reassemble the engine. Machining techniques have improved substantially over the years, and your machine shop can rebuild to a much closer spec than the mass-produced engines.

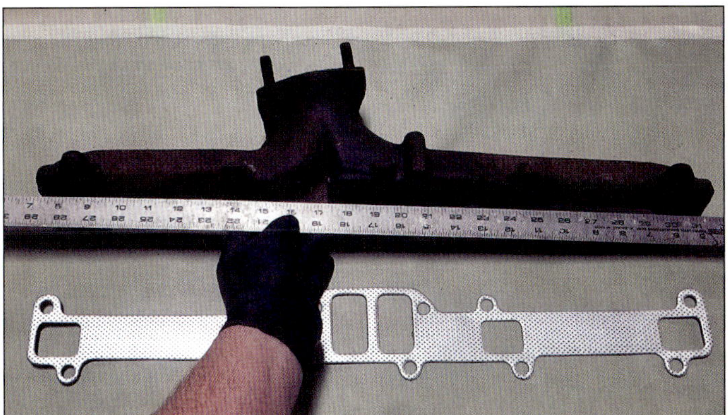

The cast-iron manifolds such as this 6-cylinder piece warped and usually leaked after the first removal from the engine. The exhaust manifolds were not installed with an exhaust-manifold gasket from the factory (lower). When reinstalling manifolds, use the gasket supplied with your rebuild kit or have your manifold mounting pads machined flat.

Engine Rebuild Tips and Tricks

See page 100 for tips and tricks to help you with your engine rebuild.

The rope-style rear seal on the left was used in most engines, as it was very good at sealing the rear main that had a lot of variance in machining. While it sealed well initially, it didn't last very long. Ford began using a two-piece design in the early 1970s, and it lasted longer. However, on some early engines, it may not seal without some shimming. You also need to remove the pins in the rear main cap that held the rope-style seal in place.

Most of these Mustang engines were built to use leaded fuels, which did not require a hardened seat installed, as the lead ash left a cushion on the seat to absorb the impact. If you are rebuilding your engine, install hardened valve seats to work with unleaded fuel.

In small-block V-8s (except the 289 HP) Ford used pressed-in rocker arm studs, which can pull out. Have your engine builder check to make sure that they won't pull up. If they do, machine the heads to accept screw-in-type studs.

Ford motors did not use exhaust manifold gaskets from the factory. The manifolds warp over time and need to be machined to lay flat against the cylinder head.

Early engines used a rope-style seal on the rear crankshaft. This allowed the machining in the seal area to be a little lax, and the rope seal didn't last long. Most likely, you will convert to use a two-piece seal on the rear, which may leak without some shimming. Also, there is a pin that held the rope seal in place: this pin needs to be removed or ground down and the hole must be sealed to avoid leaking at the rear seal.

The lead in leaded fuels served two purposes: 1) it increased the octane rating of the fuel, and 2) after it burned, a small amount of ash was deposited on the valve seat that cushioned the valve when it closed. This allowed for the use of a soft valve seat, which was inexpensive. Running unleaded fuels in these engines will eventually tear up the valve seats, so when you rebuild the engine, have the machine shop install a set of hardened valve seats in the cylinder heads.

Small-block Windsor motors came with rocker studs that were pressed into the cylinder head. All other engines have screw-in-type rocker studs or shaft-mounted rockers. The 289 Hi-Po has screw-in rocker studs. Even with stock camshafts, these studs can pull out, which can keep the valve from fully opening or they can pull out far enough to fail completely. So, have them double-checked before assembly.

On engines equipped with emissions control (smog), the Thermactor ports in the heads can really build up with crud from normal operation. Make sure the ports are thoroughly cleaned out before reassembly.

Engine Painting

You wouldn't think that painting an engine is a headache, but it can be. Using aerosols from the local auto parts store works for most engines, but for an original engine and show car, the paint is critical. Certain parts were painted on the engine, some were not. The color of the engine varied, and the off-the-shelf cans of paint are not always a good match. If you plan to paint the engine with a paint gun, the color number listed may be obsolete because some paint manufacturers discontinued single-stage paint. In general, the aerosols sold by the Mustang parts suppliers are a good match for most situations.

Early motors had their valve covers and air breathers painted separately off the engine. Later motors were painted all together. Some components were installed on the engine when it was painted, and if the engine came with a dress-up kit (for example, chrome valve covers), they were installed later. What was painted and not painted on your engine will best be determined by the group that is judging your car. Sometimes, painted parts don't look as pretty as the unpainted parts (for example, PCV hoses and valves), and it is up to you to determine the number of shiny parts on your motor.

Paint Palette

Early Ford motors were painted black until 1966, when they were painted blue. The valve covers on early cars were painted different colors to differentiate them. A chart of different Ford colors used on the motors is on page 93. Note that aerosols change, depending on batch number and manufacturer, and the PPG numbers may not be available as manufacturers are eliminating single-stage paints. Hopefully your paint supplier can switch to a brand you plan on using.

Ford Corporate Blue

Beginning in 1966, Ford distinguished its engines by painting them Ford Corporate Blue. This was used through the 1970s. The major problem with Ford Corporate Blue is that the color was not consistent from engine to engine or year to year. On

Depending on the engine, some items were painted along with the engine block. The PCV, hose and front-to-rear tubing were painted with the engine on the 1967–1969 FE engines, but some restorers leave these items unpainted because it looks "prettier." Make sure that the motor is detailed for the class in which you plan to compete (or do what you like).

Ford Engine Colors				
Year	Component	Color	Single-Stage Paint	Aerosol
1964–1965	Engine block	Black	PPG DAR 9000 Black	Any gloss black engine enamel
1964–1965	6-cylinder valve covers and air cleaner	Red	PPG 73124 GM Red	Duplicolor 1605 Red
1964	260-ci V-8 valve covers and air cleaner	Grabber Blue	PPG 2230 Ford Grabber Blue	Duplicolor 1601 Ford Light Blue
1964–1965	289-ci V-8 valve covers and air cleaner	Gold	PPG 26635 Renault New Beige Poly	National Parts Depot AP-EGC Ford Engine Gold
1966–1973	All painted components	Ford Corporate Blue	PPG 13358 Ford Corporate Blue	National Parts Depot AP-EB Ford Corporate Blue

Ford Corporate Blue was not regulated as well as the exterior paints, and as such, the color went from light to a darker blue. If you have original paint on your motor you can try to match it, and some top restorers are documenting the colors based on the time that certain groups of cars were built.

The reason the engine paint came off in big chips is that Ford used a lot of lead in the engine paint to help it stick to fresh engines that were covered in machining fluids and assembly lubes. This 1970 351W engine shows no original paint on the exhaust manifolds, but some engines had overspray on the manifolds. Check your rule book for proper painting.

some engines it was light, it was dark on others, and it depended on the plant and the supplier as to what the actual color was.

Top judges have worked hard to determine what the color was at what time and at what assembly plant. The best way to determine the correct blue for your engine is to get a sample from your engine (the bottom side of the air breather, a valve cover, etc.) and have it computer analyzed if possible. The paint code given in this chapter is a good generic match. You can get a custom blend made for your engine from automotive paint suppliers to match the color on your sample part (if needed).

Aerosol versus Spray Gun

As previously stated, most of the Mustang vendors carry an extensive line of paint for your engine that will look fine. Some restorers prefer to shoot a single-stage automotive enamel, rather than using aerosols. The reason is that the single-stage automotive paint is catalyzed, which means that it hardens better than the air-dry paints. It is also less susceptible to color change when heated like non-catalyzed paints.

When shooting engine paint, decide whether or not to use a primer first. Ford didn't use a primer under the color; it shot the paint straight on the engine. Some restorers do this as well. I prefer to use an epoxy primer under the paint to help with paint adhesion.

Carburetors

As time moves onward, fewer individuals know about the original

Engine Detailing

Engine detailing varies depending on how you want the engine to look and if you are going to have it judged. Ford was very utilitarian with its motors, sometimes painting things that normally didn't get paint. Some engines had the exhaust manifolds mounted on the engine when they were painted, and they got some paint on them. Bypass hoses and PCV tubing was painted all together on FE engines. Pretty brass parts were painted blue. If your judged class requires it, research and document what parts were painted and which were not for your particular engine. Most owners find a happy medium between what the factory did and what has eye appeal.

This example motor detail is a 351 Windsor that is going back into a 1970 Shelby GT350. The owner decided on a "pretty" detail rather than the "correct" detail from the factory. Here are a few tips on how to spray your engine.

I am shooting an epoxy primer followed by a single-stage paint (PPG/Omni 13358). You don't need a lot of primer—just enough to give the blue something to stick to. Now, I will have an even color all over the engine.

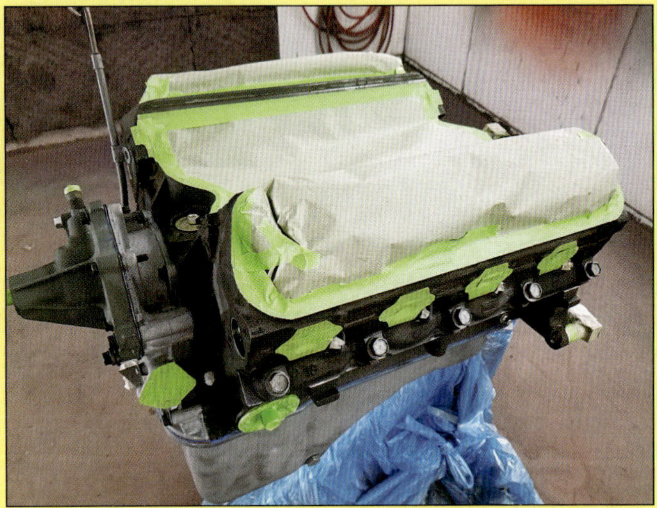

This engine is receiving a Shelby intake and valve covers, so I fully covered the open areas before painting. I covered the engine stand so that dirt doesn't get into the engine paint.

A 1½-inch rubber expansion plug works well to keep the paint out of the distributor hole.

Make sure to get into all of the tight spots. The single-stage paint should last longer without burning like the non-catalyzed aerosols.

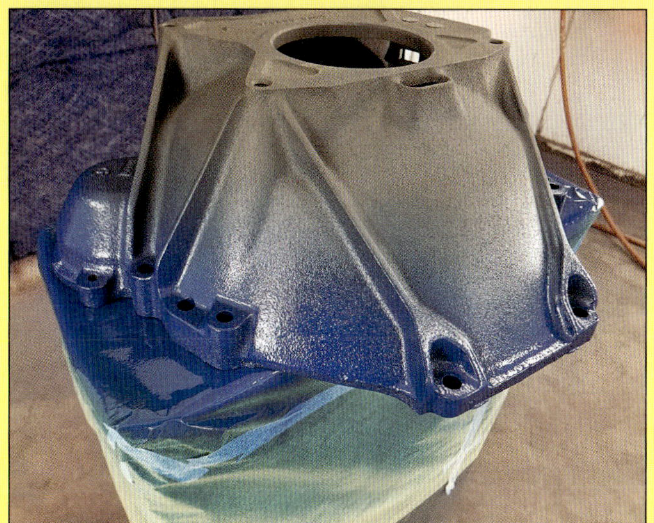

The 4-speed bellhousings appear to have been installed when the engine was painted, so I dusted some overspray on the bellhousing on this build.

With engine painted, I begin reassembly. My sources said that the thermostat housing and bolts were reused on the engines, so they were painted blue from the factory and transferred to the Shelby intake. Note that the Shelby intake received new bolts and not the ones from the factory 4V engine.

carburetors and how to rebuild them. Correct restoration of carburetors is getting harder to find, as the methods of correctly replating carburetors becomes more regulated, and many companies are dropping their ability to replicate the plating that is found on carburetors. Several years ago, there were many solid companies to help with rebuilding, but most are long gone. There are still some out there, but most come and go, and my list is dwindling.

Many books have been written on rebuilding Holley and other aftermarket carburetors. However, there is a lack of information about rebuilding and detailing Ford carburetors that were used on Mustang engines. Holley carburetors were plated with zinc chromate, and some Ford carburetors were usually left as bare cast aluminum. Hardware on the bolts were plated gold cadmium, brass, or chromate, depending on the carburetor and application. The plating varied from year to year as well, so your best bet is to look at examples of your particular carburetor at car shows or online for the correct finish and plating. Check the rule book from your judging body for additional information.

Care needs to be taken when cleaning carburetor parts for restoration. Glass-bead blasting can be used on some of the parts, but care needs to be taken on the finish. The glass beads can imbed themselves in the housing and then find their way into passages and into the bowl and cause performance problems later. If you choose to bead blast the housing, cover the ports and avoid getting abrasive on the inside of the housing.

A list of carburetors used on

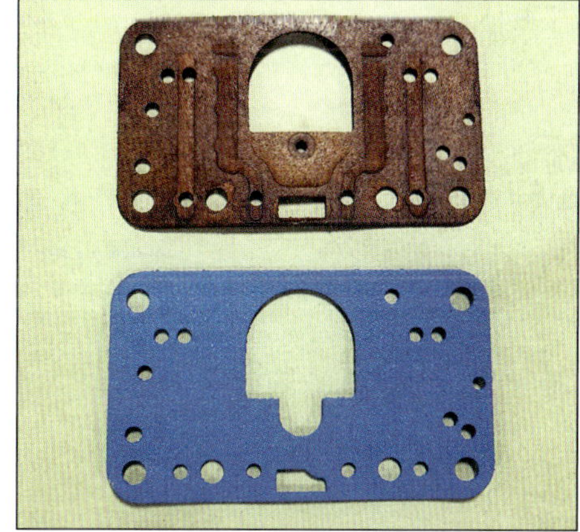

Today's ethanol-based fuels are torture on the original-style gaskets (top), which dried out quickly and caused leaks. Newer silicone and permanent-use gaskets are on the market (bottom) that work better with ethanol-blend fuels. If you plan to drive the car and they are available for your carburetor, use the silicone or permanent-style gaskets instead of the original style.

Mustang Carburetors	
Type	**Details**
1-barrel	Autolite 1100, Holley 1940, Carter YF, Carter RBS - All 6-cylinder engines 1964–1973
2-barrel Autolite or Motorcraft 2100	All Mustang engines with a 2 barrel carburetor
4-barrel Autolite 4100	Small-block V-8s 1964–1966, 289 Hi-Po, through 1967
4-barrel Autolite or Motorcraft 4300	Small-block V-8s 1967–1973
4-barrel Autolite or Motorcraft 4300 spreadbore	Some 71-73 351 Clevelands, 351 H.O., Boss 351
4-barrel Holley 4150	Boss 302, 390 GT, 428 Cobra Jet/Super Cobra Jet, all Shelby Mustangs except the 1969–1970 GT350 and 429 Super Cobra Jet
4-barrel Holley 4160	1967 GT500 (two of them)
4-barrel Rochester Quadrajet	429 Cobra Jet

I have experienced bad luck with current offshore point sets, so I seek out original points when rebuilding distributors. The two end examples are for dual-point applications (one original Autolite and one early aftermarket), and the center one is for single-point applications. The later Motorcraft service replacements work just fine. (Photo Courtesy Cunningham Archives)

Mustang engines is on page 96. The carburetor that was used depended on the year of the vehicle, the engine, and how the vehicle was equipped. The CFM rating and venturi size also depended on the engine selection.

Distributors and Alternators

The distributors and alternators have an aluminum casing, and in the old days, we would just glass-bead blast the case and put them back together. Glass-bead blasting removes the metal, and you lose some crispness on the detailing of the casting. The preferred way to detail these parts is by tumbling the parts and polishing the metal rather than blasting. Some restorers re-machine the surfaces with a clean-up cut on a lathe or mill to get the finish just right.

Most of the distributor reproduction parts are fine for most restorations, with the exception of ignition points. I have had extremely bad luck with the current offshore points sets (the only source of points in the US), so I seek out original Ford or older points sets from the 1970s at swap meets when doing tune-ups.

There are minor differences in some of the restoration parts that top judges look for, but for most cars, they work well. An advantage to using new plug wires is not relying on 50-year-old graphite wires on

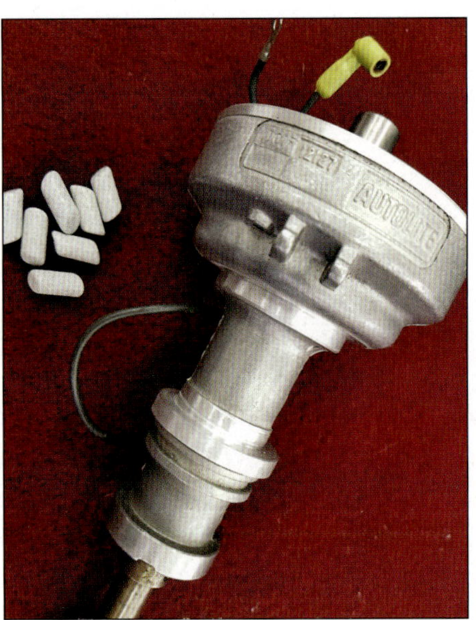

This Autolite distributor was placed in a tumbler to clean and restore the body to the correct finish. Then, it was placed in a lathe to clean up and refinish the machined surfaces. Unlike carburetor bodies, distributors can be tumbled for an amazing finish. (Photo Courtesy Cunningham Archives)

Early distributor caps were marked with a "1" only. Then, they received the "Autolite" or "Motorcraft" lettering (1972–1973) on the top. There were two different letter styles on the Autolite caps: thin (bottom) and thick (top). The thin-lettered cap is reproduced. Note the packaging for sale in department stores. There may still be some NOS caps out there. (Photo Courtesy Cunningham Archives)

Carburetor Build Tips

Carburetor wizards can rebuild a carburetor with their eyes closed, and it will run smooth on the first turn of the key. There is a touch to rebuilding carburetors that I don't have, but I'm rebuilding an Autolite 2100 from a 1970 Mustang Mach 1 351W-2V. I did not do a show-car rebuild. Instead, it is a functional rebuild that shows some tips on what to do when rebuilding the Ford carburetor. ■

I am doing a functional rebuild on this D0AE-V Autolite 2-barrel carburetor from a 1970 351 Windsor automatic Mustang. I use the drip tray from the garage to keep little parts from rolling away, and to keep solvents off the table.

Use carburetor cleaner or compressed air to clean out all of the fuel passages. Don't use brushes or anything that can scratch the passage.

It is important to keep the new needle and seat clean and free from debris. I had a professionally rebuilt show carburetor with a small amount of debris stuck on the needle that kept it from closing. It resulted in getting fuel all over the carburetor and intake. Check for proper operation after installation.

Most kits provide a gauge for setting the float level (both dry and wet), and they provide a chart to match your particular carburetor. Make sure that when adjusting the float, you bend the needle side of the tab and not the float side of the metal bracket.

External items such as the heater-line bracket can be blasted and painted because they are nowhere near a fuel port. It isn't pretty, but the carburetor fired right up and ran great with minimal adjustments.

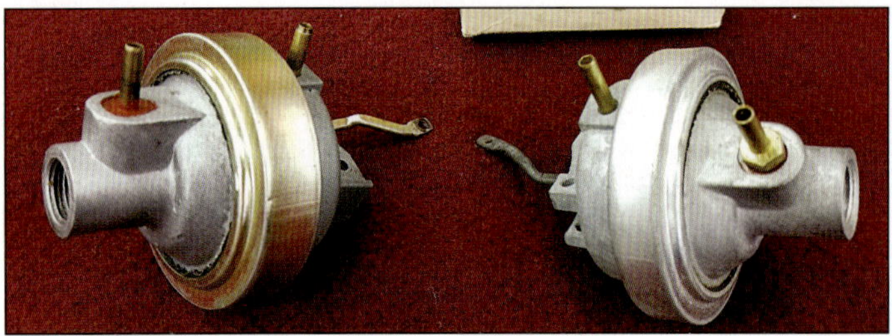

The vacuum advance can also be restored and replated, but it requires some special tools to do so. Note the bands on these two advance units: one is plated and one is not. If building a concours car, research the finish before buying NOS pieces, as Ford changed things from assembly-line to service parts.

The 1964½ Mustangs were fitted with generators, which were painted semi-gloss black and were stamped in the middle (this can't be seen when the cover is in place). The generator covers are becoming scarce and very pricey to replace. And no, that is not where the ground wire should attach.

your driver Mustang. If you plan on driving the car at all, use the reproduction wires.

Restoring the alternator is also very dependent on when it was built. Original alternators varied in output from 38 to 55 amps. Most rebuilders simply use the bigger 55-amp (or larger) core regardless of the original output. The same applies for the early generators.

Ford moved to alternators in 1965, and they went through many changes and styles through 1973. Early alternators were ink stamped with the application, and later units were stamped in the housing like this one. This unit was made by Dead Nuts On in Sewickley, Pennsylvania, and the company can include the exact detailing for your application.

Exhaust Manifolds

With the exception of the early Shelbys and their Tri-Y headers, all Ford engines came equipped with cast-iron exhaust manifolds. As previously mentioned, Ford did not use exhaust-manifold gaskets on its motors, and when refurbishing the manifold, have the mating surfaces milled flat and avoid running a gasket. Cleaning can be done with a blast cabinet or by shot-peening at the machine shop.

Besides warping, your other dangers to exhaust manifolds are heavy corrosion, cracking, and breaking tabs. Cast-iron manifolds can be repaired, but it can be expensive, and sometimes the repair will stick out on a show vehicle. Unless it is a rare manifold, it is probably best to find a new one.

Front Pulleys and Accessories

Some Ford pulleys are imprint stamped with a part number, and some were ink stamped. Pulleys and mounting brackets were either painted semigloss black or phosphated (with the exception of the power-steering mounting bracket made of aluminum on some engines—it was left bare aluminum). Some of the mounting hardware was painted the engine color if they were used to mount items such as the water pump when the engine was painted, and some are plated or phosphated.

Ford marked all its engine pulleys with an ink stamp or a stamping into the pulley. This water-pump pulley is used on 1969 302 and 351 two-sheave applications.

Although some road draft tubes were used in 1964 and even in some 1965 models, Ford's first application of emissions control was the positive crankcase ventilation (PCV) valve. Rather than dumping the oil vapors out onto the road like a road draft tube, the PCV opens when the pressure builds in the crankcase and sends the oil vapors into the engine to be burned.

In 1966, Ford began installing Thermactor smog equipment on California cars and later did so on all cars, depending on the engine. A Thermactor system injected air into the exhaust ports, and the heat from the exhaust fumes would reignite unburned fuel. This photo also shows some of the custom tools needed to restore the Thermactor pump properly. (Photo Courtesy Cunningham Archives)

Emissions-Control Systems

Starting in 1964, the industry began installing emissions-control systems on cars to reduce the amount of pollution in the atmosphere.

The first system was the positive crankcase ventilation (PCV) valve. Some early Mustangs were fitted with a road draft tube, which took the oily fumes from the crankcase and dumped them onto the road surface. The PCV system replaced the road draft tube, and the valve opens up when the pressure built up to allow the vapors to be piped into the intake system and burned. Which car received which system varied. I rebuilt a PCV system that was originally built for an April 13, 1964, Mustang, and I have seen a road draft tube installed on a December 1964 car, which was well into 1965 production.

Next came the Thermactor system. The Thermactor was a pump that injected fresh air into the exhaust gasses to help burn off additional hydrocarbons before they exited the exhaust pipe. The first Thermactor systems were installed in 1966 on cars destined for California and the West Coast.

In 1970, evaporative emissions systems were installed on some vehicles in California and later everywhere. The evaporative emissions system changed the vented gas cap to a closed gas cap. Then, a line went from the fuel tank to a charcoal canister in the front of the vehicle and was then fed into the intake to burn the vapors rather than expel them into the atmosphere.

Finally, the exhaust gas recirculation (EGR) system was installed in 1972–1973 and did exactly as the name said. It took some of the exhaust emissions and reinserted them into the intake to be burned again and reduce emissions.

In 1970, Ford began installing evaporative (EVAP) emissions control systems on California and West Coast Mustangs. The EVAP system used a non-vented gas cap, and when the fumes in the tank became sufficient, they would be sent up to the engine and stored in this charcoal cannister. Then, they'd be sent to the engine to be burned. (Photo Courtesy Cunningham Archives)

Beginning in 1972, Ford began using exhaust gas recirculation (EGR) valves. The EGR valve took a portion of the exhaust gasses and sent them into the engine to be reburned to reduce the combustion-chamber temperature and reduce the amount of smog created. (Photo Courtesy Cunningham Archives)

Engine Rebuild Tips and Tricks

Prepping the area for engine assembly can save you time in the long run. There is a lot of plastic to contain the mess and the reference material and specialty tools are ready.

Many books are available on how to rebuild your specific engine. Here are some books from CarTech that I keep on the shelf:

- *Ford Inline Six: How to Rebuild and Modify* by Matt Cox and Barton Maurer
- *How to Rebuild the Small-Block Ford* by George Reid
- *Ford 351 Cleveland Engines: How to Build for Max Performance* by George Reid
- *Ford FE Engines: How to Rebuild* by Barry Rabotnick
- *How to Rebuild Ford Big-Block Engines* by Charles Morris

Along with the factory shop manual, these books come in handy when rebuilding your motor. So, here are some tips and tricks that I use when building engines for my customers. Some of these are gleaned directly from the other books, and some are intended for the first-time builder to help get the engine right. These cover all engines, regardless of configuration.

When building your own motor, err on the side of caution. I may recommend something that your engine builder doesn't do anymore but you should.

The test subject is a bone-stock 289 C-Code engine from a 1965 Mustang. The owner has other cars with high-performance options, so for this car, he wanted worry-free drivability.

Assembly Preparation

Throwing random bolts and plugs in a box will cause you nightmares during the assembly process. Bag and tag your parts and organize them in the sequence in which you will need them. Take many photos during the disassembly process so that you know which bolts go where.

My machine shop bored the 289 0.030-over and installed the cam bearings and freeze plugs. He has the special tool for installing the bearings. If you forget an oil-gallery plug, it will ruin your day.

The assembly begins with your dry measurements. Although modern manufacturing techniques are very good, we still gap all of our rings to the cylinders to make sure that they are within the correct specifications.

Run a tap down all of the bolt holes to clean the bolt holes and to make sure that you are getting accurate torque readings during assembly.

Rotating Assembly

When installing the camshaft, fall in love with assembly lube. Most camshaft manufacturers won't warranty the cam if you wipe a lobe, so make sure that you use plenty.

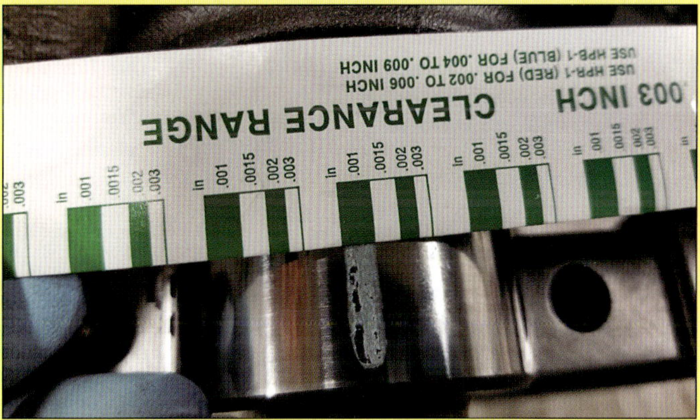

If you don't have an inside micrometer, you can still use old-fashioned Plastigauge to check the bearings on the crank and rods. Lay a small piece on the bearing surface, torque down the cap or rod, and use the printed gauge on the side of the package to measure the squeezed material.

ARP assembly lube works better than oil or WD-40 to get accurate torque readings on critical bolts. Make sure that you follow the torque sequences from your shop manual or bolt manufacturer.

Engine Rebuild Tips and Tricks *continued*

Check crankshaft endplay with a dial indicator or by using a feeler gauge. Use a few big screwdrivers to move the crank back and forth and hold while checking the distance between the thrust bearing and crank.

The machine shop installed the pistons on the rods because they are the press-on style and require heat. A soda-bottle rack is a nice way to keep the pistons and rods in order for assembly.

Masking tape helps install the rings on the pistons and to determine where the gaps should be per the shop manual. When the piston rings are installed, peel off the template and stick it on the next piston (note the notch mark used for alignment). This saves a little time because you won't have to look back at the book each time.

Use a clean, old-fashioned, metal coffee can full of break-in oil to coat the rings and grooves before installing the pistons in the bores. Break-in oils have more zinc dithiophosphate (ZDDP) in them, which offers more protection during the engine break-in.

These rod-bolt covers protect the crankshaft from damage when installing the rods in the engine. You can do the same thing with some rubber vacuum line or fuel hose.

A piston-ring compressor can be rented at some auto parts stores to install the pistons. I prefer using a serrated ring compressor (shown), as it puts less surface area on the ring and allows the rings to slide in easier. A gentle tap with a rubber hammer end on the piston is all it should take.

One of the most common mistakes that people make when assembling a motor is getting the oil-pump driveshaft installed incorrectly. The little snap ring goes up toward the distributor and prevents the driveshaft from pulling out of the pump when the distributor is removed.

Proper Sealing

The end oil-pan seals move around more than a toddler. A little weatherstripping adhesive holds it in place while you install the oil pan. Don't forget extra sealant in the corners and gaps to prevent leaking.

The gap between the timing cover and block also receives an extra amount of sealant. I generally side on using excess sealer because I hate leaks.

Valvetrain

This spring compressor is another auto-parts store tool rental. It is good for these stock springs and two-piece retainers, but it may not work well with performance springs. Don't forget to install the valve seals before the springs.

An 18-egg container works well for keeping the lifters in order if you are reusing your lifters. Keep the rockers and hardware together using a zip tie or a piece of string until they are ready to install.

Engine Rebuild Tips and Tricks *continued*

Use an oil can to soak the lifters and use an old pushrod or screwdriver to pump the lifter full of oil. Apply plenty of assembly lube after pumping the lifter full of oil.

All metal-on-metal moving surfaces get assembly lube. Don't forget the rocker tips, pushrods, and fulcrums. The assembly lube will be there longer than a coat of oil if you need to store the engine.

Final Assembly

The intake-manifold gaskets are so notorious for leaking that some builders just use silicone to seal up the engine and avoid the gaskets. Any time a surface changes angles, such as the angle of the corners of the intake to the heads, extra sealant is recommended.

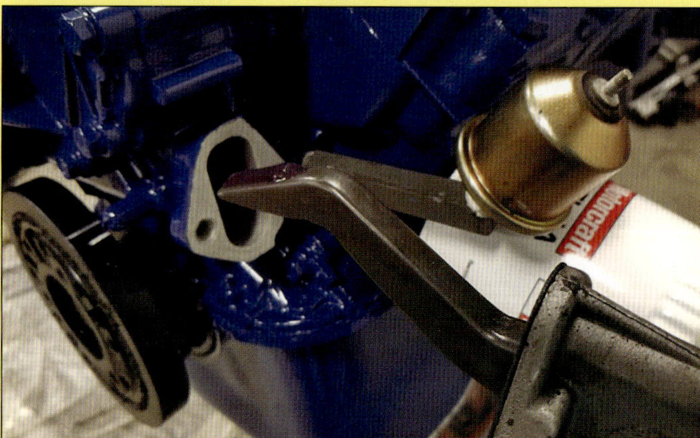

More assembly lube is shown on the arm that contacts the camshaft fuel-pump eccentric. Depending on the rotation position of the cam, it may push down on the pump and make it harder to tighten down the pump.

Stock on the inside doesn't have to mean boring on the outside. This engine was installed in a 1965 fastback and ran great in traffic and on the highway. Take your time and follow the shop manual and you will be up and running in no time.

CHAPTER 7

Transmission and Drivetrain

In 1970, Ford dropped the 390 GT engine but added the 351 Cleveland to the Mustang lineup. That same year, Ford introduced the Grabber Mustang in blue, green, orange, and yellow. This Grabber Mustang came with a C-style (or Boss-style) stripe, 14-inch flat hubcaps and trim rings, and a 302 engine. This example, which is owned by Seth Nichols, has been upgraded with appearance goodies from a 1970 Mach 1.

Only some of the Ford specialty tools that are required to rebuild Ford transmissions are shown. No, you don't need all of them. Yes, you might get by with some regular hand tools, but rebuilding a transmission may not be worth the effort without the proper tools.

In this chapter, I focus on restoration rather than rebuilding. There is a difference. Unlike engines, where once you get past the machine work, you can reassemble one with patience and tool loaner programs, transmissions are a different animal. They require tools that you can't get on loan, and they are complicated.

If you plan to restore one Mustang, the time, effort, and tool cost that is involved doesn't make sense for a single rebuild. I have rebuilt transmissions myself, but to do it right, I leave it to the professionals. If you want to rebuild your own transmission, there are some great books from CarTech on how to do it:

- *How to Rebuild & Modify Ford C4 & C6 Automatic Transmissions* by George Reid

- *How to Rebuild & Modify High-Performance Manual Transmissions* by Paul Cangialosi

Rebuilding a transmission is one thing but prepping it to go into your Mustang is another, and maintaining it requires some knowledge. Here is some basic information regarding automatic and manual transmissions and how to prepare them for your car.

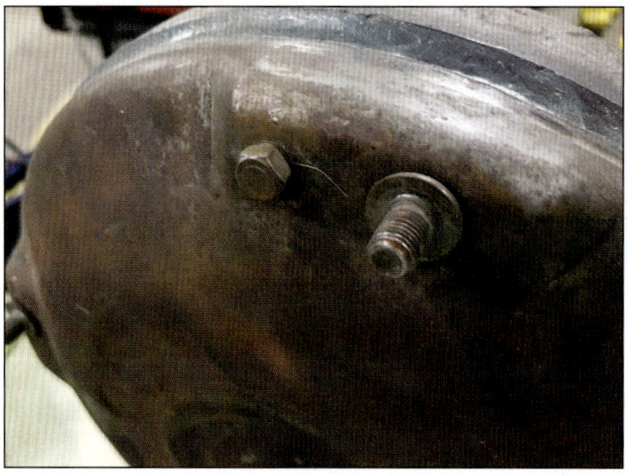

Ford torque converters have a drain plug (left of the mounting bolt) for flushing out the converter. Flushing doesn't get all of the little metal shavings and other debris that get stuck in the vanes. If you have a rare converter, it is best to have it rebuilt, and for most applications, a new converter is the best choice.

Automatic Transmissions

All three automatic transmissions that were used (the C4, the FMX, and the C6) function similarly and have a similar makeup of parts. They are all hydraulic transmissions, which means that they use hydraulic fluid (Ford Type F) to create hydraulic pressure to operate the transmission and to lubricate the internal components. They all use a torque converter to couple and decouple the engine from the transmission.

The gears are shifted through a series of bands and clutches that hold or release the gears depending on the speed of the engine. The clutches and bands are controlled by the valve body, which directs the fluid where it is needed.

Torque Converter

The torque converter, like the clutch, decouples the engine from the transmission at low speed and engages the transmission when the RPM increases. The term "stall speed" means that this is the highest RPM range before the converter fully locks in to move the transmission's input shaft. For example, a stock converter in an FMX transmission behind a 351C-4V will "stall" at 1,800 rpm. This means that the engine is fully connected to the transmission at 1,800 rpm.

The torque converter is primarily three different parts: the impeller, the turbine, and the stator. The advantage of using a torque converter is that it can multiply the torque at low RPM and help get the car moving.

When rebuilding the transmission, it is always better to replace the converter rather than flush the old one. Ford torque converters have a drain plug, but simply flushing the converter will not get all the contaminants out of the impeller and turbine. The cost of a new converter is not terribly high, and risking your freshly rebuilt transmission on a used converter is simply not worth it.

If you have a rare torque converter, such as a 428 Cobra Jet converter, and want to reuse it, they can be rebuilt. This requires cutting open the converter, rebuilding it, and then rewelding it back together. It is more expensive than replacing with a new converter, but for irreplaceable converters, it is the best choice.

Valve Body

The valve body is located just inside the transmission pan and controls where the hydraulic fluid is delivered. All of those fluid passages have the purpose of turning on valves, servos, and clutches. The

This rat's maze of passages is how the valve body directs hydraulic fluid to the clutches and servos in the transmission. There are all types of steel check-valve balls and devices, so be careful and document where everything goes during disassembly.

manual valve in the valve body is what is attached to the gearshift lever, and this valve is what directs the fluid through the correct set of passages.

The filter for the transmission is attached to the valve body and should be changed every 30,000 miles.

Band Adjustment

The bands are steel straps with a friction material on one side, and when activated by a servo, they lock down on one of the spinning drums and keep it from rotating. As the transmission gets higher mileage, the bands may need adjustment. If the bands are too loose, the transmission slips. If the bands are too tight, the components destroy themselves. Adjust the bands on an older transmission every 12,000 miles.

Adjusting the bands on a C4 or a C6 transmission can be done from the outside of the transmission. There are adjustment screws for the intermediate and low/reverse bands on a C4 as well as one for the intermediate band on a C6. On an FMX, the adjustment is made from inside the case by removing the transmission pan, and it requires special wrenches that are not available on loan, so it is best to take it to a professional.

As the transmission bands wear, they need to be adjusted to keep the proper tension on the drums. The bolts on a C4 and a C6 look like this: two on the C4 and one on the C6. The FMX cannot be adjusted from the outside.

The bands are tightened to 10 ft-lbs (120 in-lbs). Loosen the locking nut on the adjustment screw and tighten the screw to specification. After reaching 10 ft-lbs, back off the adjustment screw as follows: 1½ turns for the C6 intermediate, 1¾ turns for the C4 intermediate, and 3 turns for the C4 low/reverse band. Install a new locking nut when setting the bands.

Vacuum Modulator

The automatic transmissions use engine vacuum to shift the transmission at the correct time. The vacuum modulator connects to the shift valve, and a vacuum line runs from the valve up to the back of the intake manifold. The modulator has a pin that pushes against the shift valve, so don't forget to reinstall the pin!

The modulator is adjusted by a small screw in the vacuum-hose connecting tube. Most modulator issues occur with the vacuum line running down the modulator, rather than with the modulator itself. If the vacuum line gets a leak or split, it may prevent the transmission from shifting properly or at all. Check the lines periodically to make sure that they are not kinked and have free flow—especially the one at the modulator because it usually makes a 90-degree turn.

Leaking Front/Rear Seal

On many of the rear seals, there is a rubber lip and the tailshaft sticks out farther than the seal itself, so you can't just grab your seal installer and install the seal. I don't recommend trying to tap it in with a hammer. Use a piece of 3½-inch exhaust pipe (most auto parts stores sell a small length of conversion pipe) and press it into position with a seal installer. Liberally coat the seal on the inside with white grease or transmission fluid to prevent tearing during the first drive.

The front seal can be changed without pulling the front pump, but the front pump gasket/seal is usually leaking as much as the front shaft seal. Pulling the front seal usually requires pressing it out from the inside, unless you get lucky and it comes out easy by hand. However, it usually doesn't. If you need to change the input-shaft seal, change the front pump gasket too.

Two types of vacuum modulators were used on first-generation Mustangs. The screw-in style (upper) is more common, and the push-in style (lower) shows the modulator pin on the bottom. The C4 and C6 are interchangeable, and the FMX will not interchange.

Changing the Transmission Pan Gasket/Filter

The biggest issue by far with automatic transmissions is the transmission pan leaking. Like the engine oil pan, the transmission pan bolts are not torqued very tightly, and the pan is easily warped the first time that it is removed and reinstalled. Some of the aftermarket pans have been known to leak as well.

It is a messy job changing the pan gasket and the transmission fluid filter because Ford did not install a drain plug in the pan. Unless you have an extremely large drain pan, you will make a mess on the floor, as the fluid level is above the lip of the pan and comes gushing out once the seal is broken. To reduce the mess, snake a pump down the dipstick tube and pump out the majority of the fluid to minimize the mess under the car.

Leaks typically occur around the bolt holes because they usually get over-tightened and the pan is then distorted. Before reinstalling the pan, dolly the bolt holes in the pan flat and don't over-torque the bolts. ■

Ford transmission pans don't have a drain plug. To avoid having a lake of fluid in your garage, purchase a fluid pump, snake it down the transmission-filler tube, and pump out some of the fluid prior to removing the pan.

Inspect the bolt holes upon removal of the pan. If the pan has been over-torqued, the holes get distorted toward the transmission side. Make sure that the bolt areas are flat before reinstalling the pan.

Use a paint strainer to sift through the old fluid and look for problems. You will get some small metal shavings, and the clutch and band material is usually a dark gray muddy substance in the bottom of the pan. Expect to see some material, but consider rebuilding if you find large pieces or a large amount of metal.

The pan has been removed. The screen in this transmission is clear, and if it is clogged, you may have a problem. The screen unbolts from the valve body, and the new screen should come with a new O-ring.

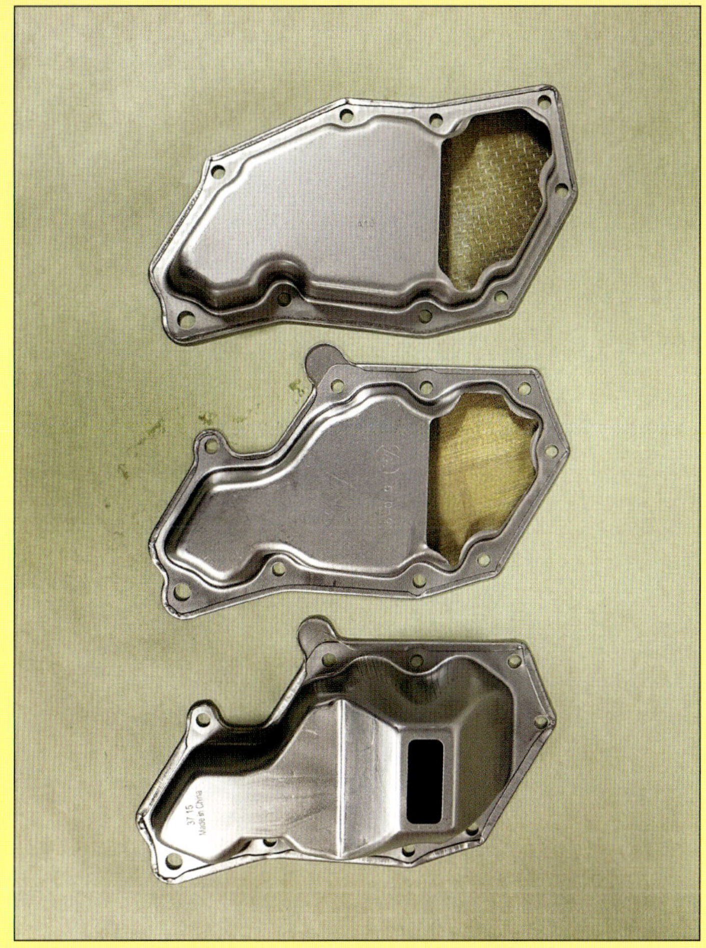

It is important to use the correct filter and screen for your application. The top filter is for an early C4 transmission, the middle filter is for an early-1970s C4 with the tab for the later pressure-relief valve, and the bottom filter is for a C4 in a Pinto with a much deeper pan.

This transmission is a 1973, so the pressure-relief spring and valve is held into the valve body by the tab on the transmission filter. Be very careful when removing and installing the filter that this doesn't fall out, roll away, and become lost. Always be careful on transmissions with springs, check valves, and other little parts and take lots of photos to remind you of where pieces are installed.

For this driver, I gave the pan a quick cleanup and a coat of cast coat paint on the pan. Then, I reinstalled the pan. Snug the bolts first and then torque them to the proper specification. Do not overtighten them and distort the area around the bolt holes.

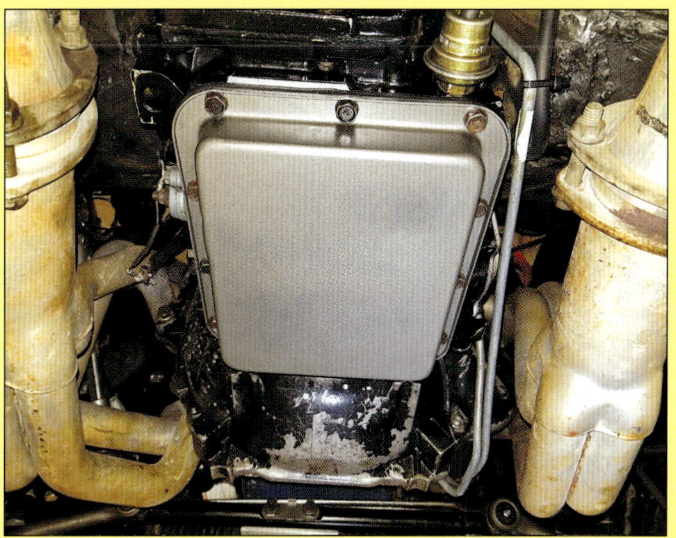

Since this was a driver, I used the newer rubber-style gasket on this install. That's all there is to changing the filter and gasket.

Pry up on the outside lip to remove the rear seal. A hard putty knife or scraper can get under the lip, but be careful not to damage the transmission end case. The seal diameter can vary, depending on the driveshaft application. Make sure that you get the correct seal for your application.

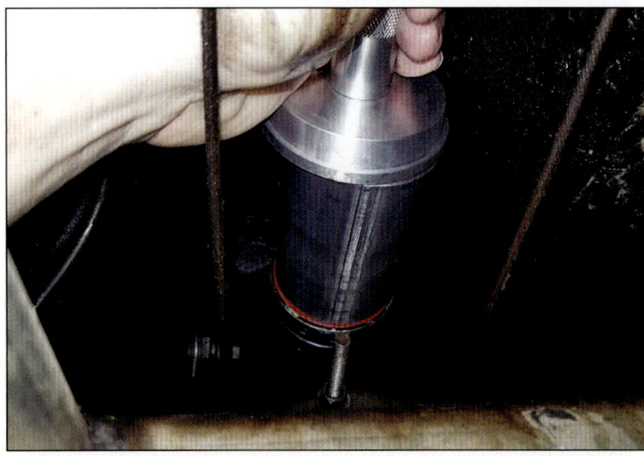

When reinstalling the seal, I use a piece of exhaust pipe and my seal installer to install the seal without damaging the rubber boot or output shaft that protrudes from the seal. A short extension pipe such as this one can be found at auto parts stores.

The front seal, which is shown here as white paper around the outside of the back of the pump and the transmission body, often leaks more than the input-shaft seal. The input-shaft seal can be replaced without getting into the transmission, but the input pump often has to be pushed out from the inside.

To properly set the neutral safety switch, put the transmission in neutral, insert a number-43 drill bit into the hole on the top side of the switch (I label my drill bit and keep it separate so that it doesn't get used for drilling), and loosen the two hold-down bolts. Move the switch back and forth until the bit falls all the way to the back of the switch and tighten the bolts.

Neutral Safety Switch

The neutral safety switch is mounted on the selector shaft and is adjusted by using a number-43 drill bit. There is a small alignment hole centered in the middle of the switch. Slide the drill bit in until it stops. Loosen the two mounting bolts and place the shifter in neutral. The drill bit should then slide through the remainder of the switch and bottom out. Once it is aligned, tighten the mounting bolts and remove the drill bits. Check the operations by making sure the car only starts in park or neutral, and make sure that the backup lamps come on (if equipped) in reverse.

Detailing for Show

The case on the C4 and C6 are aluminum, and on the FMX it is cast iron. The tailshaft housing on the 428 and 429 Cobra Jet is also cast iron. For concours restorations, carefully clean the housing to reveal as many of the factory markings as possible. While most transmissions are very greasy, which keeps them from oxidizing, you do occasionally have to remove some aluminum rust from the casing. Start with mild cleaners and work your way to stronger methods to clean the housing.

If you are planning a concours

The assembly marks and paint daubs need to be remade on a concours transmission restoration. Be careful when cleaning the transmission case because some methods remove the marks that need to be remade. The white paint daub and grease pencil marks were found on a 1969 C6 transmission.

My transmission builder allows me to clean the cases to find the marks and make the case look new. Aluminum is very porous, so be careful when cleaning. I use a big tub and start with mild detergents before moving to cleaners that can wipe away grease pencil marks or paint daubs.

restoration, see if your transmission rebuilder will work with you, and after they have disassembled the transmission, take the housing and give the outside a good scrub. Most transmission builders don't spend the time to detail the case. They just want to make it functional.

Because of the nature of the housing and all of the pressure lines and ports, it is not recommended that you attempt to blast the housing because contaminants can get lodged in the housing itself. A small kiddie pool is great for degreasing transmission housings. Once you have the transmission housing cleaned, take it back to the builder and tell them to watch their greasy hands. Aluminum is very porous, so ask them to be careful.

Most high-performance transmissions and later all transmissions had the VIN stamped on the casing. On a C6, it was stamped on this pad on the top of the casing. This transmission came out of a 1970 Ranchero with a 429 Cobra Jet.

On the left is the center housing that was glass beaded to clean the soaked-in oil and grease. Although it looks pretty, the original "as cast" surface is now gone forever. The left side of the tailshaft housing was cleaned with a nylon wheel and some mag wheel cleaner. It's a much longer process but the original casting look is retained. The right side of the tailshaft housing still shows the stained aluminum after cleaning.

Manual Transmissions

Five manual transmissions were used: two 3-speeds (the early HED 3-speed and the 3.03 heavy-duty 3-speed) and three 4-speeds (the Dagenham 4-speed, the BorgWarner T-10 4-speed, and the Toploader 4-speed).

The HED 3-speed, which can be found on 1964–1966 cars had a non-synchro first gear and was not a very strong transmission. It was replaced with the 3.03 in 1967. The Dagenham 4-speed was also a light-duty transmission that was found behind early 6-cylinder cars.

The 3.03 3-speed is a version of the Ford Toploader and can be quickly identified by its 9 bolts holding the top cover (as opposed to the 10 for the 4-speed). This fully synchronized transmission was used behind 6-cylinders and big-blocks alike, as it had some of the Toploader rugged design.

Manual transmissions are identified with a metal tag. The Toploader has a tag riveted to the front of the case (shown here). Early 3-speeds and T-10s have the tag mounted to the case with one of the rear tailshaft housing bolts. On the Dagenham 4-speed, the tag is mounted to the side cover. This transmission is a "RUG AG," which is a close-ratio 4-speed used in 1969 302s and 351Ws, and the second line is the serial number of the transmission.

High-performance transmissions had the VIN stamped on the casing in various locations: sometimes here and sometimes farther out on the mounting tab. This transmission is from a 1970 Boss 302.

The BorgWarner T-10 was used behind some small-block applications, and an aluminum version was used in the 1965 Shelby GT350. The Ford Toploader was used in many different configurations behind all Ford engines. The Toploader and 3.03 3-speed were designed to replace the BorgWarner T-10 in 1963, and the T-10 was used and slowly phased out of early production.

The BorgWarner T-10 and the Dagenham 4-speeds are loaded from the side of the case, where the shifter shafts come out of the body. The HED, 3.03, and the Toploader all load from the top of the case.

Inspection

Although you can see the condition of the transmission somewhat by pulling the inspection cover, some of the wear can only be confirmed after teardown. The obvious leaking points are the front and rear seals, shaft seals, and the top cover or side cover. Four bolts hold the front bearing/seal on the input shaft of the transmission. The gasket change is easy, but you need to inspect the front bearing for scoring on the race. Water can get in the front area and rust the ball bearings, or if it doesn't get enough oil, the race can get scored. Replace the bearing if there is anything more than very light scoring. The rear shaft housing can also be removed easily and the housing gasket changed.

Removing the cover allows for a visual inspection of the gear and blocking rings. The blocking rings are the brass pieces that help with the synchronizing of the gear. Inspect the rings and the gears for any noticeable damage from grinding the gears or the previous owners' poor shifting habits. If they look chewed up, plan on a rebuild.

With the cover off, inspect the gears and synchronizers for damage. I filter the old oil to see if there are any big metal pieces that may have come off of a gear or blocking ring. This Toploader shows some minor issues on the first- and second-speed synchronizer and a little on the first-speed gear, but it looks okay overall.

Check the blocking ring springs. Use a small pocket screwdriver or other pry tool and move the brass blocking ring toward the steel blocking ring. If they touch, things are worn out and you need to rebuild. You should have at least 0.050 inch between the two rings.

The input-shaft bearing is under the front collar and frequently gets water inside, which will begin to rust the bearing. When changing the front seal and gasket, inspect this front bearing.

This early T-10 revealed more paint marks while degreasing. Start with mild cleaners and then work your way to the harsher stuff. As I cleaned the case with stronger cleaners, these marks went away. So, take pictures of everything before final cleaning.

Cleaning and Detailing

As with the automatic transmissions, if you are rebuilding to original, find all of the markings on the transmission case before teardown. Start with light detergents and solvents. Brake and carburetor cleaners are good but can remove some of these marks. If the case is torn down, it can be soaked in Evapo-Rust, and that does not remove the markings. Document all of the markings before scrubbing the housing. Unlike the automatic case, there aren't small passages, so a brisk cleaning or

Careful cleaning of the transmission reveals the factory marks for concours restorations. These marks were found on a 4-speed Toploader in a big-block 1970 Mach 1.

This BorgWarner T-10 is being used in a street driver, so after a good cleaning, a fresh coat of cast coat paint was used to keep it nice and preserved. Special brackets are available to safely hold the transmission to an engine stand.

blasting of the case can be accomplished if you make sure to thoroughly clean it after.

Cast-iron housings were left bare, so if you plan to drive the car regularly, a cast-iron coat of paint helps to preserve the transmission. Show cars can be coated with an oil, such as Boeshield T-9, or a light Cosmoline after detailing.

Clutch

The clutch consists of the pressure plate and clutch disc. The energy from the engine is transferred to the transmission through the clutch disc, and the transmission is coupled and uncoupled through the pressure plate, which removes the pressure from the disc. Ford used a coil-spring style of pressure plate with three arms to release the pressure from the disc. While this style of clutch is generally sound, I have had them break at the small arm in high-performance applications. Most aftermarket clutches come with a diaphragm-style pressure plate, which uses a one-piece spring steel disc to push the pressure-plate ring away from the clutch disc.

I don't recommend reusing the clutch and pressure plate. If they fail, they are time consuming and expensive to replace. If you decide to reuse the clutch and pressure plate, inspect the pressure plate for cracks, severe bluing/overheating from riding the clutch, scoring from debris, and corrosion. Light bluing and corrosion can be removed with a Scotch-Brite pad (used lightly), but you should replace the clutch assembly if there is anything more severe.

Check the pressure plate with a straightedge at several points for warping along the face of the plate. If the face it not flat, replace the pressure plate. Check the face of the clutch fingers for uneven or excessive wear. The wear should be the same on all three fingers and not cover the entire end of the finger.

Inspect the flywheel not only for warping but also for cracks. Some cracks are on the surface (such as the one in the red circle), and some are deeper. Minor cracks that are removed during resurfacing are okay, but deeper ones indicate that you need a new flywheel.

New clutches come with one of these nifty clutch-alignment tools, which aids in installing the clutch. Don't throw it away! Note the wear on the fingers of the pressure plate from the throw-out bearing. If the wear has flattened the arm, replace the plate.

The throw-out bearing rides on the fork with these clips, which allows it to rotate while riding on the transmission input shaft. The fork rotation point is right under my hand and is attached with a spring or, in later applications, a riveted clip.

Throw-Out bearing and Pilot Bearing

The pilot bearing is pressed into the middle of the crankshaft and is used to hold the end of the transmission input shaft in place. Two different styles are used: the oiled bronze style and the needle roller-bearing style. Both work well, and different builders prefer certain types in certain applications. Do not grease the bronze-style bushing. This clogs the pores of the bronze and does not allow the oil to flow out and lubricate the end of the input shaft.

The throw-out bearing is mounted on the end of the clutch fork and presses against the clutch to help release the clutch disc. Most of these are sealed, but I have seen some that have a grease fitting. Good luck trying to grease the bearing after it is installed. Unless the clutch is adjusted to where the bearing is constantly riding on the pressure plate (and always spinning), the throw-out bearing is fairly trouble-free.

Clutch Linkage

Ford clutch linkage is mechanical and uses an equalizer bar, or "Z" bar, to reverse the motion from the clutch pedal back toward the clutch-release lever (fork). The upper rod is fixed, and the lower is threaded to adjust for wear in the clutch assembly. The equalizer bar is supported by brackets mounted to the engine block and the frame rail.

With the exception of performance clutches, the system works fairly well. Wear can occur at the lower equalizer bar at the point where the lower rod attaches to the equalizer bar from normal use, and as the hole increases, it affects the clutch. You usually hear a "thunking" noise as you depress the clutch. Big performance clutches can bend parts of the original system, and if you plan to use a stronger clutch assembly, consider using an aftermarket system.

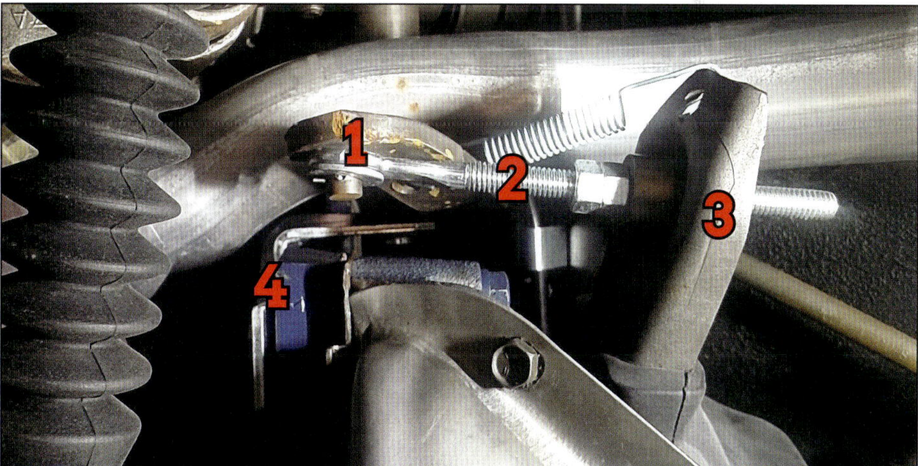

It's a tight squeeze for the big-block with a 4-speed and clutch linkage! Parts of the linkage are 1) the clutch Z-bar, 2) the equalizer rod, 3) the fork, and 4) a mounting bracket. The clutch Z-bar transfers the forward motion of the clutch pedal back toward the fork. The equalizer rod connects the Z-bar to the fork and allows for clutch adjustment as the clutch wears. The fork moves the throw-out bearing, and the mounting bracket that is mounted to the engine holds the Z-bar in place.

Shifter

The automatic shifter is a very simple lever that usually only requires new bushings to be brought back into proper working order. There is a difference between the housings for some console shifters to hold the selector dial and indicator light.

The manual shifter did vary somewhat depending on the application. From 1970–1973, Ford used

Access to the shifter bushings is made from this 45-degree-angled rubber plug. It's on the passenger's side of the shifter, which is not easily accessed. Remove the plug and remove the nut that holds the shifter together.

a Hurst Competition Plus shifter on 4-speed applications. Shifters from 1964–1968 used a reverse-lockout pull that was mounted on the shifter to allow the shifter to be put into reverse.

Most of the issues with the shifter are in the two bushings that hold the shaft to the shifter housing. A previous repair using only one long bushing failed in this shifter. A bushing goes on each side of the housing.

The early shifters (left) used an external spring and reverse lever (T-handle from 1964 to 1967, ring in 1968) to allow the shifter to be put into reverse. In 1969, Ford used an internal system (center) that is similar to the way Hurst engaged the reverse gear. From 1970 to 1973, Ford just used the Hurst Competition Plus shifter in all 4-speed applications (right). Note that the factory Hurst unit doesn't have the gear-stop bolts that the commercial units have.

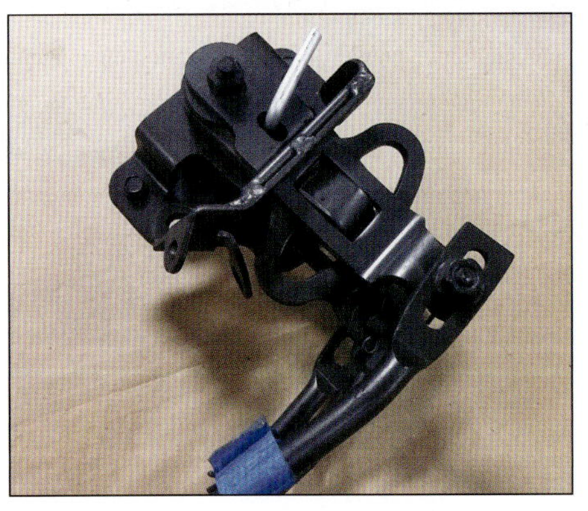

All Ford manual shifters use a 1/4-inch rod to align the shifter arms, which is shown here as the silver 90-degree tool. The rod extends all the way through the shifter body. You can make a fancy one like I did out of unthreaded rod or use a piece of threaded rod or a bolt.

Crossmember

The transmission crossmember connects the tailshaft of the transmission to the floor reinforcement under the floor pan. The 1965–1966 version was all the same and included a bracket to mount the emergency-brake equalizer bar. Most of the 1967–1970 crossmembers were the same and did not include the equalizer bar mount, and the C6 and the FMX both used a unique mount, depending on application. The 1971–1973 mounts look similar, but the driveline was mounted different in the chassis, so be careful using these in earlier cars. The C6 mount from the small-block in 1971–1973 mounts in the earlier cars if converting to a C6, but won't work for FMX applications.

Ford used the same style of transmission insulator on all transmission applications, but it came with different heights, depending on the

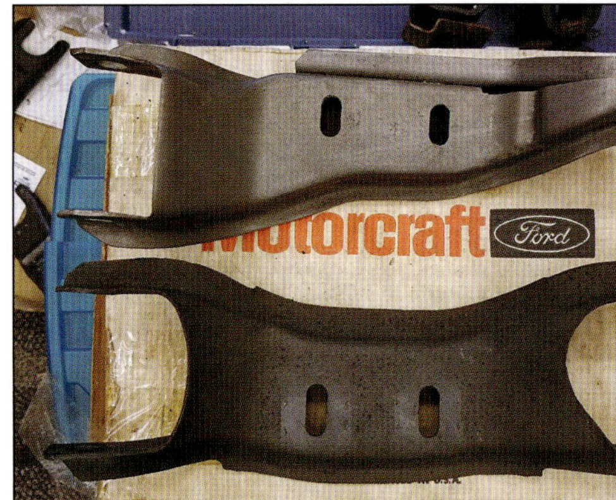

Two styles of transmission crossmembers were used on Mustangs. The top one is from later 1971–1973 small-block C6 applications, and is similar to the automatic C6 crossmembers that were used in big-blocks. The bottom one is similar to all of the other applications, with the big-block version being slightly deeper and having longer slots for mounting.

The transmission insulator came in many different heights, depending on the engine combination and body-style. They were all similar enough that they are all serviced by a single style of insulator. This insulator is for a small-block and is marked with yellow paint, some big-blocks were marked with red, and other colors may have been used. (Photo Courtesy Cunningham Archives)

Three different driveshafts were used. A solid driveshaft was used in some early 1965 6-cylinders, most used a solid tube with a cardboard inner liner to reduce vibrations, and some were equipped with the tube-in-a-tube style with rubber insulators to further dampen the vibrations (shown).

Driveshafts had specific color rings on them to help the line assembler decide which driveshaft the car received. The paint keeps the surface below from pitting like the rest of the unprotected shaft, so putting them back in the same spot is easy.

application. The service replacement part is now all the same size, so be careful with the height of the insulator. If it's too short or too tall, it can push the engine cooling fan blades into the radiator shroud.

Driveshaft

Factory driveshafts came in one- and two-piece varieties. The two-piece style damped the vibrations and smoothed out the ride but was not good for performance applications. They are made of steel with welded yokes on both ends. Driveshafts are marked with specific colors from the factory to denote the driveshaft application. There are also marks for denoting orientation, including which end goes to the transmission and inspection marks for weights. Even though the driveshafts may be close in length, it is important to get the right driveshaft for your application. The length of the driveshaft is measured from the center of the U-joints and can be measured in 64ths of an inch.

U-Joints

Although you should never reuse U-joints, the original Ford units did not use a grease fitting to grease the bearing ends. If you want an original look, use U-joints that do not have a grease fitting. If you plan to drive your Mustang a lot, the grease fittings are good.

Yoke

The yoke was a natural cast finish with the exception of the inspection marks on the U-joints. When installing the yoke in the transmission, don't use heavy grease to lubricate the splines of the yoke or output shaft. This seals the air in the yoke and prevents it from escaping, and the yoke won't go in far enough to install in the transmission tailshaft.

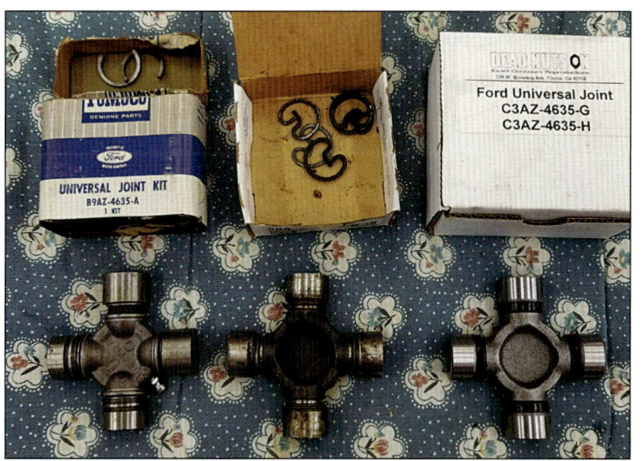

On the left is a Ford service U-joint, in the middle is a factory-original U-joint, and on the right is a reproduction U-joint made by Dead Nuts On. Note that all service replacement U-joints had a grease fitting; original factory units did not. The Dead Nuts On U-joint looks great, does not come with a grease fitting, and only lacks the Ford logo. (Photo Courtesy Cunningham Archives)

CHAPTER 8

Suspension and Steering

The Ford Mustang starred in three early James Bond films: **Goldfinger** ***and*** **Thunderball** ***utilized 1964 and 1965 convertibles, and in 1971, Bond was behind the wheel of a bright red 1971 Mach 1 in*** **Diamonds are Forever.** ***This 1971 Mustang is decked out just like the movie car, including the Nevada plate, and is owned by Doug Hvidston of Indianapolis. (Photo Courtesy Monroe Bush/ Animotion Photography)***

Most suspension items from Ford were designed to be sealed and not greased, and when the parts wore out, they were replaced. This original replacement upper control-arm shaft shows the cap that Ford installed rather than a grease fitting.

As far as restoration of the suspension is concerned, the most difficult part may be deciding to restore what you have or buy new. The original parts were not very well protected from water, road hazards and salt, so they often are not reusable. NOS parts are almost completely depleted, and some of the replacement parts are noticeably different.

Front Suspension

The original front suspension on the first-generation Mustang was an unequal-length double-arm design. The spring and shock are mounted above the upper control arm and extend into the engine compartment, unlike later designs. For example, the Mustang II placed the shock between the two control arms in a much more compact package.

In the 1950s, Ford began designing its suspension components to be sealed and eliminated almost all of the greasing of components, which was first designed into the Edsel line. Most of the front suspension and steering was designed to be replaced at regular intervals, so not much protection was applied to these pieces. The lower control arms were intended to be serviced as an assembly, so a separate lower ball joint was never offered. The upper ball joint

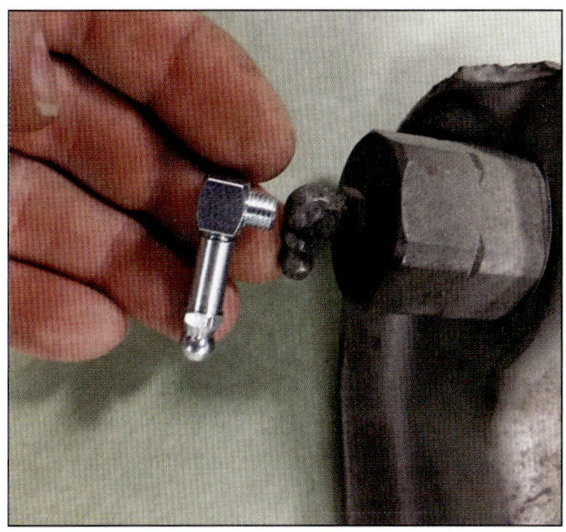

Since Ford did not intend to grease the fittings in the upper-arm shaft, there is very little room to install grease fittings on replacement parts. These special low-profile grease fittings are available from the Mustang parts vendors and work wonders over the fittings provided by the manufacturer.

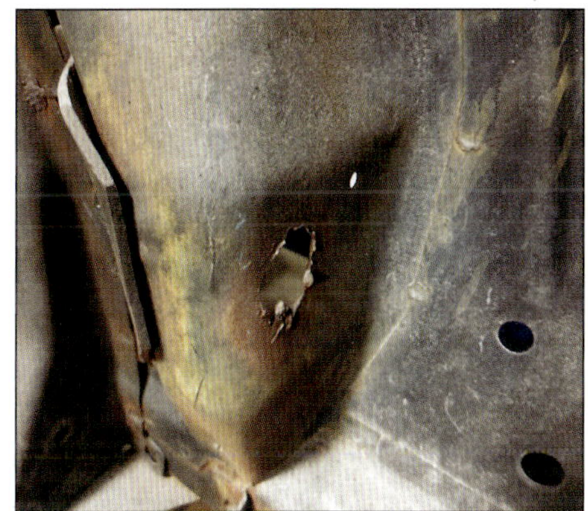

Here is the unfortunate result of no room for upper control arms and no provisions for greasing the inner shaft. Many mechanics have taken a torch to the shock tower to access the grease fittings.

This strut-rod-bushing setup on a 1969 Mustang shows how all of the pieces fit together. One of the biggest challenges in tearing apart a car for restoration is sometimes the strut-rod bushings: the inner metal sleeve rusts tight, and there is no good way to get them out other than brute force.

was replaceable as well as the inner control-arm shafts.

An item that Ford didn't think out very well was the upper control-arm shafts. They were not designed to be re-greased, but Ford put a plug in the shafts, which indicated that they were. There is not enough room to get a grease fitting and lube gun in the confined area, which led many mechanics to get out the torch and cut a big hole in the shock towers to add grease fittings and provide access to lube the upper shafts. If you plan to regularly drive the car, purchase the aftermarket low-profile grease fitting kit, rather than torching your shock towers.

Strut Rod and Bushings

The strut rods are actually called "brake reaction rods." The strut rods on your car serve four functions: 1) They triangulate the lower part of the suspension since the lower control arm only has one mounting point. 2) They absorb energy during acceleration and braking. 3) They absorb road vibrations through the bushings. 4) After 1966, they were used to help set the caster on the front suspension. The 1964½–1966 used shims in the upper control arms to set caster and camber.

During hard acceleration or braking, the inertia of the car wants to roll forward (braking) or backward (acceleration). The strut-rod bushings were intended to absorb the energy created during this condition and then return the suspension back to its normal position. When you hit a big pothole, the suspension is driven back toward the rear of the car. The strut-rod bushing absorbs this impact and returns the suspension to where it is supposed to be.

The problem is when you corner hard, the bushings give and allow the suspension to move in the car. This changes the balance of the suspension, and the car doesn't want to go through the turn. It does the same thing when you hit that pothole: the suspension moves, and the car wants to jump into the next lane, especially if you use the original alignment specifications (see Chapter 12). An aftermarket solution has been to eliminate these bushings and simply use a hard-mount strut rod. It affects the ride quality, but combined with modern tires and modern alignment specs, it eliminates the problems that were usually blamed on bump steer.

For all original restorations, you are stuck. I don't recommend anything other than stock rubber bushings for replacement. Keep the suspension rubber fresh and replace it regularly to avoid the issues with the strut-rod bushings. Don't use polyurethane in the strut rods because it can break the rods.

The rods themselves were given a phosphate finish, which means that they pit badly over time. Removing the strut rods and bushings can be difficult because the inner sleeves weld themselves to the bushing and mount point. You may be forced to destroy the bushings. Early strut rods are straight, which required two sets of holes in the lower control arm, and later rods were angled and only required one set of holes.

Upper Control Arms

Upper control arms for 1964–1966 were the same, and the 1967–1973 Mustangs used the same style of control arms. In 1970, Ford changed from a four-rivet ball joint to a three-rivet ball joint, and this became the service replacement for all 1967–1973 Mustangs. Boss 429 upper control arms have a slight difference in the spring saddle mount position. The original arm had an opening for a grease fitting, but the original ball joint was sealed. Replacements were greaseable—hence the access hole.

The upper control arms were finished in phosphate and oil and were not painted. Because of this, the original parts become very pitted over the years, and this makes the finished product not as nice as an NOS part once restored. Many service replacements were painted black. The originals can twist over time, and they can crack at the upper arm shaft and the spring-mount holes.

Upper Control-Arm Shafts

The upper control-arm shafts were subject to hot oil tempering, which made them a little darker in color than the other natural pieces in the suspension system. Very early shafts did not have a hole for any kind of grease fitting, but Ford put a plug in the shaft on later models. Ford intended the upper shafts to be replaced and not greased. The original upper shafts had an internal O-ring that was not intended to be re-greased, but new replacements come with a greaseable design. Greasing these arms does very little. When

The upper control arms were not painted or protected from Ford. However, Ford did service the ball joint and the inner shaft, so the upper arms can be reused. This is a control arm for a 1967–1969 vehicle. The upper ball joint was riveted in, and when the first rebuild occurred, the mechanic grabbed the air chisel and removed the rivets (the replacements were provided with bolts).

This is why you should not put grease fitting in the original-style components. Greaseable parts have a means for the old grease to be pushed out, but originals are sealed (such as this inner shaft cap). Greasing these components destroys the seal and will probably lead to failure of the part more quickly.

The shaft on the left is a Ford replacement 1964–1966 upper shaft, and the one on the right is an original 1964 shaft from an early-April-built car. The very earliest upper shafts used Falcon components, and they did not come with a hole for a cap or grease fitting.

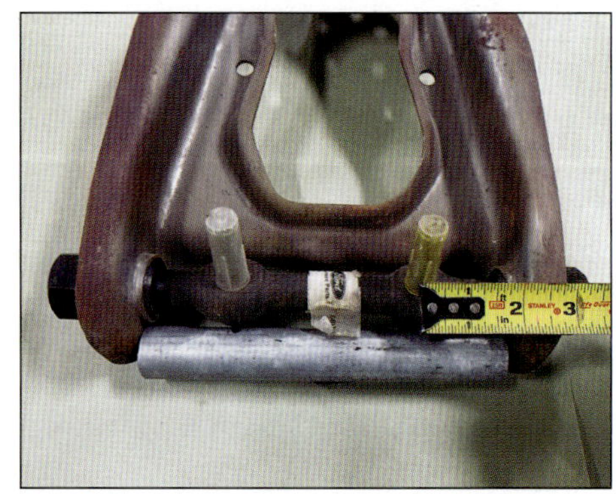

The upper shafts don't "thread" into the upper control arms, so when torquing the shafts, keep the upper arm from compressing when installing the shaft. Ford recommends using a piece of pipe between the flanges to keep it in place. Make sure the bolt-mounting holes are equally spaced from the flanges.

The original shafts were a dark phosphate or dark heat treat, and the bolts were phosphate with the chassis red dye on the assembly nuts. Many of the suspension components got a yellow stripe marking from 1967–1970, but colors and paint daubs varied from year to year.

The lower control arm was intended to be serviced as a unit, even though Ford sold the inner bushing. While the ball joint area was left bare metal, the long end was dipped in semigloss black paint.

the upper shafts begin to squeak, the damage has been done, and a shot of grease usually does not help much due to the design.

If you plan to drive the car, newer-design upper shafts are available that are designed to be greased with the rest of the suspension system. Use these in conjunction with the long grease fittings that are available from the Mustang parts vendors.

When installing new upper shafts, do not over-torque the bushings in the control arm. Depending on the year of your car, you can make a 3/4-inch pipe tool to sit inside the upper control arm to prevent it from flexing while you install the bushings. Make sure that the shaft is centered between the two ends of the control arm when installing the shafts.

Lower Control Arms

The lower control arms were designed to be replaced as an assembly, so the ball joint was never offered as a separate replacement. The control arm was dipped in chassis black up around the sway-bar-link-mount area, and this could vary somewhat, depending on the paint level in Ford's tank and how the arm was mounted. The "dip line" was at an angle, most likely because of how the arm was held in the strut-rod hole as it was dipped (my guess). The control arm was left bare from the dip-line holes to the ball joint.

Some very early 1964½ control arms came with slotted ball joints like the early Falcon units. In 1967, with the revised suspension for the big-block, the lower control arm became longer. The 1967 control

Ford installed jacking tabs on the lower control arms to prevent the jack from moving while the car was serviced. The early jacking tabs (bottom) didn't hold up very well when trying to jack up the car. Ford improved the jacking tabs (top) to keep them from collapsing during service. Replacement tabs are available from the Mustang vendors.

The angle of the black paint is most likely due to how it was held to dip it in the black paint. The underside of the control arm shows the welded washer for the stabilizer-bar mount. In addition, notice that the original control-arm ball joint is capped and not greaseable.

arms are long but have the four holes for right- and left-hand installation until Ford changed the design of the strut rod from 1968–1973 and only required two holes for the control arm. Note that Mustang and Cougar control arms in 1967 are different, so be careful if you come across 1967 Cougar control arms at a swap meet. The 1967 Cougar used an articulated strut rod, and the hole locations in the lower control arm are different.

The Ford service replacements are Granada parts from the 1970s and are electro-deposit primer (EDP) coated black. Original control arms have special tabs welded onto the bottom where the jack is intended to lift the car by the suspension to prevent the control arm from slipping on the jack. These jacking tabs frequently were flattened or damaged from the road, and new ones are available through the parts houses.

As noted previously, the ball joint was never serviced. If your originals are still tight, they can sometimes be reused or shimmed for show cars. The lower ball-joint dust boot and retainer is available, but the hard part is getting the waffle pattern on the new rivets, which requires custom tooling to do properly.

Control-Arm Rivets

New upper ball joints come with bolts to replace the original rivets that were used to hold the ball joints to the control arm. If you are refurbishing the control arms, Ford says to use an air hammer to remove the top of the rivet from the assembly. This method almost always ends up gouging the control arm. Use a cutoff wheel or grinder to carefully remove the top of the rivets without gouging the control arm and keep the cores in good condition.

Some of the parts to replace the lower ball joints are available, but you will need to find good joint internals as they are not reproduced. Lower rivets also have this waffle pattern like the upper ball joints.

Although the parts supply houses sell new rivets to install new ball joints into the upper and lower control arms, it requires some special equipment to get the rivets to look correct. First, you need a quality press that is capable of applying 8 tons of force to squeeze the rivet into place. A special set of dies are required to get the waffle pattern on top and cradle the curved back of the rivet, and the shaft on the press cannot move the slightest. Otherwise, the rivet squeezes out the side. An inexpensive press will not work well. Unless you plan to do a lot of suspension parts, purchase them from someone who already has the equipment.

Grease Fittings on Components

Several items came from Ford that were permanently sealed and not intended to be greased (only replaced). A re-greaseable component generally has a vent area to allow the old grease to flow out as it is replaced with new grease.

The original-style tie-rods were sealed with no grease fittings, and the tie-rod sleeves were straight. Service replacement sleeves sometimes neck down on the ends. All were phosphate coated, and some sleeves came with dark phosphate clamps.

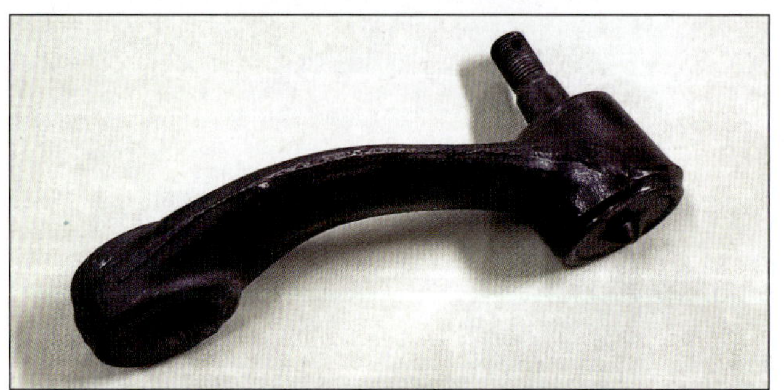

This pitman arm is for a 1967–1970 Mustang with manual steering and shows a dimple where the grease fitting should be.

Although the upper ball joint has a provision for a grease fitting, the original setup was capped. The Ford service replacements and aftermarket units are all greaseable.

Ford identified its front springs with color codes. This spring has one gold and one yellow stripe and is mounted in a 1969 Mach 1 with a 390 engine and power steering. Careful degreasing can usually uncover these marks on the spring.

If you drive your car and want to have the grease-able style of components, remember that regular maintenance is critical to keeping the parts in good condition. If parts are starting to squeak, they are worn out, and a shot of grease may quiet the component, but the wear has already occurred. It must be replaced.

Front Springs

All early Mustangs used 5-inch-diameter coil springs in the front. Although they are all similar in design, they varied based on the application. The springs can be made from different-size wire, have a different number of coils, and have more gaps between the coils when unsprung. A few dozen different combinations were used, and each one had specific ride and control characteristics.

Those that were originally installed in your car are easy to determine per the *Ford Text and Illustrations* book. Ford marked all springs with a specific color code, and this code is noted in the book. If you have the original springs and have the original colors visible, you can check this against the information in the book. Use the book in reverse to determine what color code your springs should have if yours are not readable. The marks on the springs generally (but not always) ran the length of the spring. Ford lists its springs in how much weight they are designed to hold, while aftermarket springs are rated on how much weight is required to compress the spring each inch.

Unless you build a concours car, a good set of replacement springs will work well. Only at the highest levels of judging will anyone count the coils and measure the wire diameter. Coil springs wear out in general due to the heat-treat process being applied unevenly. Heavily rusted springs can also lead to premature failure of the springs. The first thing you will notice is the sag in the front end of the car. Once the spring is gone, they should be replaced in pairs.

Compressing coil springs is very dangerous. A lot of energy is stored in a compressed spring. Use a quality compressor and never use an impact wrench to tighten the compressor (it destroys the threads on the center compressor bolt). Always compress and decompress springs slowly.

When increasing the strength of the springs (600-pound coil springs are a popular option), remember that the car will ride like a car with stronger springs: less comfortable. The tradeoff is better handling but a harsher ride.

Cutting a coil to lower the front end has been done since the 1960s, because that was the only option. Cutting a coil affects the way the spring handles (generally harsher). Lowering springs are now available to drop the front if you wish.

The spring saddles are functionally the same on all models. Unlike the replacements, they did not come with the rubber pads like the service replacement Granada parts. They were not originally painted from Ford and, therefore, they rusted quickly.

Early spring saddles did not have a Ford logo on them but were stamped with the supplier mark. Soon, the saddles were stamped with a rectangular "FoMoCo" logo before changing to the round FoMoCo logo mid-1969. Service replacements

Ford serviced the spring perch with a Granada part (right), which works just fine but is visibly different. The spring stop tab on the Granada part is longer, and the mount area for the shock is also different. Later service pieces had a rubber insulator installed. The original was phosphated and did not hold up well.

It matters on a high-end restoration to not only use the correct part but also the correct stamping. These spring perches use different logos: rectangular FoMoCo, round FoMoCo, and round Ford, depending on when they were made. If you want to drive your car, you don't need to worry about this intriguing information.

have a round Ford logo replacing the FoMoCo logo. Early saddles had a bushing that was tack welded in place, which was changed to a swaged bushing. The service replacement bushings are longer than the original bushings, which makes original-style swaged installation difficult. Most rebuilders tack weld the bushings into place.

The Granada service replacements are a different shape and style but functionally the same. All have a tab that acts as a stop for the coil spring, and this goes to the inside of the car.

Spindles

The spindles were all the same basic design, but they went through several changes throughout the run of the Mustang. The early 1965–1966 6-cylinders used the early Falcon piece with very small tie-rods and were known for breaking. The V-8 spindles for 1965–1966 were used for drum and disc brake applications. The 1967 spindles were used for drum and disc brakes, and in 1968, Ford changed the spindles to be specific for drum or disc applications.

Ford experienced some breakage on the spindles in 1969, and several different spindles were used, primarily on the Boss 302. In 1970, Ford went to an even bigger tie-rod (also used on the latter 1969 Boss 302s), and this was used throughout the 1970s and on the Granada replacement parts. The spindles were changed again in 1971 but were still split between drum and disc.

The spindles were heat treated, which gave them a dark gray appearance, and they were machined after being heat treated. The machined surfaces were left bare.

Steering

While the suspension isn't terrible, the same cannot be said for the steering. All first-generation Mustangs, with the exception of the 1971–1973 power-steering cars, used a worm and recirculating ball style of steering gear. This gear frequently became sloppy and caused problems.

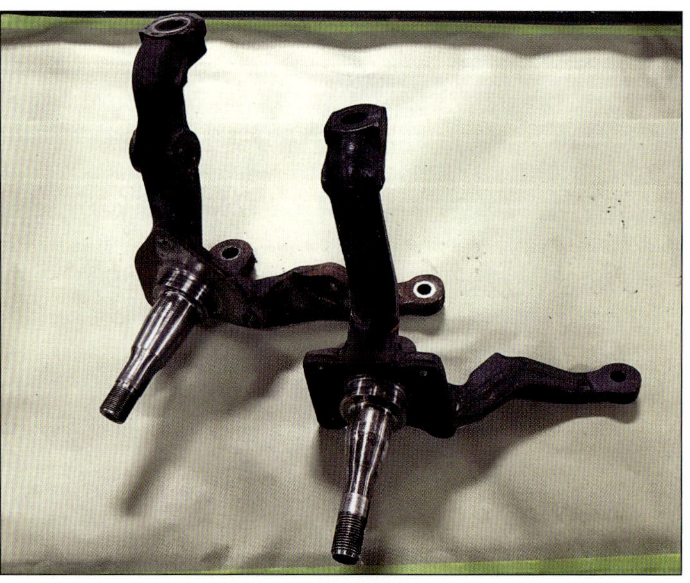

The spindle on the right is for a 1965–1966 V-8 Mustang and was used for both drum-brake and disc-brake applications. The one on the left is the much-improved 1970 disc-brake version. Note that the tie-rod size and bearing size has been increased in the latter part. Spindles were heat treated and then machined, leaving the machined surfaces bare.

The steering system consists of the steering box, a Pitman arm to connect the steering box to the center link, a center link to connect the right and left tie-rods together, the tie-rods, and an idler arm to hold the passenger's side of the steering system.

Steering Gear

Cars from 1964–1966 (and some in 1967) had a steering gear with an input shaft that was the length of the steering column, which could be a hazard in an accident. With the introduction of the tilt column in 1967 and from 1968 through 1973, all of the boxes were connected to the steering column through a coupler, which eliminated the long shaft. All of the steering boxes are of the same basic design, and the big difference is the ratio that was used. Manual steering boxes generally used a higher-ratio box to allow ease of steering over power units. Ratios that were available in the early cars included a 19:1 ratio for manual applications, and power units were 16:1 ratio (sometimes referred to as "Quick Ratio").

In 1971, Ford went to a Saginaw-style integral power steering box, which provided a much better steering system, and the fluid in the box reduced road vibration coming up through the steering column. Two models were available, a constant-ratio 16:1 unit and

Early cars received a 1-inch sector shaft (left), which was phased out in 1967 by the 1$^1/_8$-inch shaft (right). In 1967, Ford moved away from the long steering shaft and went to a short shaft with a coupler, and in 1968, the steering shaft was collapsible.

The most important aspect to look for is rust and scoring on the steering shaft (the corkscrew part) and the ball bearings. Moisture can get into the housings and rust these components. If they are scored, replace them. The gaskets and bearings needed to restore the gear are available from parts vendors.

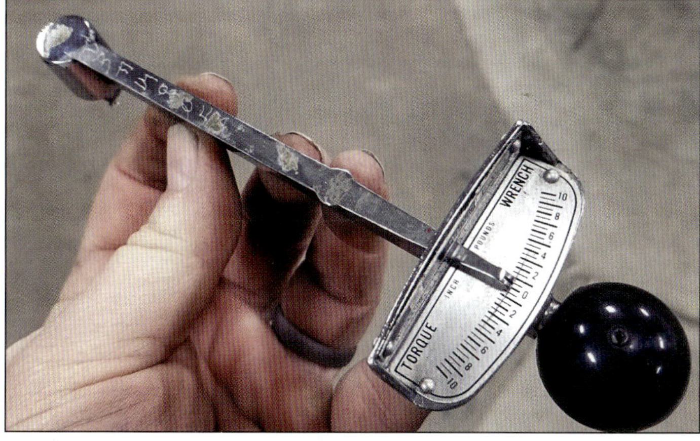

The worm bearing preload is set between 3 and 6 in-lbs. So, to set this, you need an inch-pound torque wrench that can read less than 10 in-lbs. This one reads between 0 and 10 in-lbs—very light measurements.

This is the power-steering pitman arm for 1967–1970 power steering. They were finished in a light phosphate with a yellow paint daub. Note that the paint daub is not terribly nice. Ford didn't take the time to mark things pretty in many cases.

a variable-ratio unit that was 16:1 at the center and changed to 13:1 at the extreme turns of the steering. Ratios up to 24:1 in manual-steering cars were also available to turn the bigger 1971–1973 cars.

Rebuilding a steering box requires the use of one specialty tool, an in-lb torque wrench for 1 to 10 in-lbs of torque. The steering box was prone to water leaks, which rusted the ball bearings and the steering shaft. When this happens, replace the steering unit. Most of the replacement parts to rebuild your unit are available if you want to try it yourself. The steering gears were natural cast in color and have a metal tag on top to identify the style of steering gear.

Tie-Rods

Original-equipment tie-rods were sealed and were not equipped with a grease fitting. The rods were natural or a light phosphate, and the center cover plate was shiny metal with no grease fitting. Many of the tie-rods on later models had a "B" stamped in the middle where the grease fitting would normally be. Early 1964–1966 tie-rods were solid on the bottom with no cover plate.

When upgrading tie-rods for driving purposes, it is important to note some differences. Ford tie-rods are all the same pitch (the angle of the tapered post) but have different diameters. The pitch of the mount post rises at 1 inch to the foot, but the diameter changed through the years.

The 1965–1966 6-cylinder tie-rods were the smallest and were known for breaking. The 1965–1969 tie-rods were larger and were replaced with the even larger posts from 1970–1973. This was the same size of posts that were used on the Granada disc-brake systems and other conversion systems used by some aftermarket manufacturers.

As with the other suspension components, the tie-rods did not come with grease fittings and were sealed. Some 1967–1969 tie-rods had a small "B" marked on the end cap. The finish was a natural phosphate on the tie-rod, and the cap was silver plating.

The tie-rods used from 1965–1966 varied, depending on whether the car was a V-8 or 6-cylinder and if it was equipped with power or manual steering. The 1965–1966 6-cylinder tie-rods with manual steering were 1/2-inch thread, and those with power steering were 5/8-inch thread. V-8 cars with manual steering came with 5/8-inch inner and 11/16-inch outer, and power-steering cars came with three 11/16-inch, with the passenger-side inner being 5/8 inch. Ford corrected this and made them all 11/16-18 in 1967–1973, and inners and outers work on either side, with the exception of the Boss cars in 1969.

Tie-Rod Links and Sleeves

The original tie-rod sleeves were straight in design, and in 1964–1966, they were tapped for the specific tie-rods listed previously, so the sleeves do not interchange side to side. Service replacement sleeves had a larger center section to improve strength in the sleeve. The clamps and bolts were a natural finish, and occasionally the clamps were slightly darker due to the heat-treating process. Bolts were phosphate and oil.

Center Link

The center link (also called the drag link) differed from year to year and between manual- and power-steering cars through 1970. In 1971, the center link was the same power as manual due to the new Saginaw integral power-steering gear. The 1965–1966 6-cylinder link was smaller (like the tie-rods). The 1965–1966 power-steering link had a flat plate where the power-steering-valve assembly connected to the link. From 1967–1970, the valve screwed onto the end of the link. The link is finished natural with a light phosphate from the factory.

Components that are designed to be greased, such as this replacement inner tie-rod, also have a dust cover that will allow the old grease to push out when replaced with new grease. If you are going to drive your car, a well-manufactured replacement part is the better choice.

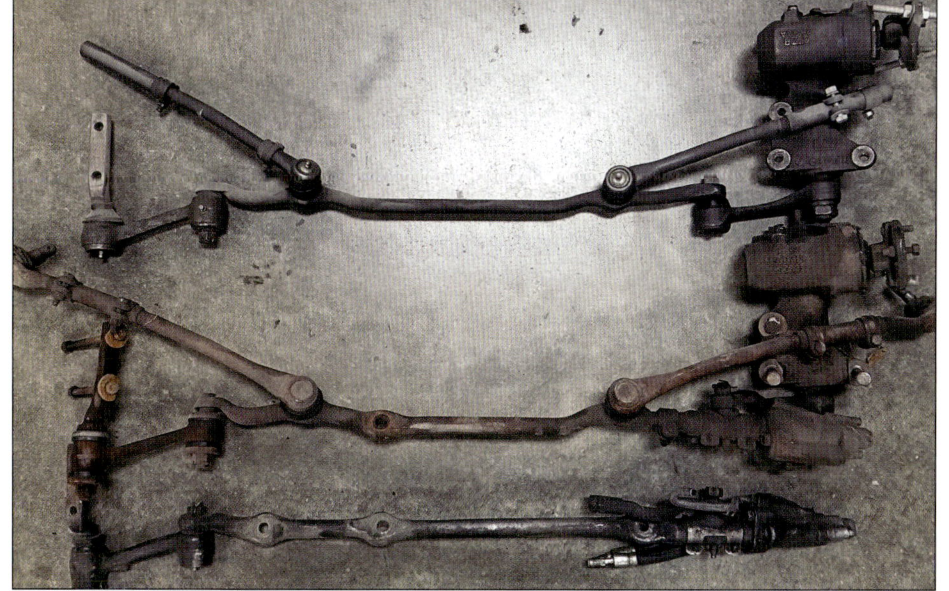

There were three basic styles of drag links. Manual drag links were pretty simple (top) and varied between years. The 1971–1973 drag links are all the same regardless if they were power or manual (not pictured). The middle setup is a 1967–1970 setup where the power-steering valve screws onto the end of the drag link. The bottom unit is a 1965–1966 unit where the valve bolts onto the end of the drag link and the control-valve ball stud is mounted in the link.

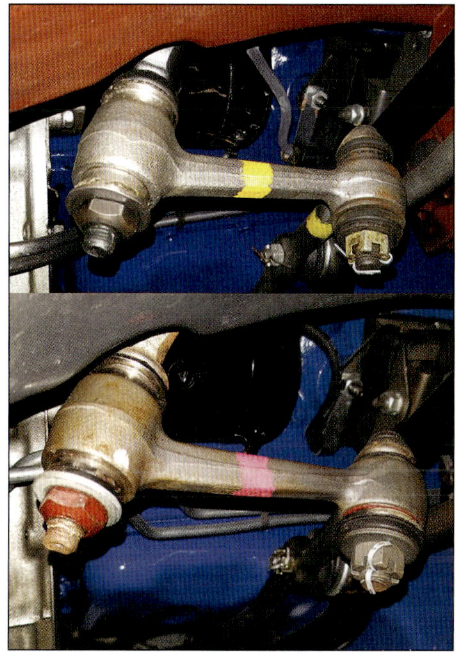

As part of the assembly process, Ford marked different parts with different colors to help with assembly. The top idler arm is marked yellow for power steering, and the lower is marked pink for manual steering. One attaching nut is red dyed, one is not. Which is correct?

Idler Arm

The idler arm attaches to the passenger-side frame rail and balances out the center link. Like the tie-rods, the original idler arm was not greaseable. The bushing for the idler arm can be replaced, and the arm itself was finished natural light phosphate.

Sway Bars and Links

The sway bar, or anti-roll bar, keeps the car flat in a hard turn. When a car is in a turn, it wants to roll over to the outside of the turn. The sway bar transfers the movement to the other side of the car, keeping the car flatter on the road. The sway bar is connected to the lower control arm through long bolts and bushings that are called the end links. The diameter of the bar and the length of the end arms help determine how the sway bar works.

The finish was either a dark heat treat or a semigloss black finish, and some were marked with a color mark. Sizes of stock sway bars ranged from 11/16 inch to 15/16 inch.

Power Steering

From 1964–1970, the Ford power-steering system consisted of a hydraulic pump, a ram cylinder, a control valve, and the connecting fluid lines. From 1971–1973, the system used a Saginaw power-steering gear instead of a ram cylinder. Some Shelby applications used a truck power-steering pump for its increased pressure and better response.

Piston

The steering piston, or ram cylinder, attaches the driver-side frame rail to the center link and pushes or pulls, depending on the pressure diverted by the control valve. The

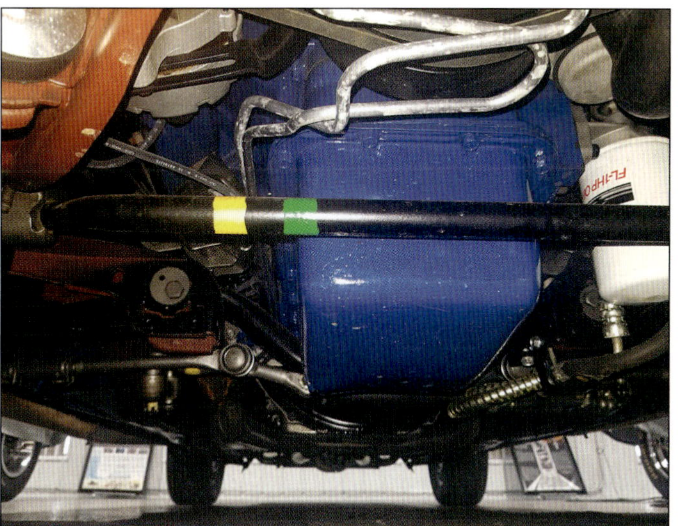

The front sway bars were color coded to denote the application. This one is in a 1969 Shelby GT500, so it is marked for the big-block 428. Note that the markings are not perfect: Ford didn't stress about how the markings looked.

piston is sealed on the end, so it can't be rebuilt, with the exception of the front seal stack. Besides leaking, the biggest problem with the pistons is having a bent piston rod. The piston body is left natural.

Pump

Two different styles of pumps were used in several different configurations. The early 1964½ pump was from Eaton, which was a simple design and was the standard since the 1950s. This pump had an external reservoir. During the 1965 production run, the Ford-designed pump replaced the Eaton pump, and the new pump mechanism was installed in the reservoir, which helped with the availability of the fluid and helped cool the pump mechanism.

The Eaton pump had two basic layouts: with or without air conditioning. The Eaton pump used an external reservoir, and with air conditioning, the reservoir was mounted on the driver-side apron to clear the AC compressor. On non-AC applications, it is

The Eaton power-steering pump was painted semigloss black, and the reservoir was painted silver. The pulley was cast iron. In a car with air conditioning, the pump reservoir was mounted remotely to the driver-side apron.

mounted directly to the pump.

Rebuilding the Eaton pump can be done, but it is best to leave it to experts because you determine the condition of the pump after tearing it down. As with the steering gears, rust is the biggest culprit in destroying the pump, and if you find egg-shaped bearings or rusted shafts, replacements are needed. The shop that does it for a living probably has extras as well as the special equipment to rebuild the pump. So, other than reservoir gaskets and filters, have the pump rebuilt by a specialist.

The Eaton pump was finished in a semigloss black, and the reservoir was finished in an argent color with a bright zinc cap.

The Ford pump, which is known as the Ford Thompson or Ford TRW pump, was introduced in 1965. Although the pump is generally the same design and was used until 1978, the configuration varied considerably. The 1965–1966 pumps had a wide filler neck and were used in two configurations: 1) a straight-up neck was used on non-AC cars and 2) a neck that angles back to clear the air compressor on AC cars.

In 1967, Ford went to the small-neck filler tube, and the low-pressure return outlet varied, depending on the engine application. The pressure outlet port was either threaded for 5/8- or 7/8-inch threads, and while most exited out the center of the housing, some were offset (like the 1965–1966 pumps).

The Ford pump is more complex than the Eaton pump, but the challenges of rebuilding it are the same. You just don't know until you tear it apart. The finish on the Ford pump was either blue/teal or semigloss

The front stack of seals for the power-steering piston can be rebuilt and the kits are readily available. Sometimes, the hardest part of the rebuild is getting the old seals out. They are in there tight and get jammed in. The Ford shop manual shows the correct sequence, which is also what is shown here.

The pump on the left is the Ford pump and was painted blue/teal. The one on the right is the Thompson pump from a 1969 Shelby and was painted semigloss black. The return-line port varied considerably between applications, as you can see here. Finding an exact pump to fit your application can be challenging.

The first Ford pumps came out in 1965 and had a wide fill opening. Cars with air conditioning, such as this one, had the fill opening angled back to clear the compressor.

black, depending on the supplier. Ford TRW pumps were semigloss black, and the tag on the back was marked with a "W." The Thompson pumps were finished in the blue/teal color.

Most Ford vendors carry both the argent for the Eaton reservoir and a good blue for the Thompson-built pumps. The biggest challenge is the reservoir. The housing takes a beating over the years, and while you might be able to knock out some of the dents, large ones may mean that the seal on the front won't seal properly and the housing will leak. Very minor dents can be filled with filler under the paint. The tag on the back of the pump is painted the same color as the pump.

Most of the parts to rebuild the Bendix valve are available. Look for rust and corrosion, and take plenty of photos as you tear down the unit to help with reassembly.

Hydraulic Control Valve

The hydraulic control valve diverts fluid and pressure to one side or the other of the piston through the movement of a spool valve. When the steering is centered, the fluid is diverted evenly around the valve. When the wheel is turned, the ball stud moves and allows the spool to move and start diverting fluid to the correct side of the piston. This also helps to center the steering system as the valve tries to neutralize.

Two primary units were used: the 1965–1966 units were bolted to the center link, and the 1967–1973 units screwed onto the end of the link. They were a natural finish, and most of the control valves were cast with "Bendix" on them. The end cap was date coded.

There were two primary adjustments to the control valve: the control-valve centering spring adjustment and the travel-stop adjustment. The travel stop is set when you rebuild the valve, and the center-spring adjustment can be made after installation. By adjusting the centering, it allows the pressure to be even when turning the wheel each way and allow the spool valve to center. The components to rebuild the valve are available from most Mustang supply houses, but, as with the other steering components, rust and corrosion are big enemies to the inside of the valve. If you replace the ball sleeve, use a bronze-coated sleeve per the original over the steel version.

Hydraulic Hoses

Pre-1970 hoses were generally single crimped. Then, Ford went to a double crimp in 1970. Some had the part number stamped on the crimped ends, and some had it ink stamped along the rubber hoses. All service replacements are double-crimp fittings, with the exception of some show hoses (most of these hoses may be single crimped for the early cars but lack the Ford logo).

For driver cars, get the double-crimp new lines. The double crimp is a safer part. In this case, NOS should only be considered for concours cars: as with tires, the silicone and oils leech out of 50-year-old parts, and they will become brittle over the years—even if they are unused. Hydraulic lines carry a lot of pressure, and cars that are driven will place a lot of stress on the hoses. Some of the aftermarket show lines have been known to leak even when cranked down hard to seal them. This is due to both the new part and the wear on the original parts.

The valve centering can be adjusted by removing the end cap and adjusting the nut to center the valve and pressures. Note that the aluminum cap has a date code—in this case, April 1964. Replacement caps are available but are not date coded.

BRAKES AND REAR AXLE

Halfway through the 1972 production, the ram-air option was limited to just the 351-2V engines. This convertible was one of those lucky cars to get the ram-air option and was painted in a beautiful Medium Lime Metallic with white interior. The car is owned by Dean Hvidston of Indianapolis, Indiana.

Ford drum brakes were essentially the same for all years of the first-generation Mustang, with the only variation being the size of the drum and shoes, and rear brakes having the emergency brake cable system installed.

From 1964–1967, the front disc brakes were a four-piston Kelsey-Hayes design, which was changed to the single-piston design from 1968–1973. The 1964–1966 had a 3/8-inch inlet line (pictured), and the 1967 had a 7/16-inch inlet. All of the 1968–1973 calipers are the same and were used on many different cars through the 1970s. All of the disc brakes were approximately 11.25 inches in diameter.

The braking system had either four-wheel drum brakes or front disc brakes and rear drum brakes. The drum system didn't change, with the exception of the size of the braking system, and disc brakes were optional in all years.

The braking system also included the pedal, the master cylinder, the lines running to the brake components, and, in the case of power brakes, the power brake booster. The biggest change in the braking system came in 1967, when the single-reservoir master cylinder was changed to a dual-reservoir system for safety reasons.

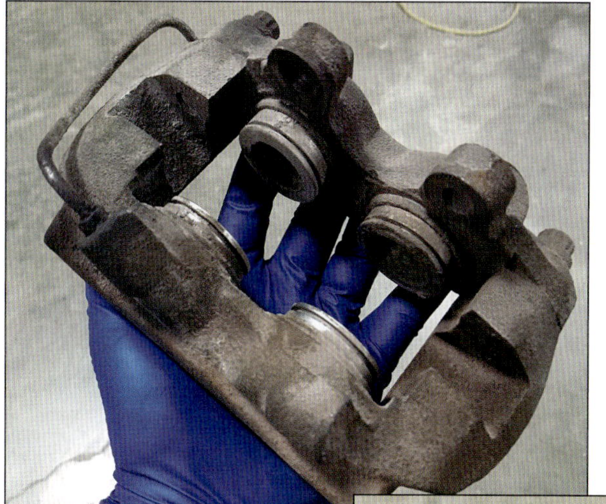

The early calipers were four piston and applied pressure to both brake pads equally. These units were "fixed," meaning that the caliper body did not move.

Drum Brakes

The drum-brake system on all cars was a Bendix/Wagner-style, single-anchor, self-adjusting system. Drum brakes require springs to pull the shoes back into place. The self-adjustment works when the brakes are activated in reverse: as the secondary shoe wears down, it gets pushed out farther by the wheel cylinder. When this happens, the brake adjuster cable gets pulled along with the secondary shoe and pulls up the adjustment lever to catch a notch on the adjusting screw. This sets the new position for the shoe to retract when the brakes are released, and the adjuster spring pulls the adjuster lever back into place.

Beginning in 1968, the standard disc-brake caliper was a single-piston "floating" caliper, which meant that the caliper only pushed from one side, and it slid on pins to pull the outer pad against the rotor. This setup was used on many applications, so rebuilt units are still readily available.

Disc Brakes

Two basic disc-brake designs were used on the original Mustang, and both were Kelsey-Hayes designs. From 1964 to 1967, Ford used a four-piston fixed caliper that squeezed the rotor from both sides. The only real change in this system came in the latter part of 1967, when the size of the crossover tube went from a 3/8-inch hose fitting to a 7/16-inch hose fitting. From 1968 to 1973, all disc brakes used a single-piston floating caliper that pressed from one side to squeeze the rotor.

The single-piston calipers are simple, and rebuild parts are readily available. Look for rust and corrosion on the caliper and the piston, as there is very little clearance between the two, and pits can cause problems and premature failure.

The worst part of rebuilding the calipers is getting the seal to sit in the rear of the caliper. Carefully, with a small pick, I put the seal over the piston and work the inside of the seal into the groove on the back side. The inner seal really limits the movement of the piston. After the piston is in, slide the piston down and install the seal in the inside groove.

Everything is available to rebuild the calipers yourself. The biggest challenge is corrosion in the piston wall area. If it is excessive, it can cause leaking around the outer seal. Stainless sleeved units are available for cars that are driven. Be patient when installing the piston boot. It is frustrating to get it to sit in the back of the caliper.

Master Cylinder

The 1964–1966 master cylinder is a single-bowl design, and in 1967, Ford upgraded to a dual-bowl design. The front brakes became the primary brakes, and the rear became the secondary braking system. This is much safer than the single-bowl system. If a single-bowl system loses pressure, all four brakes are affected, rather than just the front or the back brakes. The single-bowl master cylinder for disc brakes is larger than the four-drum system, as disc brakes require more fluid to operate. The dual-bowl master cylinder contains a larger bowl for the disc and has a bleeder valve on the drum brakes to allow the drum brake to retract.

The finish on the master cylinder varied between unpainted and painted semigloss black, depending on the year of the car. Rebuilding the original master cylinder used to be the standard procedure, but I found that sometimes the rebuilt master cylinder doesn't work or doesn't last very long. The reason is due to moisture getting into the master cylinder passages and corroding the inside of the piston wall, which can damage the piston seals. If severe, it can also allow for the pressure to be bypassed altogether and prevent the brakes from functioning.

The solution to this problem is to have the master cylinder sleeved with a stainless-steel liner. Several machine shops around the country do this and assure their customers that the master cylinder performs correctly. Rebuilt units from parts

Since disc brakes don't retract, when they wear down it takes more fluid to push the brakes out and hold them in place, so disc-brake master cylinders have a bigger reservoir (left) for the front discs (top). Since disc brakes don't self-energize, they require more pressure to engage, so make sure that if you upgrade to disc brakes you also upgrade the master cylinder and proportioning valve.

The single-bowl system in early cars means that if the brakes lose pressure anywhere in the system, all four wheels lose pressure. If you plan to drive the car a lot, consider upgrading to a dual-bowl system, which is available from most Mustang parts vendors.

Unless it is a rare, original master cylinder, corrosion like this is a replacement and not a rebuild. The pitting can allow pressure to bypass or destroy the seal. If it is a rare original part, it can be sleeved with a stainless-steel sleeve and brought back to life.

stores can fail early, as the pitting in the bore hole can tear up the new seals, so if you are going to replace your master cylinder, look for a new (not rebuilt) unit.

Power Brake Booster

The original supplier for the 1964–1966 Mustang power brake booster was Bendix. The booster was 8 inches in diameter and used a bell-crank in the passenger compartment to get the pedal ratio correct. In 1967, Ford began using a Midland-Ross booster along with a new Bendix booster. The Midland unit can be distinguished by the band clamp that holds the two halves together, as opposed to the Bendix crimped housing.

In 1969, Ford went back to using just the Bendix boosters, and to mount them, it used a spacer mounted on the back of the boosters to fit the firewall. In 1970, Ford changed the booster to use a straight booster input rod, as opposed to the teardrop-style input rod that was used from 1967–1969. In 1971, Ford went to an even bigger booster that had a different mounting-pad arrangement than the earlier units. The power disc-brake option was not available until 1967.

The 1964–1966 brake booster is small and mounted away from the firewall, which means that if you try to use it and upgrade to a dual-bowl master cylinder, the master cylinder will touch the shock tower. If you try to install an aftermarket booster mounted flat to the firewall, the ratio of the pedal with a straight pushrod will not be correct.

A note of caution regarding brake boosters: many conversion systems are on the market today to convert a Mustang to a power-brake car, but some do not work well. As previously mentioned, the 1964–1966 cars have a bellcrank mechanism that changes the ratio of the pedal. Many systems that use a straight brake pushrod do not have the correct ratio, as the pedal pin is not at the correct location for these conversions to work. Also, many of the smaller systems use a 7- or 8-inch booster, which is not adequate to operate disc brakes. If you are looking to upgrade your brakes, take a look at Mustang-Steve (mustangsteve.com). The MustangSteve team found a 9-inch

From 1967 to 1970, Ford used two types of boosters: the Bendix unit (shown) and the Midland unit, which was used in 1967 and 1968 as well as briefly in 1969. The Midland unit was more effective, but the Bendix unit was more common. On this 1970 Mach 1, the booster and master cylinder are painted black.

The bigger the booster, the more vacuum actuation for the brakes, and the 1971–1973 booster was the biggest of them all. Plenty of room and a heavier car required the larger booster.

Rebuilding Drum Brakes

The most important thing about rebuilding your drum brakes is to do one side at a time. This way, if you get confused, you always have one side to look at for reference.

If you are restoring the rear axle and don't have either side to look at, hopefully you took my advice from earlier in this book and photographed everything before you took it apart. This brake-system rebuild is for a car that will be driven daily, and an inspection of the shoes showed that they were almost new, so I reused them. There is no reason to detail the brakes unless you plan to pull the drum at shows to show your work. Hot brake-lining dust takes out any detailing pretty quickly. ■

This 9-inch rear end is going into a 1970 Mach 1 that will be driven, so there is no show detailing here. Make sure that you have a good, clean, organized area to work in if possible. Most of the items on this rebuild are available as replacements.

The brake shoes slide along these small, square, flat areas on the backing plates, so apply a small coating of high-temperature grease to these points.

The emergency-brake parking lever attaches to the inside of the secondary shoe (the front of the car would be to the left in this picture). The secondary shoe has the longer braking surface, so the smaller shoe goes to the front of the axle.

The diamond-shaped shoe guide anchor plate often gets tossed after the first brake job, and if you have yours, make sure you don't lose them, as they are only available for early 6-cylinder and 1972–1973 applications. They hold the shoes against the pins so that they don't slide at an angle and keep the shoe parallel to the drum.

This multifunction brake tool has a cup on one end and allows you to install the anchor springs safely and without tearing up the spring with a pair of pliers. As far as which spring goes on first, the Ford photo in the shop manual shows the secondary spring going on first, with the primary spring going on last. That's the opposite of what I did here.

The parking-brake link spring is usually not included in brake hardware kits, but some vendors carry it separately. The link spring goes on the primary shoe side.

Because this same style of drum brake was used for many years and applications, items such as the adjusting nut and screw are available. Whether you buy new or reuse the originals, use high-temperature grease on the threads and the stud end of the adjuster. Originals are identified by an "L" or "R," and the original pivot nuts will have one groove (left side) or two grooves (right side). These replacements are not grooved.

If you don't have a fancy shoe-setting gauge, the next best thing to do is to adjust the shoes out to the point that when you spin the tire, it makes about one revolution. This means that the shoes are barely touching the drum. When you test drive, make several stops to seat the shoes. Then, when you back up, the brakes should self-adjust.

booster that fits, and it corrects the pedal-ratio issues with the early-car pin position.

Emergency Brake

All of the emergency-brake systems are similar in design, and all are used in conjunction with drum brakes. From 1964 to 1968, a handle that mounted on the dash was used, and in 1969, Ford changed it to a foot pedal. All systems use cables to manually pull the rear brakes against the drum. Most of these components are left with a natural finish, and the length and layout of the cable system differed from year to year. The biggest challenge with restoring the e-brake system is corrosion. Commonly, the cables freeze up and lock, and getting them loose is a challenge.

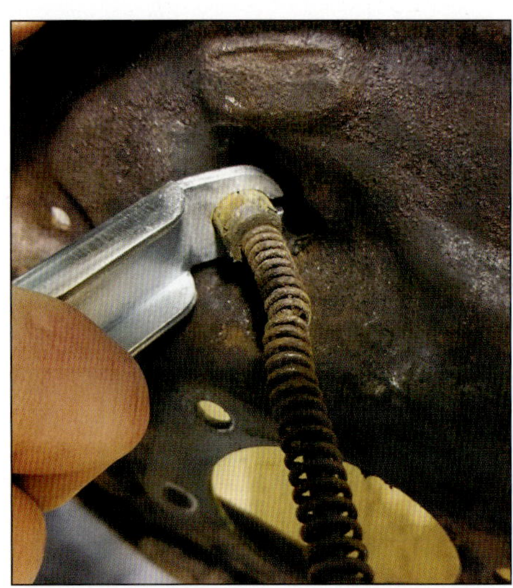

The emergency cables are held inside the brake backing plates by spring-loaded splines. Most of the Mustang vendors and parts houses sell a tool to pull the tangs inward, but in most cases, the tool needs to be modified (drilled out) to make it work. I have had about 50-50 luck using a 9/16-inch, six-point, 3/8-inch-drive, deep-well socket to pull the tangs in.

Rear Suspension

All Mustangs were equipped with leaf-spring suspension and were load rated depending on the bodystyle and engine combination. Beginning in 1969, Ford began installing rear anti-sway bars on high-performance models (starting with the Boss 429) and offered staggered rear shocks on Boss Mustangs and big-block cars with manual transmissions.

The rear suspension is not terrible, and it took very little to make it work correctly. Ford documented most of this in the *Boss 302 Chassis Modification* book. The biggest problem with the rear suspension is the leaf-springs sag, which makes the car look like it is squatting. It needs to be noted that the cars were intended to sit lower in the back than in the front, but after the springs sag, it not only effects the performance but also the appearance of the car. The original springs can be rebuilt and re-arched for show vehicles.

Leaf Springs

As with all of the underside parts, the original springs usually suffered from road debris and the fact they were only hot-dip phosphated, which didn't leave them much protection. Depending on the manufacturing, springs tended to sag after a few years. Restoring the springs can be done. The anti-squeak pads and straps are available, and the cost to re-arch the original is in line with new springs. The top leaf usually has the part number stamped into it, and if the rest of the springs are badly corroded, some owners have replaced the longer springs and installed the stamped top spring and detailed the new assembly. For cars that are driven, they can be painted with a cast-iron finish to keep them protected.

The rear leaf springs are color coded. This one is from a 1970 convertible and shows one silver and one red stripe. The silver now looks blue due to age.

The same leaf spring has the part number (D0ZA-5556-C) stamped on the top (smallest) leaf. Use the part number to cross reference with the information in the **Ford Text and Illustrations** ***manual to find the correct color codes for the springs if they are unreadable.***

Most springs are marked with identifying stripes from the factory, and over the years, these are very hard to read. When cleaning the

You can re-arch and rebuild your own springs. The anti-squeak pads are available as well as new leaf-spring straps. Note there were two types of straps used: some with square holes (shown) and some with round D-shaped holes (early cars). Document which ones your springs should have at teardown.

Most cars came with the coarse-thread spring shackles on the left. However, during the 1970 run, some cars received shackles with fine-thread studs. Some cars with dual exhaust came with studs on opposite sides. The shackles are finished in light phosphate, with some having the darker heat treat on the studs. (Photo Courtesy Cunningham Archives)

spring, it is very easy to remove the identification stripes or alter the color. In some cases, the color itself can be altered, depending on how the original stripe color pigment degraded. Use mild detergents or a mild rust remover, such as Evapo-Rust, to clean the area. Then, compare it to the strip identification found in the *Ford Text and Illustrations* book or online for your car.

Staggered Shocks

By staggering the rear shocks, most of the wheel hop was eliminated from the leaf-spring system, and Ford applied this to the Boss cars and big-block 4-speed cars in 1969. If you are looking to improve the car's handling, adding this setup works well with the leaf springs, and the parts are available in the aftermarket.

Shackles

There were two different styles of spring shackles: one with the thread nuts on the same side and one with the thread nuts on opposite sides. The one with opposite sides was used on the driver's side of some dual-exhaust cars. Some Ford replacement shackles had thinner bars than the production-line parts, and some had a different thread. Different-style locknuts were used, depending on the suppliers. The spring shackles were light-phosphate coated from the factory.

Rear Sway Bars

Ford began installing rear sway bars in 1969 on some models. They pivot on the frame rails and attach to the rear axle via a set of flat plates that are bolted on along with the leaf-spring mounting plates. As with the front sway bar, the rear sway bar transfers the movement to the other side and keeps the wheels planted in a hard turn. The plates were

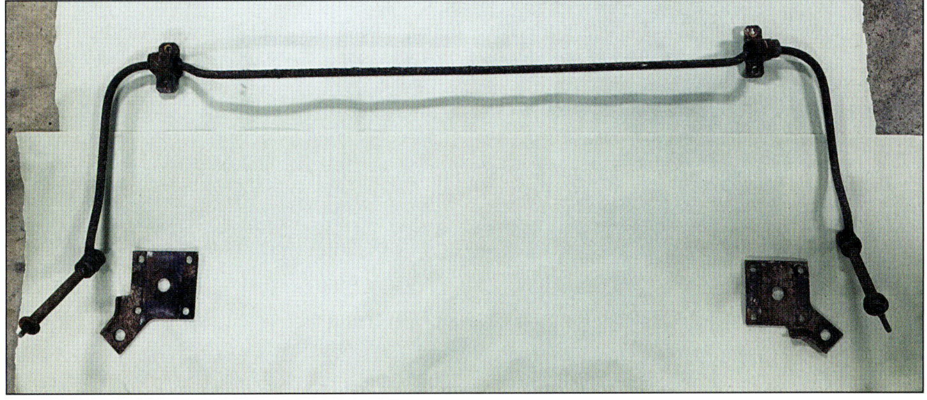

Rear sway bars began popping up in 1969, and this small bar is from a 1970 Mach 1. It is designed so that the rotation point is held at the frame rail, and the arm connects to the rear axle via plates mounted with the shock mounting plates.

Be wary of some aftermarket rear sway bars—they do not work the same as the factory bars. Some aftermarket bars have the rotation points on the axle, and the end link and arm terminate in the frame rail. That's a lot of force on the rear frame rail, and this frame rail tore out due to the forces from the sway bar.

These photos show the Ford rear axles used in the first-generation Mustangs. The 7¼-inch axle (top) was used behind 6-cylinder cars. It is easily identified by the rear cover plate and, of course, the four-lug axles. The 8-inch axle (middle) has the smooth rear center. This is an early one with the fill hole in the back of the center section. Later, it moved to the front of the gear housing. The 9-inch axle (bottom) has the center bulge to make room for the larger gearset.

phosphated, and the sway bars were semigloss black.

Be careful with some of the aftermarket sway bar kits. Some of these kits pivot on the axle and terminate on the frame rail using a U-style bolt that is drilled into the frame rail. With the Ford setup, the pressure is on the end plate on the axle, and the rotation point on the frame is relieved. With the aftermarket systems, the pressure is applied at the frame rail, and I have seen these U-bolts rip through the frame rail (in a place where you can't check the condition of the rail prior to installing the bolt). Use caution when installing this style of sway bar.

Rear Axle

Three types of rear axles were used: the 7¼-inch, the 8-inch, and the 9-inch housings. The 7¼-inch axle used an integral carrier design that was not removable and utilized an access plate on the back to service the differential. The 8- and 9-inch differentials have a removable carrier housing. The 7¼-inch housing was used for the light-duty four-lug, 6-cylinder applications through 1968. The 8-inch was used for 6-cylinder applications after 1968. The 7¼-inch used a 24-spline axle, the 8-inch and the 9-inch shared the same 28-spline axle, and the 9-inch in high-performance applications came with 31-spline axles.

Axle Housing

Identifying the various housings is fairly easy. Besides the four-lug bolt pattern, the 7¼-inch can be identified from the rear differential cover. The 8-inch housings have a smooth, rounded rear differential area, and the 9-inch has a hump to allow for the larger gearset. Early 8- and 9-inch housings had the fill plug for the rear axle lube mounted in the rear housing cover through 1966. Later housings were smooth, and the fill plug was moved to the carrier assembly. All housings were painted semigloss black.

The biggest challenge in restoring the rear housing is the pitting. Being under the car, the housing took a beating from the road, and the paint was chipped off to expose the housing to the elements, which pitted the housing. Filling in the pits before paint improves the look of the housing.

Axles

All axles used a 4½-inch bolt pattern. The 7¼-inch has four lugs, and the 8-inch and 9-inch have five lugs. Some 9-inch units had 28-spline axles, and others had 31. The easiest way to differentiate them is to look at the end of the axle: if it has

If you are unsure of which 9-inch housing you have (small or big bearing), measure the flange or bearing, and the dimensions are readily available online. These holes are 3.375 inches wide, which means that it is a small-bearing housing. A big-bearing housing measures 3.5 inches.

The quickest way to determine the number of splines on an axle is to look at the end. The racetrack oval depression on the left is a 28-spline axle, and the one on the right with the two small holes and a small center hole is a 31-spline axle.

an oval-shaped hole, it is a 28-spline axle, and if it has 3 holes, it is a 31-spline axle.

Unless the axles are bent, the only real maintenance is replacing the axle bearing and perhaps changing out a stripped wheel lug. For detailing, the axles were left in a raw machine stage, which led to rusting pretty quickly. You can have a machine shop true and replace this finish on a lathe, but for most cars, a coat of cast-iron paint prevents the axle from rusting while driving.

The axles have a dark heat-treat finish and then they were machined, leaving a bare-metal finish. If you are doing a full concours restoration, this finish can be re-created with a lathe. If you are going to drive your car, paint it with a cast-iron finish to prevent instant corrosion.

The axle plate goes on before you press the new bearings onto the axles. Make sure to document which way the plate is installed. Note that the brake backing plates don't need to be removed to service the rear axles. One thing missing here is a new axle-flange gasket.

Carrier

The center carrier on 8- and 9-inch housings was painted red oxide before the machining was performed on the center, so the machined areas were left exposed on the finished rear axle. A machine shop can duplicate this for concours restorations. For driven cars, these areas can be painted with a cast-iron coat to protect them.

The 9-inch nodular housing was first used in 1968 on the first Cobra Jet cars (and with 31-spline applications after that). It can be differentiated by its extra rib above the pinion. Not all nodulars came with the "N" welded on them. For those that didn't have the "N," there is an "N" stamped in the carrier saddles. The quickest way to identify factory Positraction units is by the carrier-bolt seats. They are countersunk on a Positraction unit and flush on a non-Positraction unit. To identify the correct ratio of the gears, divide the number of teeth on the ring gear by the number of teeth on the pinion gear.

For rebuilding, the best information comes from the factory manu-

Some auto parts stores have this tool available for rent to remove the axle seals, so don't chew up your housing trying to get it out with a screwdriver. It slides behind the seal, and you use a slide hammer to pull it out. Installation is with your bearing/seal installer.

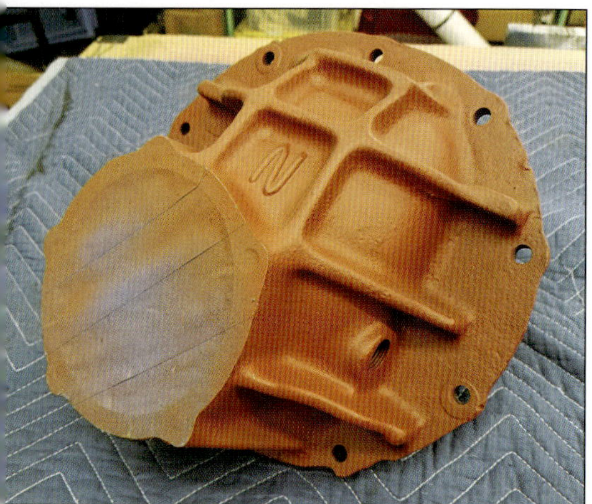

Most 9-inch nodular carriers have this "N" cast into them. Early nodular housings and "WAR" housings (for the 1967 390 engine) as well as the "WAA" and "WAB" cases were not nodular iron but have the same ribbing on the outside. (Photo Courtesy Cunningham Archives)

This is an early nodular case, which is identified by a "N" marked on the inside saddle. Note that the carrier housing and the pinion housing are different shades of red oxide: the carrier was electro-disposition (EDP) coated and the pinion carrier was dipped. Painted on two separate lines, they usually were different colors. (Photo Courtesy Cunningham Archives)

For concours cars, find as many of the original inspection marks and paint daubs as possible. With the raw machined areas, a coating of moisture-displacing oil, such as Boeshield T-9, helps to keep the corrosion away. Driven cars can use a cast-iron paint to protect these areas.

als. Access to a press and a dial indicator is needed for rebuilding. Grease for lining up the gears can be purchased at most performance outlets and online performance vendors. Noting this, in general, the center bearings in the spider-gear unit are fairly robust and usually do not need to be changed unless the vehicle has been driven hard.

Ford's friction-modifier additive for locking rear axles puts the "slip" in "limited slip." It allows the clutches to slip a little in the corners. Also, it smells terrible.

Gear oil is determined by the original Ford specification, unless you are using an aftermarket center and gears. Oil selection is determined by the design of the components, not by the latest trend. The exception is synthetic oils. They have a better molecular structure and work better than standard oils in the same weight. Ford Positraction units are clutch style, and with the factory clutch packs, Ford specifies using a friction modifier to allow the clutch packs to slip a little in corners. You'll know if the friction modifier is in the rear axle because it smells terrible!

The quickest way to identify original Positraction units at the swap meet is to look for the countersunk holes holding the two halves together. The one on the left is a Positraction unit, and the one on the right is non-locking.

Alignment grease is available from most performance parts vendors. Apply grease to the gears and then move the gears through the grease to get a contact pattern. The pinion is adjusted by shims behind the pinion-bearing housing, and the ring gear is adjusted by adjusting nuts on either side of the carrier saddles. The adjusting-nut hold downs (not pictured) prevent the adjusters from moving after adjustment.

ELECTRICAL

Just because they were built during the smog era of the mid-1970s doesn't mean that they weren't fun. Don Bierman of Baltimore is getting ready to light up the tires in his 1973 Mach 1 with a 351-4V engine and automatic transmission. Note the GoPro camera mounted on the passenger's door. (Photo Courtesy Nick Magilton)

Wiring is more intimidating to some than bodywork or paint, but it doesn't have to be. With a little knowledge and some patience, you can repair or replace your harnesses like a professional.

Grounds

I am starting with grounds because they are the cause of more angst than anything else in the wiring system. The Mustang uses the chassis to connect all of the grounds back to the battery, and the connection to the chassis is usually the culprit for many wiring problems.

One of the first places to look for an electrical fault is the grounding. Grounds get corroded and fail to pass the electrical charge. Keep your grounds clean. The battery grounds to the engine and then connects to the chassis via a small grounding strap to the firewall.

This small 12-gauge wire is all that is used to transfer the ground from the engine to the firewall and chassis, so it is very important that the contacts remain clean.

Do not overtighten the screws for the starter solenoid. The solenoid grounds through these screws, and overzealous tightening can tear out the threads, cause problems with grounding, and cause the car to not start. Other items such as engine sensors and the horns also ground directly to their mount points.

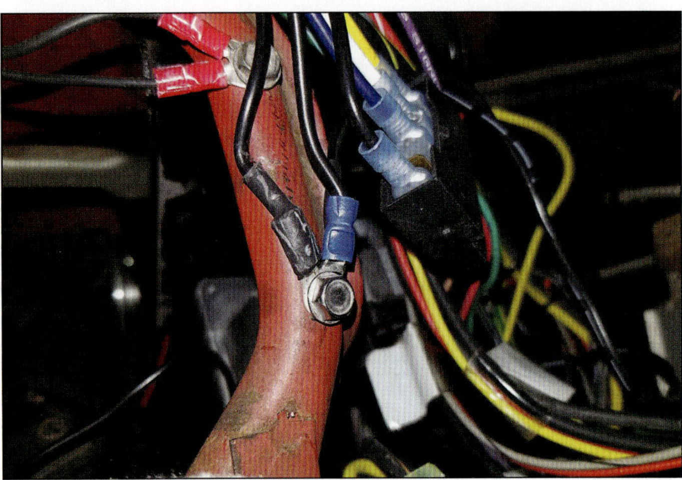

For many points on the car, Ford simply ran a sheet-metal screw to a chassis point to ground the circuit. These grounds are located behind the instrument cluster and are difficult to access. In this situation, additional accessories were added to this car, and rather than stacking five or six grounds to one tiny screw, a new ground post was started. Never use insulated connectors like these on a concours car.

Making sure that your car has clean grounds is the majority of the battle.

The ground from the battery is connected directly to the motor, and from there, it connects to the chassis via the ground strap at the back of the engine. Where the negative battery cable is a 6- or 8-gauge cable, the wire connecting the engine to the rest of the car is only a 12-gauge cable. This is because the starting system requires much more current to turn over the engine than the rest of the car, and the starter is grounded directly to the motor. It does mean that you need to keep the ground strap clean and in good contact with the chassis and engine. Most of the remaining grounds screw or bolt directly to the body to make the connection back to the battery.

Starting System

The starting system draws the most power. It includes the battery, the starter, the starter solenoid, and the ignition switch. The battery's primary purpose is to turn over the motor. It has a secondary use of running some of the electrical systems when the engine is not running. When you turn the ignition to the "start" position, the key switch sends 12 volts to the "S" post of the starter solenoid, which closes the solenoid and allows 12 volts to flow to the starter. The starter is grounded through the engine block and returns to the battery. The "I" post is connected to the ignition coil to provide a full 12 volts to the coil during startup. Simple, right?

So, what is happening when you hear a series of clicks in a row, a single click, or no sound at all?

No sound at all means that the battery is dead or something has completely broken the flow of electricity back to the battery. This may

Original starters from Ford were either ink stamped (right) or die stamped (left). You can barely see the original ink stamp on this 1965 Mustang starter (right), but it is stamped "FoMoCo" and "C4ZF-11001-A" for a small-block application. The starter on the left is "C7AF-11001-F," which is also for a small-block. Starters that have been rebuilt may not contain all of the original-style parts, as cores are thrown into big bins and used in random order.

Here are some of the various types and styles of starter solenoids: an original Autolite solenoid (left) was used in most applications from 1967–1972, the heavy-duty "C9AF" unit (middle) was found on some Dearborn cars, the Motorcraft unit (right) is shown, and a reproduction Autolite unit (bottom) is shown with incorrect hardware. The earlier FoMoCo-style units are not shown. (Photo Courtesy Cunningham Archives)

be a faulty starter, a faulty ignition switch, a poor ground connection or wire connection, or a defective solenoid. No sound could be caused by any part of the system failing.

A single click usually indicates that the starter is defective. The click means that the current is flowing down to the starter, but the starter won't move. A single click and the lights go out generally indicates that the battery is low or there is a poor connection somewhere in the circuit.

Multiple clicks usually indicate a weak battery. The battery has enough current to close the starter solenoid, but when the starter begins to try to pull power, the battery doesn't have enough current, and it drains and closes the solenoid temporarily. Then, it gains enough current to close the solenoid again, and the result is a series of clicks.

Wiring Harnesses

In general, most of the wiring harnesses that were used on the first-generation Mustangs were wrapped in black tape with no adhesive or black cloth tape with adhesive, and some were given a woven covering to prevent abrasion against body parts. Although there are specialty wires, the primary harnesses are the underdash harness, the front-to-rear lighting/accessory harness, the front-end headlight harness, the engine-feed harness, and the steering-column wiring, which includes the turn-signal switch.

Wrapping Harnesses

Rewrapping the harness is fairly simple, but the material available from the Mustang vendors is thinner than the original material, and it wrinkles up much easier. The tape used is a self-vulcanizing wrap, which means that it fuses together a little when wrapped properly. When wrapping, overlap one-third to a half of the tape width. Ford used several ways to terminate the end of the wrap: by fusing the end of the wrap by pulling it tight or by tucking it under the last wrap and by using the cloth adhesive tape. If you are not

Ford used a plastic tape with no adhesive to wrap most wiring harnesses, and most Mustang vendors carry a version of this wrap. Ford also used a cloth tape for wrapping some wires, and the wide black paper tape was used for taping down wires for things such as the fuel sender wire in the trunk.

Rewrapping the harness isn't difficult, but you need to go slow. As you wrap, keep tension on the tape and overlap about half the width of the tape on each pass. If you get wrinkles in the tape, back up and reset the tape.

A good soldering gun is a must-have item if you plan to do several repairs. A good base station (left) is best, but for some repairs, you can use a soldering gun, such as the one on the right. A small vise with clips is handy when you are trying to hold two wires, the iron, and the solder at the same time.

Ford used a weave on harnesses that might see abrasion, such as this front-to-rear harness under the scuff plates. This weave has to be done on the harness with a machine, and there are few places that can do it for a small-batch order. For non-concours cars, wiring harness covers are available to keep the wires from getting cut.

doing a concours restoration, a small amount of black electrical tape can be used to terminate the wrap.

The woven harness is much more difficult to replace. It frequently gets frayed and bunched up and cannot be repaired. There isn't a good-looking wrap that slides on the harness, so you need to send it to a specialist. Note that there are several different styles of woven harnesses that Ford used as well as different patterns on the weave itself. You may not be able to find the exact pattern that you need. If you are doing a concours restoration, NOS or an excellent used harness may be the way to go. Take care when installing the woven harnesses. The intent was to protect the harness from metal edges and cuts, and when drawing the harness through the body, it can easily snag and tear the cover.

Basic Wiring Repairs

There are two different ways to repair wiring harnesses: soldering and crimping. Soldering is the preferred method, but proper crimped connections also work.

Soldering

Soldering is generally done with the wiring out of the car, as it involves melted solder and heat, which can damage other components. Electrical solder is generally 60-percent lead and 40-percent tin (the perfect combination is 63/37), and it has a rosin core for flux that helps the molten solder flow out. Most new solders are lead free, but they don't flow out as well. The flux allows the solder to flow better in the joint.

When soldering a wire connection, the key is to heat the wire, not the solder. Melting the solder over cold wiring leads to cold connections and creates a break in the electrical circuit.

Purchasing a high-quality or low-quality soldering iron depends on how many repairs you need to make. Inexpensive soldering equipment doesn't last long, and it shows in your repairs. If you only have a few repairs, and inexpensive iron will work fine.

Crimping

Crimping connections can occur on the car if necessary. Please, with the exception of emergency repairs, do not use insulated connectors. They stick out like a sore thumb in bright red, blue, and yellow. Uninsulated connectors are preferred when making splices or fixing connector ends on original cars. Insulated connections, if they are done cleanly, look fine on a modified car.

Make sure that you have the proper tools to crimp the connectors. Some multi-tools will work, but the proper tool will make the repair much cleaner.

The key to a good crimp is to have a firm hold of both the wire and the insulation. Some crimpers fold

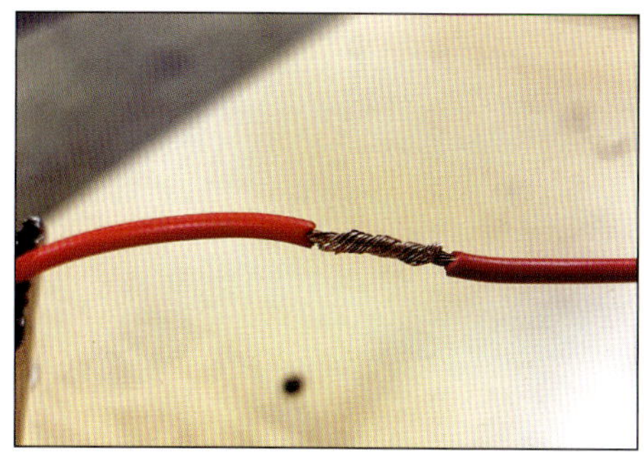

People have many different opinions on how to mesh the two ends of wire together. Whichever method you use, you don't want the wire repair to be wider than the insulation around the wire. I usually cross the two ends like swords and then wrap them around each other.

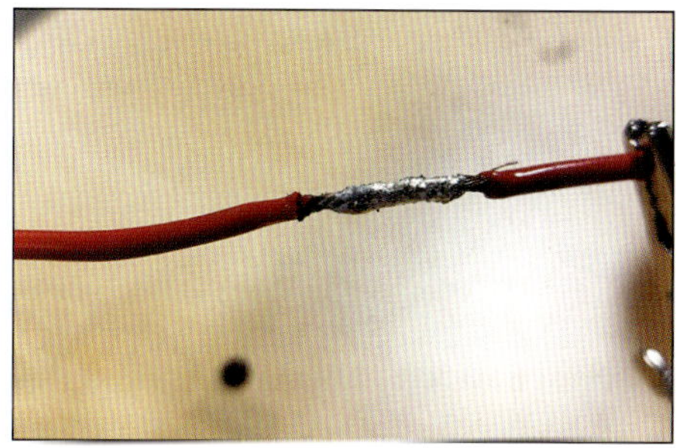

The biggest key is to heat the wire so that the rosin draws the melted solder down into the wires for a good flow. If you just use the iron to melt the solder, you will get a cold solder joint that my not hold together or flow current.

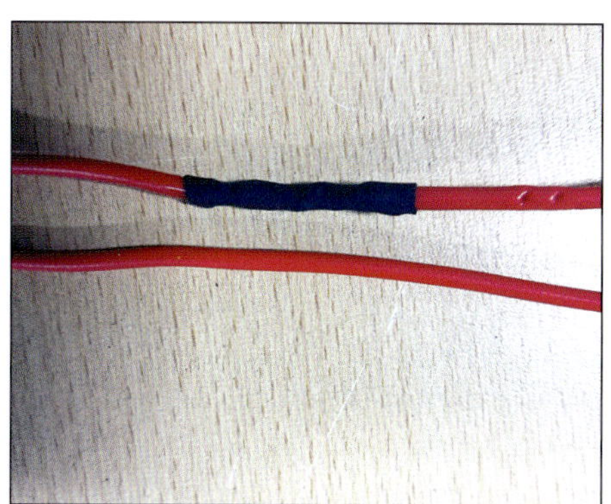

After the heat shrink is applied, the wire is not thicker than the original and won't bulge out in the wiring harness.

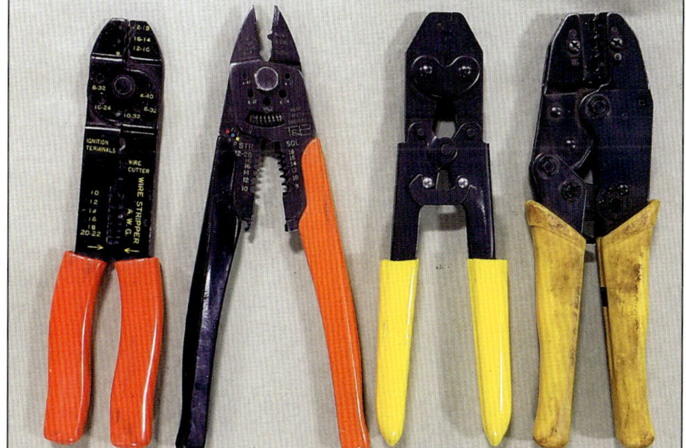

These are some of the various crimping tools that are available. The two on the left are inexpensive tools that are available at any auto-parts store. They work well for most insulated and some uninsulated applications. The second-from-the-right tool is a proper crimper for uninsulated crimps like Ford used. The one on the right is made to properly crimp red, blue, and yellow insulated ends and leaves a professional-looking crimp.

If I have to make a butt splice on a wire, I remove the insulator (the red, blue, or yellow part) and use my inexpensive crimp tool to make the crimp. The side of the tool that pushes in on the connector should face the split in the wall of the connector to drive the ends into the wire.

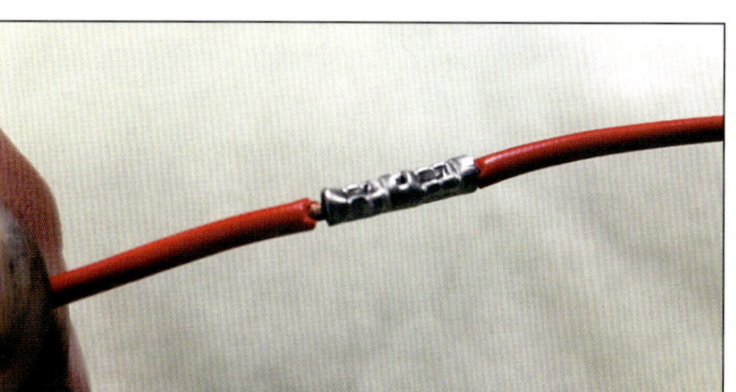

The finished crimp should be tight, but not so tight that it distorts the butt splice, making it stick out wider than the wire insulation. After the heat shrink is installed, this will not show in the wiring harness.

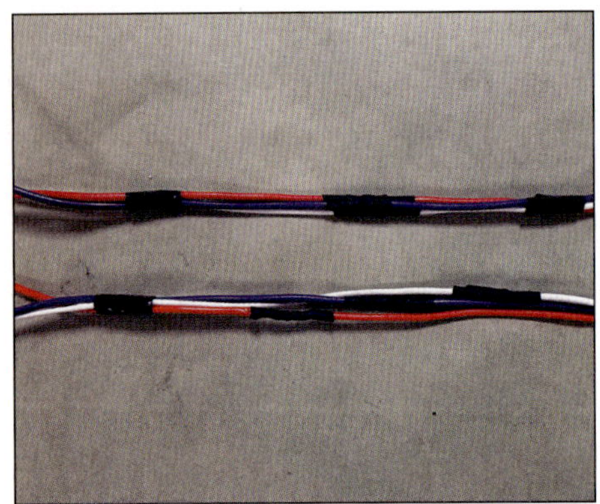

When making multiple wire repairs, spread them out (if possible) so that they don't bunch up when the harness is rewrapped. On the top, I made the crimps all in the same location and will make a huge expansion in the harness. On the bottom, I spread them out so that they won't show under the wrap.

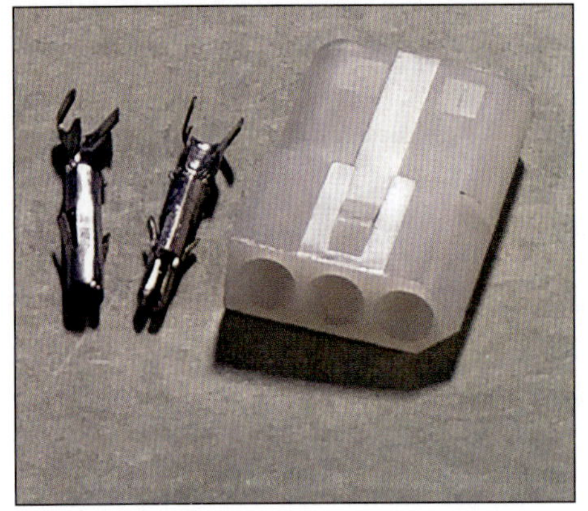

Ford used Molex-style connectors in most of its socket connections. These can be purchased from industrial supply houses. If you have several to repair, buy a proper crimping tool. They are held in place with the tangs on the side of the connector body.

the connector in on the insulation and wires, and this really provides the best connection. Be careful with over-crimping the connection. This can break some of the strands and cause the wire to disintegrate.

Ford used a variety of connector ends in its wiring harnesses. Most are available from Mustang parts vendors and industrial supply houses.

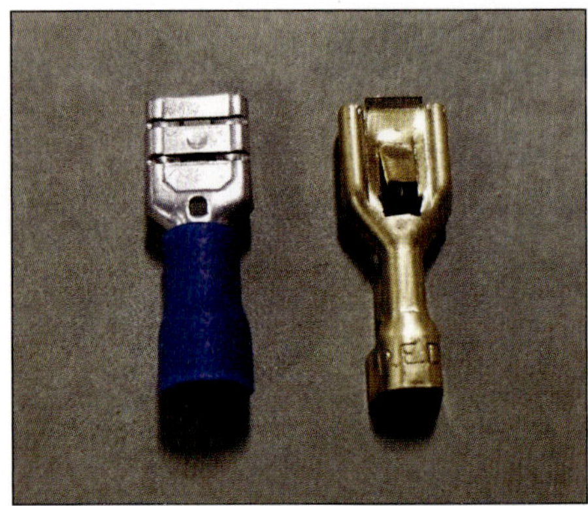

On the left is a 1/4-inch connector that you can purchase at a local parts store. The one on the right is what Ford used in connectors such as the headlight switch. The tang prevents the connector from being pushed out of the body when you connect it. This style of connector can be found at industrial-supply and electrical-supply houses.

Using the proper tool is the best way to install the Molex-style connector. This specialty tool bends and rolls the metal both into the insulation to hold the connector in place and over the exposed wires to ensure a tight connection. This tool is available from American Auto Wire and industrial parts warehouses.

To remove the old Molex connectors, most auto-parts stores sell this pin-removal tool. Find the tube that best matches to your pins, and you will have to rotate it around a little bit to get the pin tangs to push in. It can be frustrating getting the pins out, so be patient.

Cleaning

Before reinstalling the harnesses, make sure that the contacts are clean to make good connection. Commercially available contact cleaners are available that help, but it can be difficult to clean some of the smaller contacts in the molded body of the connector. The big problem with most products that you use to clean oxidation from the contacts is that they generally ruin the finish (or at least the plating on the connection). You need a milder way to clean these contacts.

We have all heard of using cola to get rid of battery acid, but for cleaning corrosion and oxidation from soft

To clean the grime from wiring harnesses, use hand cleaner (without an abrasive). It cleans the harness and doesn't remove the coloring from the wires.

There's something in taco sauce that removes the oxidation from some soft metals, such as copper and brass. The brass connector on top was cleaned with taco sauce and just needed to be wiped clean.

For years, the US Navy has used unsweetened grape Kool-Aid for cleaning mild corrosion. The phosphate removes the rust gently and does not attack the plating like other cleaners do. The connector on top was cleaned by soaking in the mix of grape drink and water.

Use a pencil eraser to clean the contact on items such as the instrument cluster printed circuit. Be very careful and go easy. If you rub too hard, you can pull the contact off of the backing plastic.

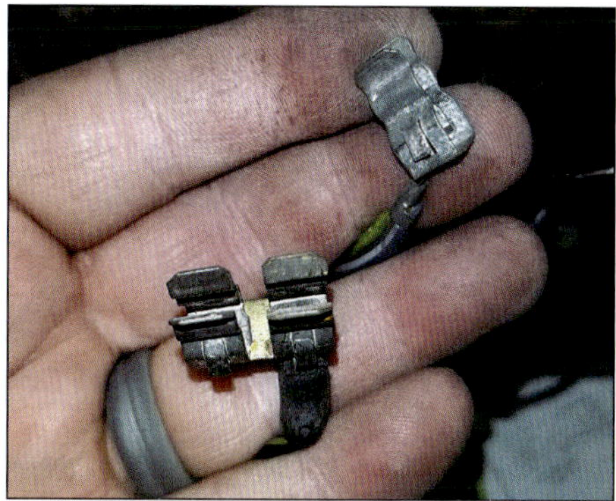

Replacement fuse-holder ends are available, but some of the combinations aren't exact because Ford used some slight offsets and several different fuse sizes. This double was replaced with a good fuse connector in a 1969 Mustang by using a donor holder from another harness.

and plated metals, I use taco sauce or Kool-Aid. The taco sauce strips the oxidation from the copper contacts, and the US Navy has used unsweetened grape Kool-Aid to remove corrosion and oxidation for years. They are both mild methods that generally don't hurt the plating. After removing the oxidation, clean the contact and apply some contact grease or spray to preserve the connection.

Cleaning the wiring harness can be done using hand cleaner with no grit. Hand cleaner also does not remove the colors from the individual wires and makes them look new.

For copper contacts, such as the instrument-cluster printed circuit on later vehicles, use an eraser to gently remove oxidation from the contact pads.

Fuse Block

Early Mustangs were woefully under-fused. The 1964–1968 models had five fuses, and 1969–1973 models had seven fuses. All years used glass-tube-type fuses and were mounted in the most inconvenient spot. It is very difficult to test the fuses in place due to the location. A good glass fuse puller is recommended when testing power issues in the fuse block. The fuse block contacts could become corroded, and they are riveted in place on the fuse block. Replacement contacts are available for broken fuse tabs, but you will need to drill out the rivets to replace them.

Gauges

Gauge clusters were individually wired until 1969, when Ford went to a printed circuit and a single plug-in connector. Ford used this style through 1973.

The fuel, oil-pressure, and temperature gauges all run off of 5 volts, which is provided by the constant voltage unit mounted on the back of the instrument cluster. The original unit had a bimetallic arm, which was connected to a small heating coil. The coil would heat the bimetallic arm and cause it to deflect and break the electrical connection. Then, when it cooled, it made contact again and would heat up and pulse 5 volts to the gauges. Solid-state replacements are available that provide a constant 5 volts, rather than the pulsing original units. However, I have had mixed success with the solid-state units and keep some original-style units around just in case.

The ammeter and tachometer are wired separately through dedicated wires not running through the constant voltage unit. When the car was equipped with a tachometer, the ammeter and oil-pressure gauges were converted to indicator lights. For the oil pressure, this meant that the sending unit was changed from a sender that put out a resistance value to an on/off switch that connected when the pressure was below a safe level. The charge indicator light illuminates if the battery is discharging and the alternator is not supplying current.

Fuel, Oil Pressure, and Temperature Gauges

These gauges work off of a resistance reading sent from the individual gauges that measures between 10 and 73 ohms. Due to the design of the gauges, these values can be off by 5 percent.

The gauges themselves can be tested with a 10-ohm and a 75-ohm resistor. Both are common values for discreet resistors. The gauge test can be performed in the car or on a bench if you have a 5-volt power supply. In the car, you can disconnect the lead from the sender (oil, temperature, or fuel) and attach either the 10-ohm or the 75-ohm resistor to the sender lead and the other end to ground. The 10-ohm resistor causes the gauge to read high, and the 75-ohm resistor makes it read low. A 33-ohm resistor allows it to read somewhere in the middle.

The fuel gauge has a potentiometer in it that measured between 10 ohms (full) and 73 ohms (empty). Check the function of the gauge by simply putting the voltmeter across the sending-wire post and the body of the sender, which grounds to the car through the fuel tank. As you move through the swing of the arm, inspect that the resistance change is constant. A failed sender may become erratic, and the resistance may bounce outside the range. A vast majority of the

In 1969, Ford began using a flexible printed circuit on the back of the instrument cluster to drive all of the gauges. Be very careful, the plastic gets brittle, and the adhesive that holds the contacts and lines in place will fail and they will pull away. The 1970 unit on top has five gauges, and the 1966 unit on the bottom has four gauges with two indicator lights.

The constant voltage regulator supplies 5 volts to run the gauges in the instrument cluster. A modern, solid-state version is available for all years, but the original works just fine.

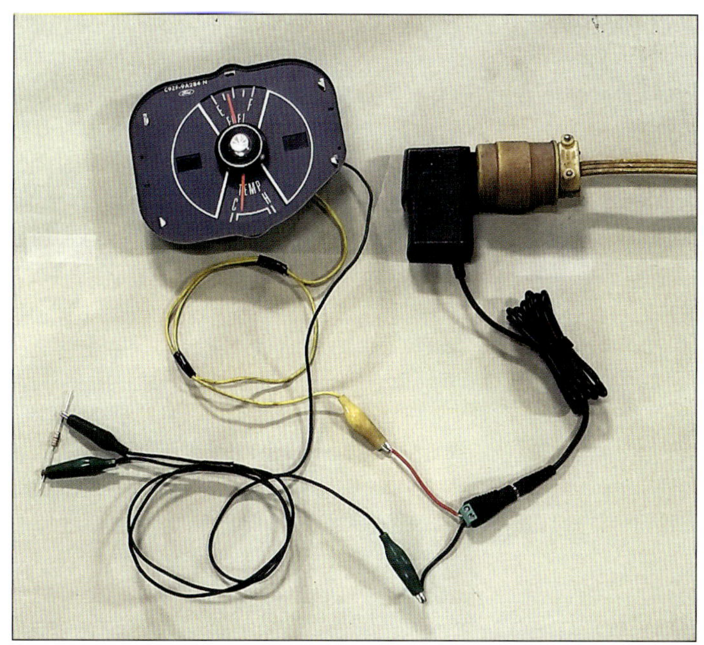

When testing gauges, the resistance is through the ground or sender side while the power is 5 volts. A 5-volt supply and a 33-ohm resistor inline on the ground side shows the fuel gauge at under half, which means that the gauge is working properly.

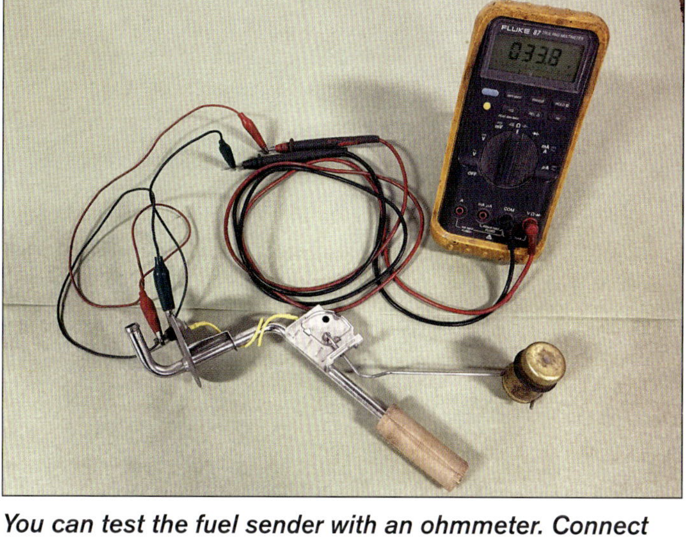

You can test the fuel sender with an ohmmeter. Connect one line to the sending post and one to the metal housing. Slowly run the arm through its cycle. The ohm range should be between 10 and 73 (within 5 percent), and it should not bounce outside of that range or stick on a reading.

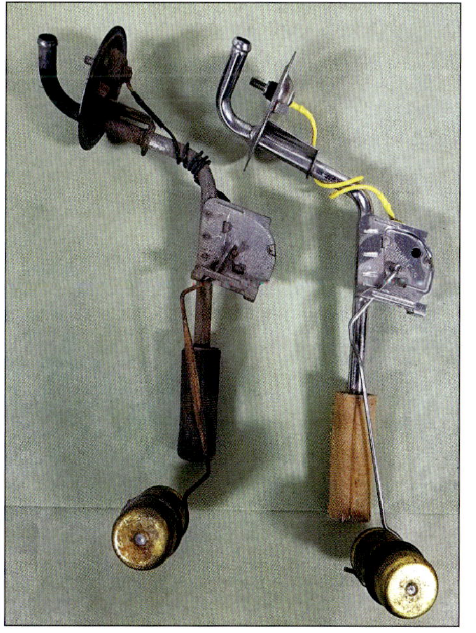

An original fuel sending unit is on the left, and a new one is on the right. Note that the float arm is different, which will give you a different reading of what is in the tank. If you still have your original fuel sending unit, use it to compare with the new one and adjust the arm if needed.

Sending units ground to the engine and send a resistance to the gauge to note any changes. On the top are the two styles of water-temperature senders. The early 1964 unit is on the left and the unit from all other years is on the right. On the bottom are the oil-pressure gauges. The gauge on the left is for an indicator light with a post-style output, the gauge in the middle is for a light with a spade-terminal slide-on, and the item on the right is the sender for a gauge.

failures have been from poorly built aftermarket sending units.

The oil-pressure gauge works off of a sending unit that sends 10 to 73 ohms to the gauge. This sending unit is not interchangeable with an indicator-light-style gauge. If you suspect the sending unit, test the gauge first with the above procedure to make sure that the gauge is reading accurately. Since the oil pressure is critical, I always have a mechanical gauge available to verify that the oil pressure is present in the engine before testing the sending unit.

If you don't have a mechanical gauge, be careful when running an engine with an unknown oil pressure!

Once you know that you have oil pressure, test the gauge-type sender with an ohmmeter. A gauge-style sender will read between 10 and 73 ohms, and an indicator-light style will close with no oil pressure and open if it detects pressure.

If your engine shows oil pressure with the mechanical gauge, reinstall the sending unit and attach an alligator clip lead or make a wire extension to avoid burning anything (including you). Then, connect the positive lead to the extension and the negative to ground. Run the engine, and the range should be in the middle range of 10 to 73 ohms for normal operation. The resistance is high when oil pressure is low, and the resistance is low when the oil pressure is high. A sending unit with no pressure out of the car can read 130 ohms or higher.

The water-temperature sensor can be checked on or off of the engine. You can bring the engine up to temperature and measure the resistance of the sender to ground (as stated above), or you can boil some water to about 180 degrees (this should be the middle of the gauge range) and heat up the sending unit in the hot water. Connecting the voltmeter probes to the sending-unit base, the connection tree should yield about 40 ohms (in the middle of the gauge). Again, a low temperature will read high resistance, and a high temperature will read low resistance.

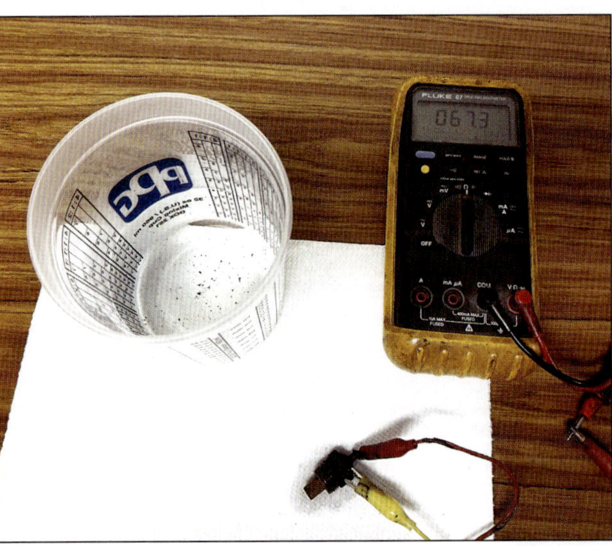

A temperature sender can be tested away from the engine with some hot water. Heat the sender and then attach the meter to the post and body of the sender. The resistance slowly changes as it cools to room temperature.

Ammeter Gauge

An ammeter gauge tells you if the charging system is charging (points to C) or discharging (points to D) the battery by measuring the amount of current (amperage) flowing from the alternator to the battery. Two different types were used. The 1965 version used an inductive loop-style ammeter that measured a magnetic field through a coil. The later units ran directly through the gauge to measure the current on the gauge. The latter gauge was not robust enough for the task and failed pretty quickly. This is why you likely have never seen the needle on your ammeter gauge move. The 1967–1968 Shelbys used a Stewart-Warner ammeter that worked better than the factory unit, and the 1969–1970 Shelbys used a Faria unit that was not very good.

Most instrument repair shops won't restore an ammeter gauge. Instead, they convert it to a voltmeter, which actually works much better than the ammeter gauge. New stock-style ammeter gauges are available from the Mustang parts suppliers, but they tend to fail at the same rate as the originals. I have purchased and know of other restorers who have purchased NOS units only to have them fail right out of the box.

Tachometer

The Ford tachometer works differently than every other tachometer on the market. Every other tachometer works off the negative side of the coil. When the points close, the tachometer counts the pulses. It's simple.

Ford tachometers run through the power feed to the coil (the resistor wire), which means that if the tachometer fails, the car may stop running. This is something that

Ford tachometers work differently than those from other companies, and it's not good. In addition, it's difficult to find a reliable source to service the originals. The unfortunate downfall to having the tachometer option is the loss of the ammeter and oil-pressure gauge, as both become an indicator light.

doesn't happen if you are counting pulses on the negative side.

Here is where I will disappoint many readers: I cannot recommend a rebuilder for the tachometer. Most rebuilders want to convert your tachometer to an industry standard unit, which means that you have to alter the wiring to accommodate their rebuild. Some of the restoration houses are no longer in existence or I have had bad experiences getting work done (or not done at all with one repair shop).

Speedometer

The speedometer is a mechanical unit that uses a gear in the transmission to spin a cable that is attached to the back of the speedometer. The cable spins a small bar magnet that creates a magnetic field that pulls the speedometer needle barrel or shell, and a resistance spring keeps the movement constant and returns the needle back to zero.

In 1967, Ford introduced the optional speedometer with a trip odometer. Standard speedometers read to 120 mph, and high-performance cars received a 140-mph unit.

Most of the issues with the speedometer setup involve the speedometer cable. The square end that inserts into the back of the speedometer can sometimes go in too far, causing a whining sound. This is especially true of the early screw-in-type cables. A speedometer that is chattering or bouncing is usually caused by a problem with the cable.

Calibrating the speedometer involves selecting the right drive gear for the transmission, which is based on a formula. To determine the correct drive gear, you need to know the following: the number of drive-gear teeth on the transmission, the rear-axle ratio, and the tire diameter. This is the base formula:

Number of drive teeth x rear axle ratio
x tire revolutions per mile ÷ 1,000
= Number of driven teeth on the
speedometer gear

To determine the revolutions per mile on the tire, use this formula:

20,168 ÷ Tire diameter =
Revolutions per mile

Say that your automatic transmission has 7 drive teeth, a 3.00 axle ratio, and a tire diameter of 24.5 inches. Calculate the driven gear:

20,168 ÷ 24.5 =
823.18 revolutions per mile
(7 x 3 x 823.18) ÷ 1,000 =
17.28 driven teeth

So, for this application, I would select a 17-tooth drive gear (round to the closest gear) for the most accurate reading. In addition, there are online calculators to help you with the math and to convert a metric tire size to a standard measurement.

Selecting the gear depends on which side the speedometer gear is mounted. Cables mounted on the driver's side typically use a right-hand rotation, and transmissions with a passenger-side mounting use a left-hand rotation. The drive gear on the transmission output shaft is typically six drive teeth for 3.50 to 4.30 axle ratios and seven teeth for ratios below 3.50. Check the specific application in the *Ford Text and Illustrations* book for the most accurate information.

Ignition Switch

Before 1970, the key switch was mounted on the dashboard. In 1970, it was moved to the steering column as part of the federal requirements for locking the steering wheel. The number and layout of the output pins varied. Some of the ignition switches came with a threaded post on the back that allowed easy access for key-on power to run various accessories. Ford even put a three-output accessories connector on some models for just this purpose.

Removing the key switch from

Driving the speedometer accurately means getting the right cable gear, and the Mustang vendors sell color-coded driven gears between 16 and 23 teeth in right- and left-hand applications. The gear on the far left is a Ford gear, and the middle four are all color-coded replacements in different tooth configurations. The gear on the far right is an original gear out of a 1970 FMX automatic. Note the longer snout on this gear.

The two biggest failures in the turn-signal switch were the plastic arms that cancel the switch and the spring-loaded horn buttons. Most replacements don't come with a new connector, and you have to snake the wires down through the column before the connector is installed.

the body requires the use of a pin and a key. Turn the key to the accessory (ACC)-on position and insert the pin to press on the release. Then, turn the key switch counterclockwise, and it should move past the ACC stop and come out. The pin hole is located on the bottom side of the key switch face on early cars. On column mounted applications, remove the steering wheel to access the removal hole inside the column.

From 1964 to 1969, the ignition switch is held in with a chrome bezel. On 1964–1966 cars, the ignition switch can be removed by holding the bezel in place and twisting the switch from the back side of the dash. On 1967–1968 bezels, there are three notches in the bezel that can be used to unscrew the bezel from the switch. In 1969, there were four. Scott Drake makes a tool for both designs to prevent scratching the dash while removing or installing the switch. Starting in 1970, the ignition switch is mounted on the top of the steering-column assembly and is a shaft-style switch with a rod to lock out the steering column while the car is parked and the key is removed.

When inspecting the key switch for reuse, check the switch and the connector carefully for signs of electrical burning and replace if either has burned. Clean the contacts thoroughly before reassembly.

Turn-Signal Switch

The turn-signal switch was never a very robust design, mainly due to the plastic return arms that can break and not allow the turn-signal stalk to center after a turn has been made. The contact under the steering wheel frequently gets a lot of debris and dirt and will fail. The horn contacts are especially susceptible. They are spring loaded and are made of soft metals that wear quickly.

Some replacement turn-signal switches do not come with a new end connector, so you have to reuse the old connector. Identify the location of each color of wire before using an extraction tool to try to remove the old wires. The matching harness may have the same color of wires, but don't count on it.

Some harnesses run on the outside of the column with a metal cover, but most run internally down the column. There is a big insulation vinyl cover that is used to reduce abrasion on the wires. If your new switch does not have the vinyl cover, transfer it from your original. It makes installing the harness much more difficult, but you need to run it to avoid shorting out wires to the column. Sometimes a little WD-40 or another light lubricant helps to get the cover back in the tunnel.

Charging System

The charging system consists of the alternator or generator, the external regulator, the battery, and the charge indicator (either the ammeter or a charge-indicator light). The battery is used to power the car when the engine is not turning (for example, at start-up). Then, the regulator checks to see if the battery is discharging. If it is, the alternator or generator begins providing power to run the systems and recharge the battery.

The industry changed to alternators in 1965 because they are more

The ground and field posts on the early 1964½ generator are the same size, and sometimes it is hard to read the generator body for which line goes where. It is stamped on the housing: the field is on the right as you look from the back.

efficient than generators. An alternator creates alternating current (A/C), and this power is converted by rectifying diodes in the alternator. Alternator output was generally between 38 and 55 amps. Depending on the application and load, some alternators were driven by a single or double pulley. High-performance applications received a larger-diameter pulley to reduce the power draw down applied by the charging system.

The generator was painted black and was stamped with white ink with the part number and date code. The generator used a two-piece heat shield with a rubber cover over the ends. The alternator housings were natural aluminum, and they were stamped until mid-1969 production, when it was changed to a die stamp at the front of the alternator housing.

Voltage Regulator

The charging system uses an externally mounted voltage regulator that limits the voltage output of the alternator. All units are electromechanical and have two different relays inside to regulate the voltage. The field relay, when energized, connects the charging system to the field circuit when the engine is running. The voltage limiter relay controls the amount of current supplied to the rotating field of the alternator and limits the voltage output.

Alternators had many variations from 1965–1973 and used different pulleys depending on the application. The unit on the left has the rounded adjustment-bolt ear of the Autolite units and a cast Hi-Po (bigger) pulley (they also came stamped steel). The middle unit is also an Autolite-style case, but it has the stamped-steel, single-sheave pulley. The Motorcraft squared-ear alternator with a double-sheave, cast pulley is on the right.

With the exception of the generator cars, all of the voltage regulators are the same basic size. Units with "AF" (standard duty) in the part number (for example, C8AF-10316-A) were printed with silver ink, and "TF" heavy-duty truck units (for example, C8TF-10316-A) were printed in yellow ink. The one that your car received depended on the output of the alternator. "AF" was used on 38- and 42-amp-output systems, while the "TF" was used with 55-amp alternators.

Most units were not adjustable, and the covers were riveted in place. Adjustable units had screws holding the cover to the base. The generator regulator is noticeably larger than the alternator version. The regulator was mounted to either the inside of the radiator support or to the inner apron, depending on application.

Horns

The horns were mounted on the inside of the engine compartment on top of the strut-rod brackets for generator applications and on the front of the radiator support for all other applications through 1970. The horns were moved to the driver-side shock tower and the driver-side inner apron for 1971–1973.

The horns are marked "Lo" and "Hi" on the case, and care needs to be taken when cleaning and detailing for restoration. The horns can be media blasted, but make sure that you don't get abrasive down in the air horn. Otherwise, it can damage the diaphragm inside the horn. The horns are painted chassis black.

Test the horn by applying 12 volts to the spade contact and grounding the horn-mounting tab. There is an

Horns for 1964½ cars (top) are noticeably bigger than for alternator cars. Depending on the application, the horns were mounted flush (bottom left) or away from (bottom right) the radiator support. Drag Pack cars had both horns mounted on the passenger's side to make room for the oil cooler.

Ford bulbs came with the Ford logo screened on them (left) or molded in the glass (right). Check your judging rules for the correct application, but I think it was a supplier change more than a transition away from the molded style. I have found molded bulbs in late 1969–1970 Mustangs, and I have found screened ones on models earlier than that.

adjustment screw on the horn that adjusts the point gap on the contacts. If the horn has a buzzing sound or a resonating tone, adjust the screw carefully to try to get the tone back. Just be careful because adjusting the gap too far either way causes the horn to stop operating. Make very small adjustments if needed.

The Phillips screw on the back of the horn is used to set the tone of the horn, as it moves the point gaps in and out, which slows or speeds up how fast the diaphragm vibrates. Urban legend says you can tweak the screw back and forth and revive a dead horn, but it never worked for me.

The early generator horns can be disassembled for restoration, but the later ones are riveted. If either design needs repair, it should be repaired by a specialist.

Generator-style horns use a separate relay that is mounted to the inside of the radiator shroud under the voltage regulator. If the horns stop working, first check the relay to see if it has failed.

Lighting

One of the big drawbacks to the lighting system is the incandescent bulbs that were used during the time period. It's very dim technology. Halogen headlamps helped nighttime driving somewhat, but it was still one of the safety concerns with the early Mustangs.

If you are not building an original car, consider upgrading to LED technology. LEDs are much brighter and longer-lasting than the original bulbs, and they are much safer because other drivers can actually see your brake lights. Note that some of the LED conversion bulbs for the dash cannot be dimmed, so they are either on or off. This may change soon as this technology improves.

As for original headlights, there are two different types of bulbs and at least two different suppliers: Tung-Sol and GE. Some headlights had the Ford logo molded into the glass, and some had it frosted in the glass. Both were used during the run; when a specific type was used in which plant could have varied. All bulbs are date coded on the back if you want to verify application.

Radio

Ford radios were terrible 1960s technology, and after 50 plus years, the capacitors leak out, and they stop working. If yours is still working, you are in the minority. Ford offered AM, AM/FM and AM 8-track radio options through 1973.

Bench testing is fairly simple. Use a 12-volt power source, an antenna, and a speaker. A few alligator-clip leads make connections to the original molded connections. If it works after you hook it all up—congratulations. You now have the awful sound of 1960s technology!

Even if the radio works, you may wish to have it rebuilt. Consider upgrading to solid-state technology. Several rebuilders can even convert your AM to FM, and keep the original AM look. The upgrade will last longer, sound better, and look original.

If you are lucky and the original paper cone speakers are still intact, they may not be for long. Use of the paper speaker after all this time will probably destroy the paper. In addition, paper cone speakers with small magnets to fit in tight places generally sound like . . . paper. If you are replacing the speakers, get a quality modern-design speaker. Some of the replacement speakers (and upgrade speakers) are still made of paper, and they sound like it. Take the time and investigate your speaker options before just buying a replacement out of a catalog.

I get into big trouble with aftermarket radios. I am not a fan of the radios and systems that are available for early Mustangs. All of the originals had potentiometers coming out for the volume and tuning, and the 1965–1966 was much narrower than the later radios, which you may be dealing with if someone hacked up the dashboard to fit a standard-size radio. Every system out there is a conversion of a radio that was intended for something else. Some of these systems are cheap in quality and don't sound much better than the originals.

I am not a fan of kick-panel speakers. My feet don't listen to music, and a piece of plastic doesn't work well as a speaker mount. In addition, they get kicked and broken while getting in and out of the car. They usually work, but I am just not a fan.

The original radio on the left shows the capacitors that usually leaked out gradually, causing the radio to fail. The unit on the right has been given a solid-state AM/FM upgrade, which is available from several online conversion companies. All of those bulky items were replaced with one small solid-state board. Units are now available with Bluetooth and universal serial bus (USB) inputs.

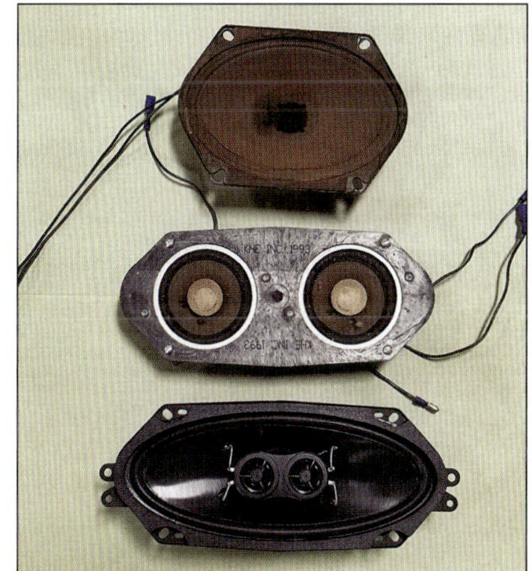

Ford speakers were awful, and after 50 years, they don't get better. At the top is an original 6x9 AM radio speaker, in the middle is an aftermarket attempt at "stereo" output from a pair of paper cone speakers, and the speaker on the bottom is well-made and sounded very good when installed in the 4x10 space for an early car.

While becoming more prominent toward the end of the first-generation run, the AM/FM radio was an uncommon option, and if your car came with one, it was special. An AM radio/8-track player is even rarer.

CHAPTER 11

Interior

Besides a few one-offs, Shelby officially got into the convertible game in 1968, with big- and small-block versions available. These made up about one-third of the production run. This GT350 is finished in Highland Green with a 302-4V engine and automatic transmission. The car is owned by Steve Schonegg of Indianapolis, Indiana.

Interior restoration to make a first-generation Mustang look like new can be done with a small investment in tools and a good weekend. Most of the reproduction parts are pretty good, and with patience, you can achieve good results.

Convertible tops should be left to the professionals, and even within the professional ranks, very few know how to install one properly so that there aren't leaks or wind noise. Headliners are something that you can try, but the professional with the steamer and experience usually does

The dash takes a lot of abuse from keys, knees, and other sources of chips and scratches. Painting the dash of an early, assembled car can look like you're fogging for bugs, but everything needs to be covered because the overspray goes everywhere.

a much better job. However, if you are careful, you can get a nice result.

Dash Pad

Regarding some of the NOS soft trim that you may see for sale at a local swap meet or online, many of these pieces were sold and sent back to Ford because they didn't fit well. When a part went "4R," which is Ford lingo for "last chance; there ain't no more," many of the NOS items, such as dash pads, were purchased, but when they didn't fit well, they were returned or exchanged. This process repeated itself, and the last ones to go were the ones that didn't fit well. So, sometimes that dashboard on the table at the swap meet isn't in a car for a reason.

The biggest mistake made with most dash installations occurs with 1968–1970 Mustangs. The VIN tag is in the dash area, and it is frequently jammed underneath the dash pad as it is being installed. On 1971–1973 cars, it was mounted in the actual dash pad itself, and it was not mounted in the windshield prior to 1968. When fitting a new dash pad, notch it for the VIN plate to clear (if needed).

A small piece of tape to mark the original dash-pad-mounting holes helps when poking around to find the holes after the dash is in place. The 1971–1973 cars do not have these screws and bolt into the front edge of the dash support.

The dash pad will require several fittings before it is ready to install. The pads are generally slightly oversize and require some trimming to fit flush in the car. On 1964–1970 cars, the dash is secured near the base of the windshield, so long-shank screwdrivers and non-scuff pry tools are good to have on hand. On 1964–1968 cars, there is a pair of trim pieces that press against the pad and the windshield seal to hold the pad in place. On 1969–1973 cars, they all have butyl-seal-installed front windshields, and the dash doesn't press up against the front window seal. Sometimes, it is easier to see and fit the later-car dash pads without the windshield in place because there are no trim moldings.

Make sure that your defrost ducts align with the openings in the dash

Starting in 1968, Ford installed a VIN tag in the window area of the car. The flimsy aluminum tag gets smashed and sometimes gets covered by the dash pad (or partially, as shown here). When installing the dash pad in 1968–1970 cars, make sure that the VIN tag is clearly visible through the windshield.

Hopefully, you took photos of how items such as the defrost ducts and speaker are stacked in the dash during disassembly. In the early cars, they go over the top of the pad.

pad and take small snips, rather than big ones, when fitting the pad. Once you have the pad in place, using a small awl or screwdriver to hold the dash in place while securing the other screws works wonders to keep the trim in place.

Carpet

The carpet was not originally glued down, although some restorers like to keep it in place with adhesive. I prefer to not glue it down because you inherently need to get under the carpet for something. The carpeting was used along with a sound underlayment that needs to be used to allow the molded carpet to fit properly.

The carpet was originally made of an 80/20 loop that was 80-percent rayon and 20-percent nylon. This was used in most carpet before 1974. It was sewn in nice rows, and the replacement carpeting has been changed regarding the material and how the loops are sewn together. The original 80/20 was not terribly durable and would fray fairly easily.

Sometimes the molding of the replacement carpet does not quite work correctly, or the gluing of the jute padding causes a wrinkle in the carpet. If this occurs, try getting them out by using a steamer and some weights, a heat gun, or pulling the jute pad off the back of the carpet and resetting it on the carpet properly. Be very careful when applying steam or a heat gun because the carpet can be damaged fairly easy. I use a heat gun for remolding corners and steam for removing wrinkles.

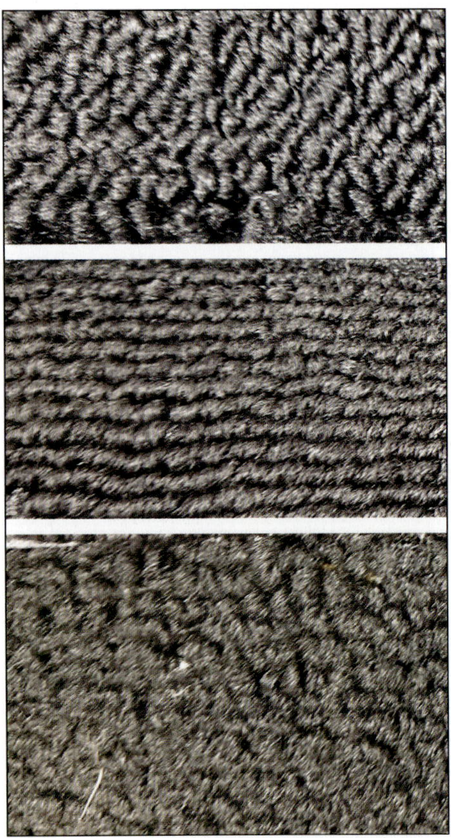

Some replacement carpet looks different than the original carpet. On the bottom is an original carpet weave with horizontal individual bulbs of carpet. In the middle is an older replacement carpet with horizontal bands. On top is a newer carpet with a diagonal pattern of mixed-sized strands. For a concours car, find and restore an original carpet set.

A common source of wrinkles in the carpet is from the pad, as it can get bunched up when it is being applied to the back of the carpet. This won't smooth out and needs to be reapplied.

Headliner and Convertible Tops

Hopefully, you marked or stored your headliner bows in such a way that you can install them back in the correct positions. If not, check the factory interior installation book to denote the colors on the end of each bow to get them in the right order. You may need to snip the ends of the aftermarket headliners a bit to get the bows to fit properly. With the bows in place, start from the middle of the front and rear glass openings and work your way to the corners. Old pieces of windlace work great for holding the headliner in place.

If you didn't store or mark the headliner bows properly, you can figure out the position of the bows by the color that the bows are marked. This paint can become very faded (as these are), so I don't recommend relying on that to identify them later. The factory interior assembly manual shows the sequence of the bows.

With the headliner bows in the proper position and the rear retainers (if used) in place, begin at the front and back windshields in the middle and work your way toward the corners. Repeat this process for the door openings. Note the old piece of windlace used to hold the headliner in place (center).

Many people claim to be able to install convertible tops, but very few can do it without improper folding or causing bad wind noise. You can watch videos online all day, but it really takes experience to learn to install one properly. Find a professional and hire him or her to do this task.

Seat Re-Covering

When re-covering seats, it is easier to re-cover the low-back seats than it is to work on the high-back seats from 1969–1973. With some patience and a good set of hog-ring pliers, you can do this yourself with very nice results.

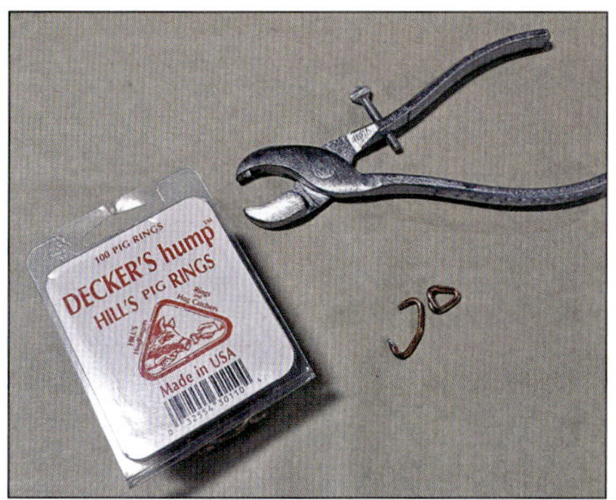

Hog-ring pliers and hog rings are used to secure the seat-cover wires to the frame. They are available from the Mustang vendors, online, or a local farm-supply store.

Door Panels

Early door panels were cardboard backed, and Ford later added metal uppers and lowers to later years. The reproduction panels fit well, but be careful installing and removing the panels because repeated installations weaken the cardboard areas where the mounting clips are located and will pull the clips out of the cardboard. An inexpensive tool to remove the

For most restorations, reproduction door panels are the best choice. There are companies that can restore the older panels, but if you are building a full concours car, check that the grain finish and color is correct before committing to the extra expense. Judges can tell the difference.

clips without damaging the panel is highly recommended.

Interior Side Panels

The interior side panels were made from metal, fiberglass, or plastic, depending on the application.

If you find yourself having to remove your panels after installation, be very careful and use tape, a rag, or other means to protect the paint on the door. If you used a lacquer interior paint from a Mustang supplier, it chips very easily.

1969 Mustang High-Back Seat Repair

I used this high-back seat as a "donor" to repair some original seat covers for another build. I'm using it to show you how to install a reproduction cover and foam on the original frame.

The large mounting wires on the seat should lay right under the valleys of the padding. This is where the hog rings attach for the padding and the seat cover. Install new frame-edge padding with hog rings to protect the seat foam from the frame.

If you can avoid replacing the burlap on the seat, do so. If not, use 0.035 music wire (not annealed) and 5/32-inch kraft rope to anchor the ends. The kraft rope can also be unrolled and used to repair the larger mounting rods under the foam.

The front seat-back trim panel was either vinyl-covered cardboard or plastic. Use an awl to prep the holes in the frame. Then, press the clips through to install.

Secure the pad to the under wires with hog rings and be careful to not allow the ring to drive/rip through the pad. The listing wires go into the sewn pockets of the seat cover. Turn the cover inside out to install the wires to the frame. This is the hardest part of the job, and having an assistant really helps.

Re-graining the interior panels is a difficult process, and these panels take a beating, especially from the fold-down seat. I made some molds out of latex rubber from a nice set of panels, and after prepping, I use a two-part epoxy to fill in the top layer after repairs. Use a simple mold release and some pressure, and the molds will reinstall the grained finish.

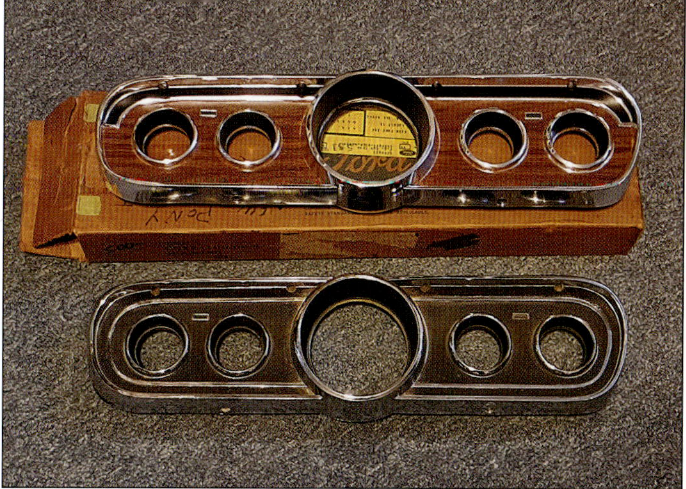

The aftermarket instrument housings (bottom) are a good choice for most restorations. NOS units (top) are getting scarce, and for most concours applications, you most likely will have to re-plate an original unit. Replating small-batch parts can be expensive.

To repair chips such as this in fiberglass, I first build the back side with fiberglass and then fill in the front with fiberglass most of the way. Then, I re-grain the area with one of my molds. Finally, sand down the back-side fiberglass smooth so that the panel fits flush.

Instrument Housing

The instrument housing (gauge cluster) has some chrome appointments on it. Replating the original plastic chrome is becoming expensive, and it is difficult to find a company that does it. The companies that I used to use are long gone. Check out the model hobby sites because plastic chrome shops pop up occasionally in the hobby world. If your car is not a thoroughbred, the reproduction clusters are much cheaper than re-chroming an original.

For clusters and dashes that get a wood-grain finish, wood-grain appliques are available for refinishing. Make sure the grain matches your original. The 1969–1970 appliques were available with both walnut and teak finishes.

Different vendors make different parts, and the colors usually don't match up. This brand-new instrument housing, original glove-box door and original transmission-shifter base were all masked and painted to match. The 1967–1968 wrap-around dash design really stands out if all of the pieces don't match.

When doing a color change on panels, you usually don't have to strip them down before refinishing, but these particular panels had several layers on them and I was losing the grain in the panel. Some people recommend using oven cleaner to get the old dye out (left), but I recommend lacquer thinner, even though it takes a little more work. It is safer to work with. Always use proper safety gear and work in a well-ventilated area.

Installing Carpet

Reproduction carpet comes pre-molded and typically has the jute backing already installed. Some tools to consider when installing carpet are a sharp carpet knife, an old soldering iron, a steamer, and a heat gun. Before using these tools, test them on a scrap piece because the carpet can be damaged if they are used improperly. ■

Take the carpet out of the package and let it sit out for a day to allow it to unfold. This is a 1964½-style carpet with no molded heel pad, and it does not run up the sides of the rocker panel.

Use a spray adhesive to install fold-down-area carpet to the fold-down components. Work from the middle out and trim it after it has dried.

This carpet set had the jute pad glued on improperly. To get it to sit down, the padding had to be reseated. Once the pad was smooth, the wrinkles went away.

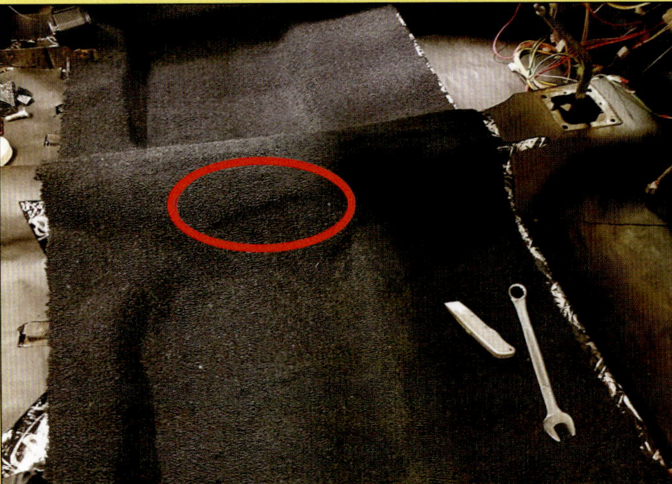

The molded carpet usually fits fine on aftermarket pieces, but the big wrinkle in the center of the transmission tunnel (red oval) was what went away when the pad was reseated. Some wrinkles can be removed with a steamer and some heavy weights to reshape the carpet. The rear carpet section is installed first.

Be careful when trimming the carpet. Several smaller cuts are preferred over one big cut because you can go too far and then the carpet doesn't fit under the trim anymore. Areas such as the rear corners require several slits to allow it to sit beneath the interior side panels.

With extreme care, use a soldering iron to open the holes for the seat belts and seat holes. Test on a discarded piece first to make sure that it doesn't cause more damage (be careful with the padding) and make sure that nothing smolders or catches fire. If you put the hole in the wrong place, you now have a melted nylon mess on your hands.

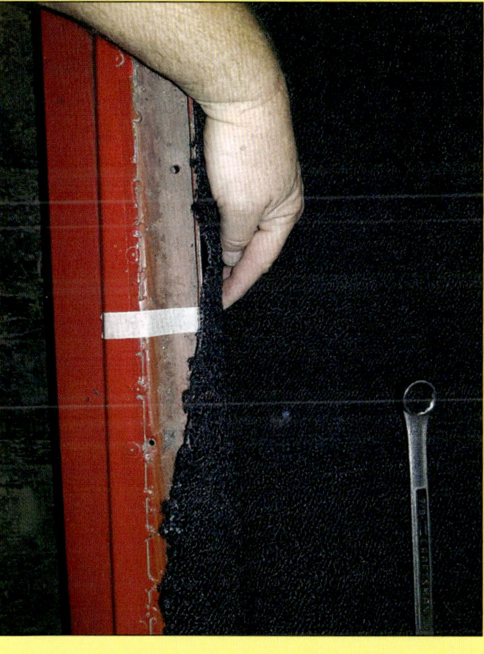

Use a piece of masking tape to locate the holes in the rocker panel for the seat belts and the sill-plate screws. This saves your carpet when you are poking around for the holes with an awl.

With the wrinkles out and seat holes located, this 1969 carpet did not come with a precut hole for the shifter, which will be made along with adding the screw holes for the console. Be patient and know that it may take several fittings to get the carpet to lay down properly.

Most of them have a grained finish that is difficult to re-create, especially when repairing fiberglass panels. Paint buildup can reduce the look of the grained surface, so when repainting, be careful of the buildup. The original paint was actually an enamel or a dye on fiberglass panels. Most parts houses sell a lacquer replacement paint which doesn't hold up as well. Be careful stripping these panels because abrasive scratching reduces the grain look.

With some of the aftermarket panels, try to purchase all of them from the same supplier. Sometimes when mixing and matching, the grain pattern may not be the same from panel to panel. Even from the same supplier, the grains may not match, depending on what was used to make the original molds, and often they might be acrylonitrile butadiene styrene (ABS) plastic, rather than fiberglass.

Heater Box

The heater box that is mounted under the dash became larger and more complex as the years passed (and with the addition of air conditioning). In general, the biggest issue with the heater box was the failure of the heater core, and the first indication of a problem was a puddle on the passenger-side floorboard. Over the years, the foam seals inside the box disintegrate into powder, so when refurbishing the interior, now is the time to refurbish the heater box.

The early defrost plenum chambers were made of pressed cardboard, and with condensation and boots, they took a beating. Finding a nice original unit is difficult. The reproductions are made from plastic and are good for all but concours cars.

This is the original color of the heater casing: a mottled gray/dark gray. This one got painted black, so I spent some time cleaning it off with lacquer thinner and super-fine steel wool.

Two types of foam are available to reseal the case: the original-style open cell (shown here) and a denser foam rubber style. Both work well. Use spray adhesive and trim as necessary, especially the swinging doors, as they can bind up the control-cable operations.

Most people won't crawl under their dash to see the restoration of your heater box, but don't skimp on the small details. This box is ready to go back in a 1964½ coupe.

CHAPTER 12

Reassembly and Completion

Ford had to build at least 500 cars with the Boss 429 engine to qualify the motor for NASCAR racing, where it was installed in Talladega Torinos. However, street versions of the Talladega had 428 Cobra Jet engines: Ford decided to stuff the Boss 429 into specially equipped Mustangs instead, and in doing so, created an instant legend. This 1969 version is owned by Jeremy Feller of Indianapolis, Indiana.

The white powdery residue on new seals is the mold release, and it can be removed with rubbing alcohol. It must be removed for the adhesive to work properly.

When reassembling the vehicle, my best advice is, "Don't drive past the end of the hood ornament." This means that it is tempting to grab your wrenches and start bolting parts onto the car because the end is in sight.

However, by not taking the time to properly prep your tools, the parts, and yourself, this is where most of the damage is done. Take your time and think about the steps that are required to install each component. This chapter is not a step-by-step sequence about how to reassemble the car. Instead, it features things I have learned over the years when completing a Mustang project.

Soft Weatherstripping

Weatherstrip adhesive is very stringy, so protect the area around the weatherstripping so that you do not have to peel off stringers later. Run a piece of automotive tape along where the seal will be installed. Apply sealer to the edge of the seal and to the surface that you are attaching it to and let the adhesive tack up. Then, apply more adhesive to the seal and set it in place. On items such as the

Assembly Tips and Tricks

Keeping everything that you have just restored in the same condition after it is installed takes patience. Here are just a few tips and tricks for keeping the finish on your parts and the car looking like new.

When installing and adjusting body panels, tape off the edges so that you aren't chipping the fresh, new paint. Wax paper on the right also helps with the occasional brush-by and items rubbing up against painted parts.

Washers tend to dig into paint, so when making adjustments, I use little U-shaped pieces of cardboard or foam while I am adjusting items such as the front fenders. Once you have found the right spot, pull out the cushions and tighten the bolts.

Sometimes the door strikers use a shim, and the shim digs into the paint. I made these pads out of an old antifreeze jug. Once the striker is in place, they can be removed without damaging the finish, and the striker can be tightened down.

Weatherstrip adhesive is very stringy and gets everywhere, so I run some tape on each side of the weatherstrip when possible to pull off strings and adhesive when the weatherstrip accidentally shifts. Then, peel off the tape and save time cleaning off the adhesive later.

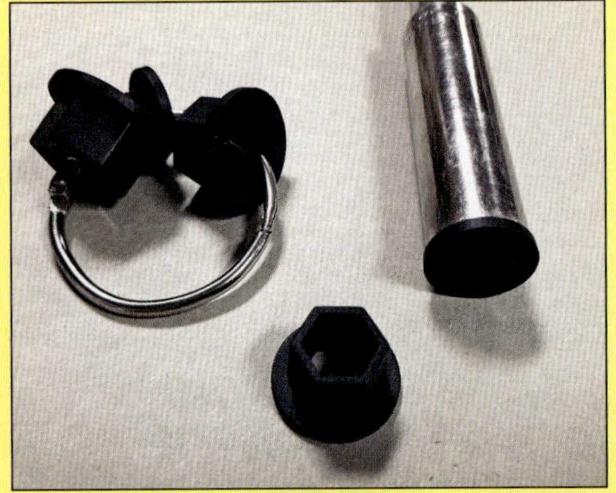

For show cars, the judges assess at the finish on the hardware. These plastic inserts help keep the finish on the bolts clean while assembling. I purchased mine online, but some of the parts vendors may still carry them.

When installing your hardware, try to keep from pressing down on the bolt because the socket will leave a ring on the washer and may damage the finish. Always try to keep the socket just off the washer when tightening the bolt.

Keeping bare and phosphated parts rust-free is done with a waterproof oil, such as Boeshield T-9. These oils displace water and are clear. This product can be used with a rag or towel for normal maintenance after the parts are attached.

Strip caulk was used throughout the car: under the fenders, under the gas-tank lip, and under the drain plugs. It was also used to hold the water shields in place on the door. If you didn't photograph the location of the old caulk, the correct pattern is found in the factory interior assembly manual. Dip your fingers in water to keep the caulk from sticking to your fingers.

trunk seal, your assembly manuals indicate where to start the seal. Hold the seal in place until it grabs firm. Then, continue to move and apply additional adhesive.

The new seals have a different durometer rating than the original seals. A durometer rating is the measured hardness or softness of the material, and the originals tend to be softer than the current replacements. This means that you will get your doors lined up, but when the seals go on the doors, they stick out because the seal is not compressing properly. It may take much longer for the new seals to compress enough to allow the door to fit properly. You may also have to adjust the doors again (primarily the striker plate) to compensate for the new seals. The seals often come too long, and in the case of the door seals that are affixed with specific fasteners at each end, some restorers have had to cut them in the middle of the bottom of the door to remove the excess material and make them fit tightly.

Strip Caulk

Strip caulk is used on items such as the fenders and around the drain-hole covers in the floors. It is a soft caulk that stays soft, and it came in black and light gray, depending on the year and application. When applying the strip caulk, have a small cup of water on hand to dip your fingers in so that the caulk does not stick to your fingers and you can lay it down smoothly.

Door Beltline Weatherstripping

Before snapping in the door beltline weatherstrips (the outside rubber and the inside felts), make sure the slots that the parts snap into are straight and flat. Sometimes, taking the old ones out causes the door metal to pull and then the new pieces will not sit flush. The little tangs on the new strips pull out very easily, and then you have to buy new ones.

Radiator Support Seal

Some cars received a hard rubber seal on the top of the radiator-support shroud. This seal was power stapled to the shroud at the factory. The new seal typically comes with staples but no means to install them. Drill out the original staple holes with a small drill bit. Then, after you slide the seal on, use a right-angle dental pick or an awl to poke through the holes and through the new seal. You may have to reshape the new staples, but once they are the correct width, you can push them through and then bend them over with a pair of needle-nose pliers.

New seals that are supplied with staples can be installed by drilling a hole with a drill bit the size of the staples and then running the staples through the hole and bending them over on the back side. These were used on early splash shields and the radiator-support upper seal.

Glass Alignment

Unfortunately, there are no shortcuts when it comes to aligning the side glass. Be prepared to settle in and take your time because there will be a lot of back and forth when aligning the glass. It is a little easier on the 1969-and-up cars that do not have a vent window, but after many years of bending and tweaking, nothing fits very well, and you will need patience

The 1964½–1968 cars have front side vents and four bolts to adjust them to the car. The vent gets adjusted before the roll-up window. Bolts 1 and 2 (the top two) adjust the height and length along the door, and Bolts 3 and 4 are used to move the frame in or out from the seal.

The 1964½–1966 cars have a rear glass channel that is adjusted by removing the caps and loosening the bolts from the doorjamb area. The 1967–1968 cars have this outer bolt, but the lower track is adjusted with a set screw and nut that is behind the door panel. The 1969–1970 cars have dual bars that are adjusted from undeath the door and inside and behind the door panel. The 1971–1973 cars are the easiest, with a single bar adjusted from behind the door panel.

The front and rear glass can be installed with the help of a small cord laid in the body-lip side of the weatherstripping. Set the glass and weatherstripping in the lower window opening lip. Then, gently pull the cord to peel the lip of the gasket up and over the glass-opening lip. Light pressure on the outside of the glass helps to seat the gasket.

to get the fitment correct.

On 1964–1968 cars, align the vent window first, as this sets the position of the window glass. If you have a coupe or convertible, then preset the rear quarter glass before setting the actual roll-up window. Start by aligning the vent window to the roof seal, making it parallel to the seal vertically and in and out. Then, follow the directions in the body-assembly manual (there is one available for all years). Be careful when installing the vent glass that you don't over tighten the pot-metal tabs to hold the vent window in place. They can break easily.

In 1969 and 1970, Ford dropped the vent window and mounted the side glass on a pair of slide bars, and from 1971 to 1973, it went to a single slide bar, which helps with the alignment process. In 1971, Ford also added power windows that can interfere if you don't take your time. The 1969 side glass was glued in, which didn't work very well and was upgraded to bolt-in-style glass in 1970. Conversion kits are available to upgrade the 1969 glue-in glass.

The 1964–1968 front windshields use a rubber seal to set the glass, and 1969–1973 front windshields use a urethane sealer to set the glass. Although Ford installed alignment braces for setting the latter windshields, the thickness of the sealer is more important in the installation. The depth of the glass installation determines how well the windshield trim sits against the glass. Ford recommends a 3/16-inch bead when

For windshields with butyl tape, the tape goes just out to the edge of the body lip. Use a piece of masking tape to note the location of the windshield-trim-clip posts so that when you install the trim, you know where to press.

applying the adhesive, which allows the trim to set flush on the car. If you choose to go with a butyl tape instead of the urethane, make sure that you find it in 3/16-inch thickness.

Chrome and Brightwork

I typically leave chrome and brightwork installation as one of the final tasks because it keeps some of the potential damage to a minimum.

Although Ford chrome and brightwork fits better than aftermarket chrome, it looks terrible. Ford's chroming process wasn't stellar, and the quality of the chrome shows it. Top restorers know this, and if you have nice, shiny, pretty chrome on your car, they will know that it isn't original! Top-end cars tend to not have nice chrome work because they use NOS components.

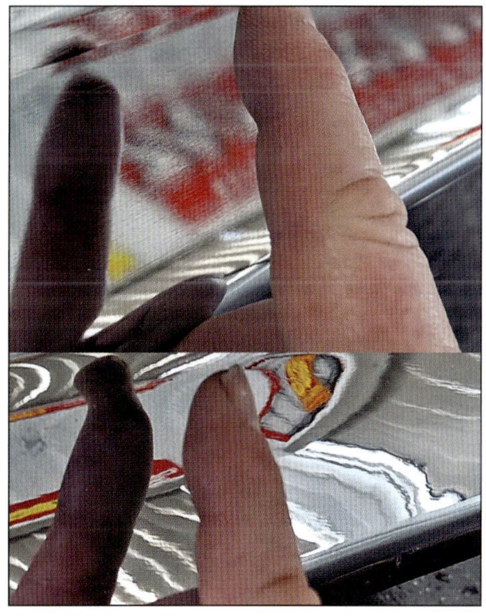

NOS Ford chrome is on top, and reproduction chrome is on the bottom. Believe it or not, some judges in some classes want to see the Ford chrome, as it is not as pretty as the reproduction chrome. The best-fitting, prettiest chrome is usually a rechromed original.

If you have nice, original emblems and chrome work that needs to be painted, the red and blue are a translucent color, and the white is solid. These Krylon Stained Glass paints work perfectly on the red and blue, and model-paint white works for the middle.

Aftermarket chrome looks much nicer but does not fit as well as the original pieces, which can really show. The bumpers tend to stick out farther on aftermarket chrome. The aftermarket chrome is the most cost effective, and aftermarket chrome is perfectly fine for all but original and show cars.

When installing the drip rails, start in one of the upper corners (not the end). This helps to align the drip rail better than the ends. The trim will hook over the rail and then snap underneath as you go. Don't use a hammer because it will dent the trim. An open palm can be used to gently snap the trim into place. If you painted the car and you have a large buildup of paint on the drip rail, you may need to take some of the paint down to the primer to get the drip rail to fit (especially with some of the aftermarket drip rails).

Use caution when installing the windshield and rear glass trim. It may take some influence from a hand palm, and it is very easy to damage the trim. The trim usually goes in with hand pressure, but be very careful if you need to influence the trim. Always run automotive tape around the outside edges of the paint to avoid chipping or scratching the paint. Mark the location of the trim clips so that you know where to press after the trim is in place.

Engine Start-Up

The first few minutes of any engine fire-up helps determine how long the engine will survive. The initial metal-on-metal contact before the oiling system is warmed up determines whether or not the engine will be scored or damaged, so use extreme caution. Hopefully, you took my advice in the engine chapter and used liberal amounts of assembly lube when reassembling the engine. This lube generally breaks down after start-up, and the oil takes over.

Engine Break-In Oil

I am a big fan of break-in oil because of zinc and phosphorus. Zinc dithiophosphate (ZDDP) is one of the best anti-wear additives in oil. Because of some of the hazards, it is being phased out, but I recommend that you use a good break-in oil that will help with the engine start-up. Some camps use a straight-weight oil over a multi-viscosity and synthetic/organic oil. Whatever you use, make sure it is a break-in oil with ZDDP. Once the break-in is complete, use oil that has been designed for your engine (as recommended by Ford or your engine builder).

Breaking in an engine results in the most raw metal-on-metal contact before the oil pump gets going. All break-in oils have one thing in common: lots of zinc. You can buy oils that are ready to go (left and center), or you can buy a quart that is meant to blend with your oil (right).

Priming the Engine

The most important item on the pre-fire list is to prime the oil pump. The oil pump is driven by the distributor, so it requires removing the distributor and using an oil-pump priming tool. Mount the priming tool in a drill and run the drill counterclockwise. You should feel the pump bind when the oil starts flowing. Give it a minute or two to get oil flowing through the block.

Ford used two different sizes of oil-pump drives: 1/4- and 5/16-inch hex (depending on the engine). The aluminum disc on this oil-pump priming tool sits down in the distributor hole to keep alignment. I put tape on the outer side of the shaft, as it keeps the shaft from sliding out and down into the oil pan.

Mechanical Oil-Pressure Gauge

Every time that I fire a new motor, I temporarily install a mechanical oil-pressure gauge. Your Mustang came with an electric gauge or just a light, and if something is wrong with the gauge or wiring, it could give a false reading when starting up the motor. If you fire the motor and see no oil pressure on start-up, shut it off right away before the engine is damaged. A mechanical gauge reduces the possibility of a no-read on the startup, and once you break in the motor and you know that there is oil pressure, reattach the gauge (or light) and confirm its operation.

On first fire-up, I usually install a mechanical oil pressure gauge so that I can watch for the proper oil pressure. If the dash gauge isn't working or is not hooked up correctly, it can give you a false reading—or worse, it may not let you know you have an oiling problem.

Set Initial Timing

To reinstall the distributor, bring the engine crankshaft around to the compression stroke and then to your timing mark. To find the compression stroke on the engine, pull the number-1 spark plug and put your finger over the spark-plug hole. Turn the crank manually, and as you get to top dead center (TDC), you should

The timing grooves on the damper or pulley can be hard to read while timing the engine, so I use a white-out pen to mark both TDC and the timing point to which I want to set the engine. If it is a show car, it wipes right off after timing the engine.

feel air pressure on your finger from the compression stroke. If you don't feel pressure, you are on the exhaust stroke. Bring the crank to your timing mark (for example, 6 degrees before top dead center [BTDC] for a 1968 302).

The distributor gear is curved, so it will rotate about 20 degrees before it slides into place. Sometimes the oil-pump driveshaft is not aligned to allow the distributor to slide into the tooth that you want to engage on the camshaft. If this happens, use the oil-pump primer and manually turn by hand the oil-pump driveshaft slightly to allow the distributor to engage both the camshaft gear and the hexagon driveshaft socket. If you have the distributor pointing at the number-1 spark plug and it backfires when you try to fire the engine, you are 180 degrees out of timing. Simply pull the distributor and turn it 180 degrees, and you should be close.

To make sure that you are close on the timing, install the spark plugs on all but the number-1 plug.

Marking the number-1 plug location from the distributor cap on the distributor body with tape helps when you are trying to get the vacuum advance pointing straight forward while lining up the rotor. Remove the tape after you find the correct spot.

Install an extra plug on the end of the number-1 spark plug and ground it to the engine somewhere on bare metal. Then, have a helper turn the ignition to "on" but not "start." With the crank set at the ignition timing mark, you should be able to move the distributor body back and forth and get a spark out of the grounded plug. Once you find the spark, lock down the distributor because that is very close to the timing point for running your motor. This will also tell you if you have spark coming through the coil and distributor. You can now hook up the number-1 plug.

To get the distributor advance diaphragm to point straight forward, put the engine right at your timing mark on the number-1 cylinder. Mark the position of the number-1 plug wire on the distributor housing, and install the distributor so that the number-1 wire is at the one o'clock position and the diaphragm is facing straight forward. Make sure that the rotor is pointing at the number-1 mark. This will get you close.

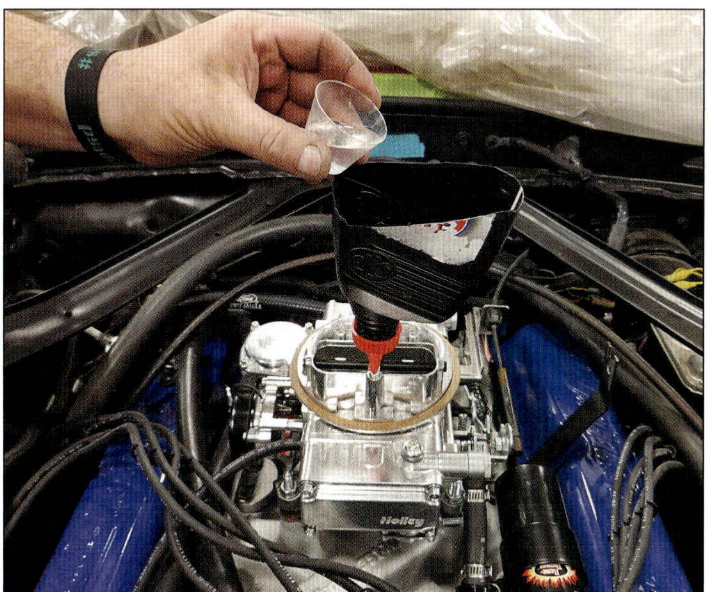

You can pour about a 1/4 cup of fuel slowly down the bowl vent of the carburetor to prime the fuel system. A Holley, such as this, can also be primed by filling through the float sight port.

Carburetor Priming

Please heed this advice: never use a starter to prime a mechanical fuel pump. This tends to damage starters and cables, and your engine is turning at low RPM, so no oil pressure is building. Never pour raw gasoline down the throat of the carburetor because this washes down the cylinder and can damage the cylinder. Never use ether (starting fluid) to prime the engine. Continuous shots of ether can damage the motor, and it acts as a solvent, which can strip oil away from an already oil-starved start-up engine.

The carburetor can be primed without taking it apart. Locate your carburetor's bowl vent and, using an eye dropper or a very small funnel, pour about 1/4 cup of fuel in the vent to fill the bowl. If you have a Holley, pull the primary bowl sight glass and fill it from the side. Be very careful to not spill fuel on the engine and to allow sufficient time for the fuel vapors to disperse before trying to start the engine. This should provide sufficient fuel to run the engine and prime the mechanical fuel pump.

Engine Break-In

Follow the engine break-in guidelines from your engine builder and/or your camshaft manufacturer. Typically, you should run the engine for about 20 minutes and run it between 2,000 and 3,000 rpm. Watch the oil pressure continuously and make sure that it doesn't go too high or too low per the engine specifications from your shop manual. Look for fuel, oil, coolant, and transmission fluid leaks during and after engine runs. After engine break-in, re-torque the intake and exhaust manifold bolts per Ford specifications and look for other bolts that may have vibrated loose. This is almost impossible to do on an FE big-block.

Transmission Break-In

Here are some tips for breaking in manual and automatic transmissions.

Manual

Never run any type of transmission fluid other than what Ford recommended for the transmission. I have heard of people trying to run Mercon in their old Toploaders. Don't do it. As with the engines, the gearbox is designed for a certain weight

The manual transmissions are difficult to fill or top off after they are in the car. The inexpensive hand pump on the left is helpful to fill the transmission, and you can make a siphon tube from some of the manufacturers' caps to remotely fill the transmission. The automatic transmissions are filled through the dipstick tube.

of oil, and running a lighter oil can cause big problems.

For newly rebuilt manual transmissions, get the rear wheels in the air when you run the transmission, and run it in reverse for 10 minutes or so first. This helps to push out some of the assembly grease in the gears.

Automatic

The automatic transmission is a large hydraulic pump, and it is designed to work with Type F fluid, so don't try Mercon.

Make sure to put a quart of fluid in the torque converter prior to installation. The biggest need on startup is to get fluid in the converter. With a new rebuilt engine and transmission, I generally have a second person on the transmission while someone else is concerned with the motor. Your transmission is not going to hold all of the capacity until it starts pumping it through the transmission and torque converter. A C6 transmission holds 11 quarts, but for a new start-up, you will probably only get 4 or 5 quarts in there before it is full.

When first starting the engine, have the transmission inspector ready to put in additional quarts of fluid on startup, when the pump starts. Keep adding quarts until it registers on the dipstick. Once the motor is broken in, raise the rear tires off the ground if you can and carefully run the transmission through of all the gears, making sure to come to a complete stop before changing gears. Check the dipstick frequently and fill the transmission to the recommended level.

Before the torque converter is installed, put a quart of fluid in it so that it doesn't run dry on start-up. During start-up, continuously check the fluid level in the transmission, and, if possible, raise the rear wheels off the ground and run it through the gears to get fluid into all the passages.

Tires

Bias-ply tires should only be used on show cars that are never driven. Several of my customers have requested me to install them, and they all ended up trading them out for radials. They just do not track as well as a modern radial. Radial versions of some of the early-style tires are now available (for example, red-line tires), and you should select these if you are going to drive the car. Reproductions of some of the early radials are available and are fine for drivers. If you plan to drive the car on a regular basis, a good radial with a modern tread design is the best choice.

If you are building a show car and are seeking original tires, know that they are almost nonexistent today and

Reproduction radial tires are great for show cars and drivers, and radial versions of bias-ply tires are available for show cars. If you intend to drive the car a lot, a modern radial is a better choice.

This car still has its original spare in the trunk, and for anything but a thoroughbred, that's where it belongs. Fifty-plus-year-old tires are not safe to use on the road.

those that are available probably need a tube installation to hold air. Tires, even NOS tires that sit on a shelf, will leech out silicone and other components and will dry rot and crack. New tire dealers are generally restricted to 6 years to sell a tire as new. Fifty-year-old tires are dangerous to use on the road, even if they look brand new and hold air. They should only be used on show cars. Plus, they are really expensive, and once you drive on them, they lose all of their value.

It is getting more difficult to find qualified alignment personnel. Some shops will only do what their computer tells them, and some shops won't mess with 1964½–1966 cars that use shims on the upper control arm to set caster and camber—and I don't blame them! Look for a shop that really knows alignments, especially on older cars.

Alignment

The primary job of the front-end alignment is to keep as much of the tire patch on the ground in all situations. Before active suspension technology, this was difficult because suspension components don't move exactly parallel to the road surface. All manufacturers made designs for the best compromise of handling and ride comfort.

Alignment on the early cars is something that Ford got wrong. Some blame it on bias-ply tire design, and that may be true, but the alignment didn't change much from 1964 to 1973. Although radial tires began entering the Mustang fleet in 1967, the specifications didn't change much to compensate. As with the suspension geometry, the alignment is part of the reason why the cars often handled poorly and bounced into the next lane.

For cars that are pure stock and never driven, use the alignment specifications in your shop manual for the vehicle. They are great for getting the car on and off the trailer. For those who wish to drive their cars and want to use modern radials, look for something better. We have 50 years of advancement to utilize, and alignment equipment is much more accurate, so let's take advantage of the newfound knowledge.

I do not recommend a specific alignment specification for your vehicle. My recommendation is to seek out a shop in your area that really knows alignment and to discuss with the people at that shop the best place to set the front suspension. Don't hire a shop that just does what the machine says to do. Seek out a real expert who is used to seeing many strange combinations.

The three major alignment specifications are camber, caster, and toe.

Camber

Camber is how much the tire leans in and out. If you were looking at the tire straight on, this is how much the top of the tire would lean away from the car (positive camber) or leans in (negative camber).

The suspension doesn't move straight up and down; it moves in an arc. In a turn, the outer front wheel compresses, and the weight of the car wants to roll outward over the side of the tire. This means that the tire tread is no longer touching the road. Correct engineering pulls the wheel in toward the car by adding negative camber as the suspension compresses, keeping the tread on the road.

The Ford design, based on the Falcon, adds positive camber in a hard turn, which makes the problem worse. Ford discovered that lowering the upper control arm added negative camber to the system in a turn and kept the tire on the road. It is now referred to as the "Shelby drop." Either way, too much camber affects tire wear.

The Ford specifications for camber range from 0 to 1½ degrees of positive camber. Yikes! Most aftermarket manufacturers now recommend around 1/4 to 1/2 degree of negative camber. With the design already pushing the tire in the wrong direction, positive camber doesn't help.

Caster

Caster is the angle of the spindle in relationship to the ground surface.

Caster is used to help re-center the wheels after a turn and keep them going straight. Positive caster is how far back the spindle is leaning (the more it leans, the more caster in degrees).

The best way to visualize caster is by picturing the front fork on a bicycle. The fork angle on a bike helps the front wheel re-center. The more caster, the more the wheels want to center, but the harder it is to turn the wheels. A unicycle has no caster and turns on a dime but relies on the rider to re-center the wheel. A chopper with long forks rides very straight but is difficult to turn. Cars with little caster can bounce into the next lane after hitting a bump, which is usually blamed on bump steer.

Ford's caster specifications ranged from negative numbers to plus 1 or 2 degrees. That's why when you hit a chuckhole, the car jumps into the next lane. More caster controls this but makes the car harder to steer. Most performance-suspension manufacturers want to see 3 to 5 degrees of positive caster, and you want yours to be on the positive side as well. Talk with a local expert and find out where he or she recommends the setting based on the parts you purchased.

Toe

Toe is the amount that the front wheels point in toward the center of the car. In a rear-wheel-drive car, the front suspension is pushed along, which causes the suspension to push back toward the back of the car due to the resistance caused by friction with the road surface. By pointing the tire in, they actually track a little straighter when the car is moving. Toe-in can also help reduce oversteer and improve high-speed stability. Too much toe can cause premature wear on the tires and instability because the tires are not pointing straight at speed. If one tire hits a puddle, you can have erratic movement in the front.

Toe in on early cars started at a whopping 1/4 inch to 5/16 total toe (preferably equal on each side). This got down to 1/16 of an inch and back up to an even wider 3/8 toe in 1973. With stock components, your alignment specialist will probably try to keep you in the 1/8 to 1/16 total toe, and the new equipment should allow them to make it equal for both tires. If you are using non-stock components, use the recommendation of the manufacturer.

Insurance

The most important aspect of insuring a car is knowing that it is your responsibility to prove that your car is worth what you say it is. You may find an insurance policy that pays out guaranteed, but it always comes down to having proof of the true value of the car. Don't assume that just because an insurance company says something that it is the truth. Be prepared in the case that what the insurance company says is not true.

Even though your policy holder may only require a photo or two to assure coverage, I highly recommend that you document everything. The more you document, the easier it is to prove that what you have is what you say it is worth. Also, do not pay for more coverage than you need. If your car is worth $30,000, don't pay premiums for $50,000.

Most plans are a variant of a stated value policy. This means that either you state the value of the car or you provide appraisals and documentation to prove the value of the car. For example, say that your 1972 Mach 1 is valued at $30,000, you get hit, and the car gets totaled. Some insurance companies (not all) may find a car that is similar to yours for sale for $10,000. So, the insurance company writes you a check for $10,000 instead of $30,000. It is up to you to prove that your restored car is worth more

What happens if you hurt your pride and joy? Make sure that you have all of your documentation ready to go. This all-original car took a hit, and with proper documents, NOS parts were approved for its repair.

Find a friend who has a lift or a nice repair shop and document everything on the car. This helps you determine the correct value of the car so that you are not overpaying or underpaying for insurance. It also helps when issues might arise after a claim has been filed.

Judging sheets compiled from qualified judges are an asset to your restoration and its value. Good judges tell you what is right with the car and do not just look for the flaws.

than the one that the insurance company used for comparison.

Even if your insurance policy is with one of the big, national classic car insurance companies, which are very good and probably know what your car is worth more than you do, always assume that the burden of proof lies with you. If something happens, don't find out the hard way that you weren't covered like you thought you were.

Your documentation checklist should include an appraisal, a video, and more.

Appraisal

A professional appraisal should be kept up to date at least every two years. The value of vintage Mustangs swings up and down a lot, but the cost to repair and the parts don't, so make sure that your appraisal is up to date.

The more that you invest in the appraisal, the more value you will have if you have a problem. An appraisal that is sent in to an insurance company with two 3/4 shots is not worth as much as one from a professional who looks the car over well.

I had a customer who paid someone to look at a car before he bought it, and let's just say that I rebuilt the entire car. A reputable appraisal is critical. An appraisal from five years ago for $30,000 doesn't do you much good if the car's replacement value is now $40,000. You also don't want to overpay for a policy if the situation is reversed.

Video

Take a quality video of the finished product—and not just of the outside. If you don't have a lift, find a friend or a shop that will let you use one to get footage of the underside of the car in detail. It's much easier to prove to an insurance company that your car doesn't need floors like the one that it compared your car to when you can go right to the video. As with the appraisal, keep the video updated. It may also help you find areas that need attention.

Documentation

Keep all of the photos that you took as well as all of your receipts. Do this not only for your brag book but also to prove the quality of your work. Note that parts purchases will vary wildly on the value of the car. Some insurance companies don't care about them.

Values

You probably already researched the web, looking for cars like yours and seeing what they are worth. Keep doing that. Prices fluctuate, and if it shifts a bunch (they went crazy in the late 1980s and the mid 2000s and then sank in the late 2000s), you may want to update your information and insurance policy.

As I stated at the beginning of the book, it is always cheaper to buy a car that has been restored than to restore one yourself. So, just because you did a thorough job on a 6-cylinder coupe and spared no expense on the restoration does not mean that it will bring Shelby prices. Understand that something is only worth what someone else is willing to pay for it.

Consider the cost of replacing the car if it is destroyed, and that is something you need to make sure that you and your insurance agent fully understand. Just because you paid a lot for your restoration doesn't make it worth that much, and some cars, such as family heirlooms, are irreplaceable. Make sure that you understand exactly what your policy is covering and that it may be possible to replace your car with one that you value less.

Source Guide

American Auto Wire
150 Heller Pl.
Bellmawr, NJ 08031
800-482-9473
americanautowire.com

Boeshield T-9
PMS Products Inc.
76 Veterans Dr. #110
Holland, MI 49423
800-962-1732
boeshield.com

CJ Pony Parts
7461 Allentown Blvd.
Harrisburg, PA 17112
800-888-6473
cjponyparts.com

Classic Industries
18460 Gothard St.
Huntington Beach, CA 92648
800-854-1280
classicindustries.com

Dead Nuts On
P.O. Box 279
Sewickley, PA 15143
510-903-1059
deadnutson.com

Dynacorn
4030 Via Pescador
Camarillo, CA 93012
805-987-8818
dynacorn.com

Evaporust
800 Enterprise Rd., Suite 101
Horsham, PA 19044
800-272-8963
evapo-rust.com

Fuel Safe
1550 NE Kingwood Ave.
Redmon, OR 97756
800-433-6524
fuelsafe.com

Ididit
610 S. Maumee St.
Tecumseh, MI 49286
517-424-0577
ididit.com

John's Mustang
5234 Glenmont Dr.
Houston, TX 77081
800-869-6894
johnsmustang.com

JR1 Racing Oil
722 W. Pearl St.
Lebanon, IN 46052
765-483-9371
jr1racingoil.com

Lucas Oil Products
1310 E. 96th St. Suite 200
Indianapolis, IN 46240
800-342-2512
lucasoil.com

Marti Auto Works
13238 W. Butler Dr.
El Mirage, AZ 85335
623-935-2558
martiauto.com

Mustang Project
300 Brushy Creek Road
Cedar Park, TX 78613
800-631-0507
customcarlight.com

Mustang Steve
info@mustangsteve.com
817-415-2793
mustangsteve.com

National Parts Depot
900 SW 38th Ave.
Ocala, FL 34474
800-874-7595
npdlink.com

POR-15
800-457-6715
por15.com

Pro-Strip Indy (Formerly Redi-Strip)
4020 Millersville Rd.
Indianapolis, IN 46205
317-545-2088
prostripindy.com

Roller Hoop
DSK Auto Products
712 W. Cornhusker Hwy.
Lincoln, NE 68521
402-475-9968
rollerhoop.com

Royal Purple
One Royal Purple Ln.
Porter, TX 77365
888-382-6300
royalpurple.com

Scott Drake
Holley Products
holley.com/brands/scott.drake

TMI
1493 E. Bentley Dr.
Corona, CA 92879
888-460-0640
tmiproducts.com

Virginia Classic Mustang
195 W. Lee St.
Broadway, VA 22815
540-896-2695
virginiaclassicmustang.com

Year One Inc.
354 Front St.
Cornelia, GA 30531
800-932-7663
yearone.com